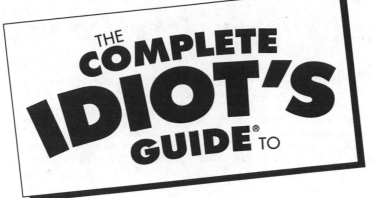

THE COMPLETE IDIOT'S GUIDE® TO

The CIA

by Allan A. Swenson and Michael Benson

ALPHA

A Pearson Education Company

To Wilson—A thinker, mentor and friend whose ideals live on in this book and beyond. AAS.
To the Soaring Eagles—MB

For marketing and publicity, please call: 317-581-3722

The publisher offers discounts on this book when ordered in quantity for bulk purchases and special sales.

For sales within the United States, please contact: Corporate and Government Sales, 1-800-382-3419 or corpsales@pearsontechgroup.com

Outside the United States, please contact: International Sales, 317-581-3793 or international@pearsontechgroup.com

Publisher: *Marie Butler-Knight*
Product Manager: *Phil Kitchel*
Managing Editor: *Jennifer Chisholm*
Acquisitions Editor: *Gary Goldstein*
Development Editor: *Jennifer Moore*
Production Editor: *Billy Fields*
Copy Editors: *Heather Stith*
Illustrator: *Chris Eliopoulos*
Cover/Book Designer: *Trina Wurst*
Indexer: *Julie Bess*
Layout/Proofreading: *Megan Douglass, Mary Hunt, Brad Lenser*

Contents at a Glance

Contents

Foreword

A one-time intelligence operations professional and a long-time author of over 50 books, Allan Swenson knows the CIA and the U.S. Intelligence Community from experience. *The Complete Idiot's Guide to the CIA* is a landmark contribution to the story of U.S. intelligence, not only for "idiots" but also for intelligence professionals. His use of the fictitious "Wilson McLean" disguises the real life stories of numerous intelligence operatives, who have responded to his requests for their first-hand experiences, providing many intriguing asides. The result is a fascinating account, not only of the history and realities of the CIA, but also of the entire U.S. Intelligence Community as well as selected foreign intelligence organizations. Not only does this book offer CIA's human intelligence (HUMINT) collection, but also the National Security Agency's signals intelligence (SIGINT) collection, and the photographic and other kinds of technical collection by spy planes, satellites, and drones.

No other book has covered such in-depth coverage of the CIA as this one. Particularly fascinating are: CIA jobs, the qualifications for them, and how to apply, including by Internet: www.cia.gov/cia/employment. Also within the chapters of this book are discussions of each of the Directors of Central Intelligence from the first (Admiral Sidney W. Souers) to the current (George J. Tenet); some of the names are well-known, e.g., George H.W. Bush, but others far less so. Topics range for The Berlin Wall and CIA's tunnel to the tapping of Soviet phone lines and mind control, sometimes called "brainwashing."

Topics that make the book especially timely and up-to-date are its coverage of anti-terrorism, Osama bin Laden, and Afghanistan; and the unique new role of CIA's Special Activities teams in Afghanistan and elsewhere. All in all, an extremely fascinating book on a fascinating subject, made even more so by the breezy style geared to an *Idiot's Guide*.

—E. R. Thompson, Maj. Gen. (Ret), former Assistant Chief of Staff for Intelligence, U.S. Army

Introduction

In March 2000, as President Bill Clinton was travelling in Asia, CIA officers learned about a massive cash transfer that they interpreted as a payoff for an assassination. Whose assassination? Analysts weren't sure, but they weren't going to take any chances, particularly since previous reports had linked a threat on Clinton's life with Osama bin Laden (this a year and a half before the September 11 attacks).

Because of the report, President Clinton changed his travel plans. Instead of using Air Force One, the president's Boeing 747, he traveled in a smaller and more agile jet from New Delhi to Dhaka, Bangladesh. The smaller jet, it was felt, would be less apt to be hit by a shoulder-held missile launcher on the ground. The president also cancelled a trip to a Bangladeshi village.

We'll never know for sure if the CIA's intelligence report saved a president's life, but it might have. Quiet situations and successes like this are part and parcel of the CIA's business.

A Lot of Headaches, But Very Few Headlines

The incident, by the way, appeared in U.S. newspapers a full week later, and then only as a small item toward the back of the news section. You can't make the front pages with something that didn't happen.

When the CIA has a success, it is quiet. Everything goes on normally, and no one is aware of the horrible consequences had the CIA not prevented them. Sometimes the truth doesn't come out until many years later. Sometimes the public never finds out at all.

On the other hand, when a national security force and intelligence gathering arm like the CIA has a failure, America's security is damaged, and everyone usually finds out about it—and starts pointing fingers—immediately.

In some ways, working for the CIA is a lot like being an umpire in a baseball game. If no one is paying any attention to you, chances are you're doing a pretty good job. However, America's security is no baseball game, and the CIA rarely gives terrorists and others who seek to harm the United States three chances before striking them out.

Playing for Keeps

A lot of what you read about the CIA or see in movies is heavy on drama and intrigue but light on the truth. Sure, the CIA has its cloak-and-dagger aspects, but a lot less of them than most people think. This book gives it to you straight. In **Part 1, "The World's Second Oldest Profession,"** we try to offer you as straightforward a picture of the CIA as we can (many aspects of it are classified, after all). We shine the light on the agency's purpose and how it is structured. From there, we'll look at the best ways to start a career with the CIA and provide an overview of the intelligence community in the United States (there are probably a lot more intelligence agencies than you think!).

In Part 2, "Fathers of Intelligence," you'll learn about how the CIA developed out of the Office of Strategic Services, an intelligence-gathering organization that supported the efforts of the Pentagon during World War II. You'll meet the men who have served as the Director of Central Intelligence over the years and take a look at some foreign intelligence agencies upon whom the CIA will be increasingly reliant during the current global crisis.

If you're looking for intrigue, then you need look no further than **Part 3, "The CIA on the Frontlines of the Cold War."** We highlight some of the CIA's shadowy activities during the Cold War, including some that belong in the Hall of Shame. The CIA took the threat of communism seriously and engaged in hundreds of covert operations in dozens of nations around the globe, a few of which we detail in this group of chapters. We'll also take a look at brainwashing experiments conducted by the United States and examine the technology behind spy planes and satellites.

The CIA's secretive nature caught up with it in the 1970s. **Part 4, "Watergate and Other Black Eyes,"** takes a look at Watergate and the bum rap the CIA received in the scandal that led to the downfall of the Nixon administration. The CIA deserved a few of its black eyes, and you'll find out about those, too. We'll also consider traitors and the ongoing problem of weeding out those who have betrayed their country and are giving or selling secrets to the enemy.

Finally, we conclude with **Part 5, "Keeping the Terror at Bay,"** a detailed look at the CIA's role in the war on terrorism. Hopefully, by the time you've finished this book you'll have a solid understanding of who works for the Central Intelligence Agency, what the agency does, and why it does it. You can't ask for better intelligence than that!

Wait, There's More!

Along the way you'll find the following boxes filled with secret and not-so-secret information about the CIA and intelligence in general.

Spookspeak

Like the rest of us, spooks have their own jargon and technical terms, which are defined here.

Top Secret
Okay, so maybe these "secrets" aren't so classified after all, but they're still worthy of note!

Tradecraft

These tips are straight out of "Being a Good Spy 101"— neat little tricks spooks use to confuse the opposition and get on with their jobs. Some of these may seem obvious, and others may sound foolish. Nevertheless, they are a compilation of little lessons learned in training, in the field, and from friends and associates who have survived by relying on such techniques.

McLean Says ...

Don't be troubled by the fact that fictitious CIA Officer McLean is at the Berlin tunnel on one page, hiding near a mountain in Afghanistan the next, and touring Saigon on the next. By attributing these real-life adventures to McLean, we can protect those operatives out in the field who have not yet come in from the cold.

Special Thanks to the Technical Reviewer

The Complete Idiot's Guide to the CIA was reviewed by an expert who double-checked the accuracy of what you'll learn here to help us ensure that this book gives you everything you need to know about the Central Intelligence Agency. Special thanks are extended to Major General Stephen Nichols, U.S. Army (Ret.).

Trademarks

All terms mentioned in this book that are known to be or are suspected of being trademarks or service marks have been appropriately capitalized. Alpha Books and Pearson Education, Inc., cannot attest to the accuracy of this information. Use of a term in this book should not be regarded as affecting the validity of any trademark or service mark.

Part 1

The World's Second Oldest Profession

Spy novels, big screen thrillers, and even occasional media reports often give people a distorted picture of the CIA. In the following chapters, we'll set the record straight. You'll find out what the CIA's role is, who it answers to, where it's located, and how it operates.

By the time you're ready to move on to Part 2, you'll be able to distinguish between information and intelligence; agents and officers; and the NSA, FBI, and DIA. Heck, you might even be ready to apply for a job at the CIA—which you'll also learn how to do in this part of the book!

Chapter 1

The CIA's Mission: Intelligence

In This Chapter

- ◆ How the CIA fulfills its mission
- ◆ Making sense of the many kinds of intelligence
- ◆ Learning about the intelligence cycle
- ◆ Putting intelligence reports to the test

It's not by chance that the United States government has very friendly relations with United Kingdom and Canada but is suspicious of China and Russia. Furthermore, policy makers didn't just wake up one morning and decide to be openly hostile towards Iraq and North Korea, yet on good terms with Pakistan. And although it sometimes seems like it, policy makers don't simply throw a dart to decide how much money to budget for military spending or the types of weapons and technology to research and develop.

In order to determine the most appropriate policy toward another country, to set the military budget, and to make thousands of other decisions that impact the nation's security, government officials must know what other countries are up to. It's only after they are aware of potential threats to the United States that they can determine what we need to do to protect ourselves and how to interact with other nations. For example, if officials suddenly discover that one of the nations with which the United States is on friendly terms is openly supporting groups that are hostile toward us, our policy toward that country will shift accordingly.

The CIA's mission is to support the United States in determining its national security policy. The CIA fulfills this mission by gathering intelligence on foreign soil that could impact our national security and undertaking other special activities at the request of the president. You'll find out how the CIA goes about fulfilling the first part of this mission—intelligence gathering—in this chapter. As for those other "special activities," check out Part 3.

Increase Your Intelligence IQ

Intelligence gathering is one of the primary functions of the CIA. You probably already have a pretty good sense of what intelligence is; however, when it relates to the CIA's job, we can define intelligence as information needed by our nation's leaders, such as the president, the National Security Council, and other policy makers, to keep our country safe.

Some of that intelligence is overt, or publicly available. The president, for example, doesn't have time to read newspapers from all over the world to find out about what's going on. It's the CIA's job to do that, and to keep the president informed of the things he should know. Other sources of overt intelligence include foreign broadcasts, periodicals, and books. Anyone who has access to the Internet and can read foreign languages (or find someone to translate them) more than likely has access to this kind of information.

McLean Says ...

There is no typical intelligence officer. We are operations officers, scientists, analysts, and a hundred other kinds of professionals. There is a natural and healthy tension between the multitude of disciplines as they interact to provide our government with the information it needs to succeed. Furthermore, the CIA isn't the only intelligence bureau in the federal government. Nearly every cabinet department has its own intelligence gathering function. Each department approaches intelligence from the perspective of its own needs. Coordination of these efforts can be a daunting task as each struggles to provide for perceived needs. The CIA isn't the largest nor the most complex, but is likely the most important.

Then there is covert intelligence—that is, secrets—that other countries won't share with the United States but that we want anyway. CIA operations officers collect such information in a number of ways, including relying on information from agents abroad, intercepting communications, taking satellite pictures, or even interviewing defectors. The average Joe isn't going to have access to this information, and the CIA and other countries want it that way. Some examples of covert intelligence might include the military budget of another country, the kinds of weapons it has under development, and whether it has access to materials to build nuclear weapons.

Tradecraft

During the American Revolution, General George Washington said in a letter to one of his officers, "The necessity of procuring good intelligence is apparent and need not be further urged. All that remains for me to add is that you keep the whole matter as secret as possible."

What the CIA Knows

Intelligence is categorized both by the nature of the information and how it is gathered. The CIA distinguishes between the following kinds of intelligence:

- **Current intelligence:** follows day-to-day events.

- **Estimative intelligence:** looks at what might be or what might happen.

- **Warning intelligence:** gives notice to our policy makers that something urgent might happen that may require their immediate attention.

- **Research intelligence:** an in-depth study of an issue.

- **Scientific and technical intelligence:** information on foreign technologies.

Top Secret

The CIA is allowed to spy inside the United States; however, the subject of the spying has to be foreign.

How the CIA Knows What It Knows

Intelligence agents gather intelligence in different ways, sometimes relying on the old stand-by—people, or what it calls "human assets"—and other times employing sophisticated technologies to get the job done. Read on to find out more about these intelligence-gathering methods.

Human Intelligence: Guys (and Gals) in Trench Coats

Human intelligence, called HUMINT in spookspeak, is information collected by means of human beings (agents, also known as assets, or informers). It involves relying on the skills of people trained in numerous areas, including linguistics, economics, and technology. For example, the CIA recruits and trains linguists who speak the language of countries where they will be assigned. Those operatives are then able to use their language skills to gather both overt and covert intelligence.

Top Secret
The CIA has always relied on human intelligence, although in recent years it has neglected this aspect of intelligence in favor of more technology-based intelligence gathering methods. Veteran CIA officers and others in the intelligence community realize that sky-high satellites have their value, but it takes people on the ground to look, listen, and get the feeling or intent of enemies and potential enemies. That requires recruiting and training linguists who speak the language of countries where they will be assigned. It takes time to learn languages and work operatives into place in foreign countries, but is essential to learn what the leaders in those nations may be thinking about doing that would harm the United States.

Electronic Intelligence: Plug-In and Know!

Electronic intelligence is information gathered using electronic listening devices, also called bugs. Contrary to popular belief, CIA officers can't place bugs anywhere they please. Before a bug is placed, Langley (CIA headquarters) has to sign off on it—and they refuse all the time. They also decide which type of device should be planted, and where. Bugs take many forms, including taps on phone, microphones in walls and furniture, recorders in hollow books in a library, or a minirecorder in a pocket.

Top Secret
People often worry that their phones might be tapped, but the CIA is much more likely to bug a room, where a greater percentage of the conversation can be heard. The CIA doesn't usually conduct such activities within the United States—their primary mission is overseas. The FBI conducts investigations within the United States.

Officers often place bugs in foreign embassies, because they are often a hotbed of intelligence activity. For example, if the CIA finds out that a country is going to change embassy buildings, agents might try to find out what building is going to be used as the new embassy, and place bugs throughout it before the embassy people move in.

More Acronyms: COMINT and SIGINT

When CIA gadgets and gizmos are used to intercept a target's communications, this is called Communications Intelligence—or COMINT. COMINT overlaps with SIGINT, or Signals Intelligence, which is knowledge gained from the interception of a target's electronic emissions, transmitted communications, radar systems, etc. Whereas electronic intelligence allows us to listen in on things that we ordinarily would not be able to hear *through electronic means*, COMINT's primary function is to intercept a subject's electronic communications.

Protecting Our Own Secrets: Counterintelligence

The CIA isn't just involved in gathering intelligence, though. It also spends a lot of time preventing others from learning the United States' secrets. They do this by either making sure that our secrets are very difficult to discover, or by impeding the efforts of those who want to uncover the secrets. This is called counterintelligence, the art of keeping others from spying on you.

A lot the individual pieces of information the CIA gathers is pretty mundane or otherwise uninteresting on its own. But when all of the pieces of the intelligence puzzle are put together, the resulting "picture" can provide policy makers with crucial intelligence and help them steer the United States over the ever-shifting sands of international relations. The CIA puts together the various pieces of the intelligence puzzle by following the steps of what they call the intelligence cycle.

Spookspeak

Moles are bad in people's lawns. They are worse in the world of intelligence. A mole is someone who gets inside an enemy's intelligence or security system and, for whatever reason, makes that information available to those who shouldn't have it.

The Intelligence Cycle

The intelligence cycle is the development of raw information into intelligence-for-use. There are five steps: planning and direction, collection, processing, all source analysis and production, and dissemination.

Let's look at those steps one at a time:

Phase 1: Planning and Direction

The first phase of the intelligence cycle is called planning and direction. It begins when policy makers request intelligence information, also called tasking, from the CIA. Once the CIA has a task, officials need to figure out the best way to manage the mission and identify the kinds of data they need to provide to the person or group who made the request. So before they actually begin to gather information, they determine what they already know about the topic and, just as importantly, what they don't know. The whole process depends on guidance from public officials (see Chapter 7, regarding the House Permanent Select Committee on Intelligence.)

Spookspeak

If an agent's real affiliation is discovered, it is said that his **cover is blown**.

Phase 2: Collection

Collection is the phase of the intelligence cycle that most people think of when they imagine what the CIA does. Once the CIA determines the kind of information it needs, the raw information must be collected. It is from this raw data—both overt and covert—that finished intelligence will be produced.

Spookspeak

Technical collection is information gathered via electronics and satellite photography.

Phase 3: Processing

The processing phase of the intelligence cycle involves taking the vast amount of information CIA officers collect and converting it into a form usable by analysts. This phase can involve decrypting encoded information, translating material into English, describing satellite photos, and summarizing lengthy documents.

Phase 4: All Source Analysis and Production

The fourth phase involves the conversion of basic processed information—the translations, decrypted documents, and so on—into what's called "finished intelligence." All available data is integrated, evaluated, and analyzed. Much of the information will be fragmentary or contradictory and so experts weigh the quality of sources during this phase.

When possible, previous experience in similar situations is used to make predictions, or forecast developments, based on the data. Finally, the information is packaged into an intelligence report providing the information requested in the original task.

Spookspeak

If an agent is deliberately sacrificed by his own agency to protect an operation, it is said that the agent has been **burned**.

Phase 5: Dissemination

Finally, the finished intelligence report is distributed to the interested party. If the report is useful to the policy maker, it will influence future national security policy and, hopefully, help keep the United States safe from attack by enemies.

A Glowing Report from Afghanistan

Now that you know how the CIA produces intelligence and what it does with the information once it's been gathered, let's watch some raw data go through the intelligence cycle. As is often the case, the raw information in this real-life example looks very different from the finished intelligence.

Part of the mission of the intelligence officers in Afghanistan was to search all Al Qaeda/Taliban sites to find out exactly what they were up to. One of the biggest fears on the part of the United States and its allies was that Al Qaeda was developing nuclear weapons, and so officers wanted to find out if this was true and, if so, how close they had come to developing them.

After clearing the Taliban Ministry of Agriculture in Kabul and a site at an Al Qaeda compound in the Kandahar region, officers and soldiers searched the sites. They obtained raw data in the form of canisters filled with radioactive substances at both sites. Of course, the immediate assumption was that these were materials for building a nuclear weapon. The material was taken back to the United States, where the third and fourth phases of the intelligence cycle kicked in. The canisters were carefully analyzed, and the information obtained was considered in relation to what else was known about the Taliban and Al Qaeda.

By the time the analysts were through with the material, they drew a very different conclusion

Spookspeak

If you want to sound like you know what you are talking about, because you do, then remember that a CIA **officer** is a staff employee of the Agency, whereas an **agent** is an outsider hired by the officer to spy. The agent is often a citizen of the country being spied upon. Another term for agent is **asset**.

from the one first considered. Analysts found that the material could not be used to build nuclear weapons. As a matter of fact, Osama bin Laden probably thought he was getting the raw material he needed to build nukes, but had been ripped off. Analysts concluded that the radioactive substance in the canisters was counterfeit nuclear material, with just enough radioactivity to fool a Geiger counter—and Osama bin Laden!

Top Secret

Intelligence rumors intrigue the public. One that surfaced after September 11 may surface again during upcoming Congressional investigations. Insider scuttlebutt is that a French-Algerian had been captured in Boston the week before September 11 with piles of Boeing flight manuals and construction documents. The French identified him as a bad guy—probably a leader of top suicide mission volunteers. Word has it that this information was misplaced or overlooked. Could action on it have thwarted September 11? That and other hard questions undoubtedly will be asked during the Congressional hearings. Stay tuned. You can bet all spies will!

Tradecraft

CIA analysts say that the vast majority of the trade in "nuclear materials" is initiated by swindlers. In its own way, that's very good news.

Bin Laden appeared to have been duped by black-market weapons swindlers. The analysts in their intelligence report, however, resisted an urge to say that this meant that bin Laden did not have nuclear weapons—and the finding certainly bolstered the theory that bin Laden was attempting to purchase weapons of mass destruction.

International Spy Museum

If you are fascinated by the intelligence-gathering process, then check out the recently opened International Spy Museum in Washington, D.C. It is located at 800 F Street NW, adjacent to FBI headquarters in a block of five buildings.

"We think that it's a good idea to better inform the public on the true mission of the CIA and intelligence gathering. Most of what's out there is Hollywood's perception and what you read in novels. The vast majority is not true," agency spokesman Tom Crispell said. "I think it will give individuals a more realistic understanding of what the intelligence business is all about."

Among the features is a section on celebrity spies, like Moe Berg, the major league baseball player who worked for the OSS; Josephine Baker, the American singer who worked for the French Resistance; and Julia Child, who cooked for the Nazis with her ears wide open.

The Least You Need to Know

- Intelligence is evaluated information needed by our nation's leaders to keep our country safe.

- Human intelligence, also called HUMINT, is intelligence collected by humans (agents or informers).

- Intelligence officials do their best to keep other countries from finding out their secret information by providing counterintelligence.

- The intelligence cycle is the development of raw information into intelligence-for-use.

Chapter 2

A Who's Who of the CIA

In This Chapter

- ◆ Where it's located
- ◆ Who runs the operation
- ◆ How it's organized
- ◆ What it does

Want to find out how many people work for the CIA or what its budget is? You're out of luck—that's classified information.

You see, the CIA doesn't want other countries to know how extensive it is or what it's capable of doing. For example, if the CIA published its budget every year, and one year there was a 50 percent increase in spending, that would sound off alarms in intelligence agencies around the world. China, Iraq, and anyone else who's interested (and believe me, a lot of people are interested) would know that some new operation is in the works or a major research initiative is under way. So, the less anyone knows about the CIA, the better.

That said, we do have a pretty good idea about how big the CIA actually is, and how much money they spend. There are some things that are just too hard to keep a secret in an open society like the United States. In this chapter, you'll get the scoop on how the CIA is organized and the kind of work they do.

Spying on the CIA

The CIA employs about 22,000 people full-time, and many more than that if you count contract employees, who are the intelligence version of temps. They won't acknowledge the total number of employees officially, but this figure is probably accurate based on Congressional Oversight Committee and budget records. The agency maintains stations in more than 130 countries, but the vast majority of its employees actually remain stateside. In fact, 85 percent of them work in the Washington, D.C. area. Most have offices in the old and new CIA buildings in McLean, Virginia, a.k.a. Langley. A variety of other buildings around Washington, D.C. also house CIA offices. (For more on CIA headquarters, see Chapter 6.)

The CIA needs so many people because it doesn't just spy. It also has to determine what and who needs to be spied on. It needs people to interpret the information its intelligence officers have provided. It needs people to make sure the right agents are in the right place to do the spying. And it needs people to make sure that the company stays on the cutting edge of technology. All this, without going over budget.

Here is a quick look at the structure of the Central Intelligence Agency. The Director of Central Intelligence oversees four directorates, or divisions, of the CIA:

+ Operations

+ Intelligence

+ Science and Technology

+ Administration

Top Secret
Because of a lawsuit, the CIA released its overall annual budget for 1997 and 1998, the only two years it ever did so. The budgets for those years were $26.6 billion and $26.7 billion, respectively.

In addition to the four directorates, the fifth functioning section of the CIA is the Office of the Director of Central Intelligence. Let's visit that office first.

How the CIA is organized.

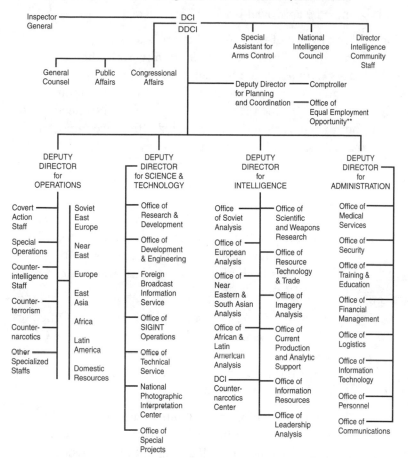

Director of Central Intelligence Command Responsibilities*

*DCI Counterintelligence Center, DCI Counterterrorist Center and DCI Counternarcotics Center

**Also serves as Special Assistant to the DCI for Affirmative Employment

The Man with All the Secrets: The Office of the Director

You've just entered the office of a very powerful person. The Director of Central Intelligence (DCI) is not just the head of the Central Intelligence Agency. His role is actually much bigger than that. He oversees the entire U.S. intelligence community, so is therefore the supervisor of the National Security Agency, the military intelligence services, and the intelligence-gathering wing of the FBI. He is also in charge of many interagency groups and committees. These include the National Foreign Intelligence Board, which includes representatives from all of the U.S. intelligence agencies (for a thorough look at the intelligence community, check out Chapter 4). The

DCI is hired and fired by the president of the United States. Before a president's choice may serve as DCI, he must be approved by the U.S. Senate.

Portions of the CIA don't belong to any of the four directorates and are part of the office of the director. These include the Intelligence Community Staff, the National Intelligence Council (which does estimates), the Special Assistant for Arms Control, the Comptroller, the Congressional Affairs Committee, Public Affairs Committee, and the Office of the General Counsel, which is the CIA's legal office. No need to go into most of these sections, but the lawyer's and public affairs' offices are important aspects of the DCI's office that you should know about.

Are You Really a Lawyer, or Is That Just Your Cover?

The legal division of the CIA is known as the Agency's Office of General Counsel. Consisting of about 90 attorneys and their staff, the OGC advises the Director of Central Intelligence on all legal matters relating to his role as head of the CIA, and his role as head of the U.S. Intelligence Community.

Thus, the General Counsel, who heads the Office of General Counsel, is both the top lawyer at the CIA and the DCI's Community Management Staff, which helps the DCI oversee the other agencies in the U.S. Intelligence Community.

The Office of General Counsel also advises CIA officers and employees who may need legal advice when it comes to conducting U.S. intelligence operations.

The OGC also handles numerous tasks one would expect attorneys to do, such as handling the agency's contracts and reviewing foreign and international laws.

Because the CIA, in order to do its job, must sometimes break laws—but only the laws of other countries—a lawyer working for the company can have some pretty tricky work trying to determine what a CIA officer can and can't do. The legal offices at the CIA now have 125 employees, and 60 of them are lawyers.

> **Tradecraft**
>
> Because the CIA is a foreign intelligence agency, not a law enforcement agency like the FBI, it is forbidden to make arrests or to conduct investigations of domestic subjects on domestic soil. That is the FBI's job.

> **Top Secret**
>
> There's one division of the CIA you can't join unless you meet very specific criteria (hint: you need four legs): The CIA Canine Corps. It was first created in January 1991, when a terrorist attack on the agency was feared because of U.S. involvement in the Persian Gulf War. A squad of bomb-sniffing pups have been on duty ever since.

The Office of General Counsel, which once spoke only when spoken to, can now be a pain to officers who are trying to break the rules, as the office now has lawyers assigned to all of the directorates.

Tradecraft

Ever since 1990, the CIA's inspector general has been in a position of power nearly equal to that of the DCI, some people believe. The inspector general, like the Director, needs to be nominated by the president and confirmed by the senate. The inspector general inspects, audits, and investigates CIA activities to make sure that everyone is spending as little money as possible and following all CIA rules.

Publicizing Privacy?

For such a large organization, the CIA devotes very few of its human resources to public relations, but that makes sense when you consider that most of what the CIA does is a secret. The CIA division that communicates with the media, the general public, and the CIA's own work force is called the Office of Public Affairs. The PR department, if you will, has only been around since 1990.

Only two Office of Public Affairs employees are in charge of responding to press requests. Public Affairs personnel also scour newspapers and broadcasts for items concerning the CIA, and this is also the office that reads and sometimes edits all published information coming out of the CIA.

The Director of the Office of Public Affairs serves as spokesperson for not only the CIA, but also the U.S. Intelligence Community. He or she reports directly to the DCI, provides public affairs support to the Director of Central Intelligence and his deputy in both their CIA and intelligence community roles, and is their senior advisor for media and public policy issues.

The Spy Guys: Directorate of Operations

Formerly known as the Directorate for Plans, the Directorate of Operations (DO) is the part of the CIA that does the actual spying. Sometimes referred to as Clandestine Services by those on the inside, it puts officers into the field to recruit agents and gather information.

Spookspeak

Operations, in the vernacular of the shadows, always means clandestine, or secret, operations unless otherwise noted.

The DO employs about 5,000 of the agency's 22,000 full-time employees. Operations (or ops, for short) officers clearly have the CIA's most dangerous job. They travel to or live in foreign countries and try to find out things the countries' officials don't want them to know. Sort of like being an unwanted houseguest, except it can get you killed … or worse.

Officers in the Field

Officers in the field—say, in Afghanistan—recruit agents from among the locals. These agents spy on the Taliban or on Al Qaeda and return to the CIA officer with information, which is later compiled with other information to become polished intelligence.

Contrary to popular belief, ops officers cannot recruit at will. They select the people they are considering as agents carefully, and they okay their every move with headquarters. Officers give HQ everything they know about prospective agents and HQ runs a check, called a trace, to see if the agency has information indicating whether they are a good risk or not.

If everything looks good, HQ okays the subject, and the officer approaches him or her, usually offering money in exchange for information.

Weeding Out Double Agents

The CIA isn't a very trusting place. The primary reason for not using a potential agent in the field is that the CIA suspects he or she is a double agent—that is, they are already working on the other side.

Top Secret

The United States' intelligence operation is overseen by two panels that report directly to the president. One is a citizen's panel called the President's Foreign Intelligence Advisory Board, and the other is the President's Intelligence Oversight Board, a three-person panel consisting of nongovernment people appointed by the president.

If the potential agent seems overly eager to supply information, the CIA will be particularly suspicious. Experience has taught the CIA that eager beavers are sometimes being paid by the enemy to give false information.

Tradecraft

The CIA learned the hard way that polygraph machines—so-called lie detectors—can be beaten. The CIA used polygraph examinations in the past to try and weed out double agents, but they had to give up the practice when they found that almost all of their agents inside Cuba who had passed lie detector tests were actually also working for Castro. Because the agents had been taught not to believe in the polygraph's ability to read their minds, they did not have the sudden jump in nerves when they lied, and the machine failed to screen them out.

One Paperclip, Two Paperclip ...

There is no contest: The CIA keeps a closer watch on the dollars and cents it spends than almost any other U.S. tax-dollar-financed organization. Just because the public isn't privy to the CIA's budget numbers does not mean that the agency has a blank check to work with. The struggle for a sufficient budget is ongoing and all efforts are made to see that the CIA accomplishes as much as possible with its given budget.

Getting an adequate amount of money out of Congress hasn't always been the CIA's forte, so it remains the sort of company that counts its paperclips. The accounting system is huge. It's called the Evaluation and Plans Staff, and it's part of DO.

Analysis: The Directorate of Intelligence

The Directorate of Intelligence (DI) is the analytical arm of the CIA, and as such it is charged with, as the CIA puts it, "providing timely, accurate, and objective intelligence analysis on the full range of national security threats and foreign policy issues facing the United States." It is also the smallest of the Directorates, with only about 3,000 employees.

Again quoting the agency, "the DI provides integrated, multidisciplinary analysis on key foreign countries, regional conflicts, and issues that transcend national boundaries such as terrorism, weapons proliferation, and narcotics trafficking." It has unique analytic capabilities that exist nowhere else inside or out of government.

Tradecraft

Have several pair of glasses, each of a different style. Change them regularly. By doing so, you change your appearance, making it very difficult for people to describe your face accurately.

The DI provides analyzed intelligence for people responsible for setting national security policy, who the DI refers to as its consumers, including the following:

◆ The President

◆ Vice President

◆ Cabinet members

◆ National Security Council members

◆ Many subcabinet officials

◆ Several Congressional committees and specialized government departments, including the FBI, U.S. Customs Service, and the Drug Enforcement Administration

The directorate responds to the requests of its consumers, no matter how specific. The intelligence supplied by the agency (which, keeping with the consumer metaphor the intelligence community has adopted, they often called a "product") might come in the form of briefings, quick-reaction papers, or in-depth analyses. Diplomatic negotiations and military operations are also apt to be supported by the efforts of the DI.

The Directorate of Intelligence analyzes all of the information gathered by the agency.

Top Secret
Eighty percent of the intelligence gathered by the DI is overt.

Keeping the President in the Intelligence Loop

The Office of Current Production and Analytic Support, a division of the DI, produces what is known as the President's Daily Brief. Since its inception, the CIA has given the President a daily written brief of what is new in intelligence around the world. The brief has become increasingly sophisticated over the years. At first, the president was given a summary, then this was expanded into something called the National Intelligence Daily—which was disseminated to the president and 250 other government officials who were among the in-crowd.

McLean Says ...

The average President's Daily Brief is 10 pages long and is laid out like a newsppaper, with a combination of text and illustrations. The most important news is on the front page. Who, what, where, when, and why go on top, followed by a steady unfolding of detail, from most to least in importance.

During the Kennedy Administration, the National Intelligence Daily was rearranged, made to read more like a daily newspaper, and renamed the President's Daily Brief—or, more commonly, the PDB. Think of it as a top-secret version of *USA Today*.

Because it is in charge of keeping the president abreast of the latest developments, the Office of Production and Analytic Support is also the CIA's news center, where tabs are kept on global events.

On the Cutting-Edge: The Directorate of Science and Technology

The Directorate of Science and Technology (DS&T) is the arm of the CIA in charge of technical operations and tradecraft. In that capacity, it has a hand in all phases of the intelligence process.

The scientists and engineers of DS&T, according to the Agency, "create and implement technologies and analytic tools that can close gaps in the access, processing, and exploitation of information." It is this directorate that uses satellites to spy. We will be learning more about the work of DS&T in Chapter 5.

The DS&T is partnered with other U.S. government organizations, major universities and other institutions of learning, and private industry to stay one step ahead of the global information revolution.

Tradecraft

In the hit single "Secret Agent Man" Johnny Rivers sang, "They're giving me a number and taking away my name"— but this is not the way it works. CIA officers usually use their real names. It is their professional affiliations that are changed.

Top Secret

During the Cold War, the DS&T didn't just create technology to spy on the Russians from space. They also worked on spying on them from the bottom of the ocean. The Glommar Explorer was a ship built by the CIA designed to raise a Russian submarine that had sunk three-miles deep off the coast of California in 1968. The operation was not a complete success.

The sub broke in two when being pulled to the surface, and much of it settled back down onto the bottom. It was not a total loss, however. In the operation, the CIA recovered Soviet code machines, parts of missiles, and portions of nuclear-tipped torpedoes.

The DS&T is the portion of the CIA in charge of using developed technology—as well as inventing new technologies—that can be used for intelligence-gathering functions. These inventions and techniques may collect, process, translate, or disseminate information.

The directorate directly supports the National Reconnaissance Office, which has been assigned to meet U.S. government needs through spaceborne reconnaissance by designing, building, and operating satellite spy systems through their Office of Development and Engineering.

Pussycats and Gerbils

During the 1960s, one of the DS&T's primary assignments was to find a way to get surveillance bugs inside the Kremlin, where several key Soviet government officers were located. They learned that cats were allowed to wander the Kremlin's halls—presumably to eliminate a rodent problem—so the clever scientists at the DS&T, for a time at least, planned to implant surveillance bugs in cats. The bugged cats would then be released in the Kremlin area with the hopes that they would get inside the building. The plan was eventually scrapped as impractical, as it would have been impossible to know where the cats were in the Kremlin at any given moment. Nor was there a way to keep the cats in the vicinity of people who were discussing sensitive subjects.

The CIA went so far as to actually operate on one cat and implant a recording device in it. The cat, unfortunately, was run over and killed not long after that, the listening device still functioning inside its body.

The plan may seem a tad silly, but it seems downright sober compared to a plan that British intelligence once tossed around. The Brits considered training gerbils as counterespionage agents. Gerbils, it was believed, could smell the change in the scent of a human's sweat, caused by secretions in the adrenaline gland, when a person was lying. Therefore, a gerbil could become a lie detector that would make a polygraph obsolete.

Tradecraft

To demonstrate how fiction, especially comedy, imitates life, in 1966 the British released a comedy movie called *The Spy With a Cold Nose*, about a dog that is used to record Russian communications.

The gerbils could also work, it was thought, at security checkpoints, where relaxed people could be distinguished by the gerbils from those who were in the throes of an adrenaline rush. Trouble was, although the gerbils could smell the change in scent fine, they had trouble telling the scientists that.

Tradecraft _____

The use of animals in spy work has not always been silly. Carrier pigeons were used to deliver messages extensively during World War II. British intelligence referred to the birds as "pigeon agents." The British thought Hitler was using the pigeons as well. During the days when the British expected an invasion of England by Germany would commence any day, the Brits were convinced that carrier pigeons were being used by the Nazis on mainland Europe to communicate with Nazi agents inside England. To prevent this, the British intelligence services developed a fleet of falcons.

Falcons eat pigeons. So the falcons were assigned to cover the coast of England and intercept any pigeons coming inland from over the channel. Did it work? Who knows? But there were undoubtedly "dogfights" over England during World War II that didn't have any humans involved.

Office of SIGINT Operations

Silly ideas from a long time ago aside, the DS&T applies state-of-the-art technologies to support the collection of vital intelligence in a clandestine manner; and, last but not least, they research, develop, and apply advanced technologies that provide the nation a significant intelligence advantage. The Office of SIGINT (short for Signal Intelligence) Operations, a component of DS&T, uses radar and state of the art sensors to pick up radio transmissions and electromagnetic waves from unfriendly countries and groups, as well as details of any missile tests that might be occurring in a hot spot.

The DS&T is the office of the CIA that works most closely with the National Security Agency. While the NSA does a lot of SIGINT work as well, their duties are more general: to maintain, as best as possible, global surveillance. The CIA's SIGINT office has more specific missions, usually designed to support particular CIA operations.

Office of Technical Services

The Office of Technical Services, a subsection of the Directorate of Science and Technology, comes up with all of those great spook toys. (You'll learn more about the Gadgets and Gizmos of the CIA in Chapter 9.) They are in charge of providing disguises for agents, too. If the CIA needs something bugged, officers from the Office of Technical Services do the job. If you need a pickpocket or a safecracker, this would be the place to look as well.

A Picture's Worth a Thousand Words

The National Photographic Interpretation Center (NPIC), also within the DS&T, is where reconnaissance photos, no matter what the source, are brought so that they can be analyzed. Experts in image interpretation (they know which circles are bomb silos and which are barn silos, for example) examine the photos with what amounts to state-of-the-art magnifying glasses. Even back in the 1950's, good photo officers could spot real tanks from fakes, identify the caliber of artillery pieces, and give a fairly accurate assay of local battlefield conditions for commanding officers.

> **Tradecraft**
>
> If you want to wear a disguise that involves fake skin covering the face, or any prosthetic part that needs to be glued on, be sure to use a material that allows your skin to breathe. If you don't, such disguises will become uncomfortably hot no matter what the weather.

Today, with satellites and much more modern camera equipment, the people doing photo interpretation are armed with exceptional high-tech equipment. Back in the Civil War, soldiers with telescopes in hot air balloons watched for enemy troop movements. What would they think if they saw the CIA Photo Interpretation Center today?

The CIA Is Listening, Even If No One Else Is

Housed in Washington, D.C., the Foreign Broadcast Information Service, also part of the DS&T, listens in to all radio and television broadcasts throughout the world. Broadcasts for almost 50 countries are monitored. It's a funny job.

Watchers and listeners have to sit through a lot of *Gilligan's Island* reruns in Chinese and *I Love Lucy* episodes dubbed in Iraqi before they come up with overt intelligence that might be useful.

> **Top Secret**
>
> The Directorate of Science and Technology was also responsible for the spy planes that played a large part in the Cold War: the U-2 and the SR-71 Blackbird. (For more about spying from above, see Chapter 15.)

Office of Special Projects

The Office of Special Projects, within the DS&T, is in charge of determining the location of every nuclear facility or device in the world. They have other tasks as well, which remain classified—the "special projects" after which they are named—but the bulk of their work has to do with the nuclear proliferation.

The Publishing Wing

The CIA's publishing division, which functions independently from any directorate, is known as the Center for the Study of Intelligence.

The CSI sponsors independent research and publishes books, including several on the Cold War. It also publishes oral histories and reference works on CIA history and the history of intelligence more generally.

CSI promotes public understanding of intelligence. It provides a forum for practitioners and scholars, makes important research widely available, commemorates major historical events in the intelligence world, and interacts with academic specialists. Its university programs encourage and improve the teaching of intelligence production and sponsors a CIA Officers-in-Residence program on college campuses.

CIA headquarters in McLean, Virginia, has its own printing plant. The plant is equipped to print in any language and in any alphabet. It is from here that the agency's top-secret documents are printed and where, each day, the written version of the President's Daily Briefing is prepared. In the basement is a smaller printing plant where fake birth certificates, passports, and other documents are prepared.

It is also from this printing press that the CIA produces its propaganda. During the Cold War the CIA propaganda program focused on sending books to the Soviet Union offering the American viewpoint of the world and Cold War history.

Another printing job the CIA regularly ran during the Cold War years was a list of Soviet military hardware, along with the amount in dollars that the CIA was willing to pay for it.

This program worked very well. By disseminating this list in key places, the CIA was able to buy a Russian missile during the Vietnam War. Because of this, the United States was able to render that type of missile useless by disrupting its guidance system.

Top Secret
Many articles originally published in *Studies in Intelligence* have now been declassified and are available in book form. Edited by H. Bradford Westerfield, and published by Yale University Press, the book is called *Inside CIA's Private World*. It contains articles written between 1955–1992.

Top Secret
All CIA intra-agency communications are according to importance. From most crucial to read-it-when-you-get-a-chance, those classifications are: ◆ Critical ◆ Flash ◆ Immediate ◆ Priority ◆ Routine

Office of Military Affairs

The CIA's Office of Military Affairs (OMA) is in charge of making sure that all U.S. military operations receive the maximum possible support from the agency. Employees from all directorates, as well as all branches of the service, are apt to work in this office.

Spookspeak

Psy-War is short for Psychological Warfare.

OMA supports military exercises and sends representatives of the DCI to advise the commanders in chief of the major unified commands, and the faculty of major military universities, as to how the CIA can best serve their needs.

The Office Manager: Directorate of Administration

The Directorate of Administration, or DA, functions as the CIA's office manager. It makes sure that everyone has enough paper clips and that their phones are working. In terms of number of personnel, it is the largest of the directorates. The DA has about 9,000 full-time employees. When there is a world crisis, the DA is the least effected of the directorates. However, that doesn't mean that the DA is devoid of intrigue. On the contrary, it contains the Office of Security, the molehunting section of the CIA, where the counterespionage takes place. (You'll learn more about people who have been caught attempting to spy on the United States in Chapter 17.)

Allowed to Work Domestically

The DA is also the only directorate in which the employees are allowed to investigate U.S. citizens. That's because it's the DA's job, through their Office of Security, to run background checks on prospective CIA employees. The DA has also been known to work with the FBI on espionage cases.

The DA is in charge of internal security. The guard at the front gate works for the DA. The night watchman with hi-beam flashlight—and many TV screens—works for the DA.

> **Tradecraft**
>
> Be a good writer. And I don't mean be Ernest Hemingway or Robert Frost. I mean be a good communicator. A misunderstood report can sink an operation. Written communication is essential to any spy. When an officer in the field believes he has learned something important, he files an intelligence report. The report consists of a cover page upon which he puts his cryptonym—his code name—and the source of his information, and a second page, which contains the info, along with the officer's best estimate of its reliability. In CIA headquarters, that info is then weighed and, if it is deemed appropriate, action is taken.

Pest Control

The DA is also the home of intelligence's version of the exterminator. These are the guys and gals who sweep rooms for bugs before an important meeting, to make sure that no one is listening in.

The DA's *debugging* crews do *sweeps* both in the Langley headquarters and in CIA outposts elsewhere in the world.

Within the Office of Security is the Technical Security Division, which not only does the debugging for the CIA, but also installs white-noise machines in CIA headquarters and other pertinent locations. The machines create a steady sound, nonannoying to people who are near the machine, but designed so that any bugs that might still be in place will hear only the white noise, and not the intelligence-laden conversations that might be taking place in the room.

> **Spookspeak**
>
> A **bug** is a small electronic listening or recording device that can be planted in a room and monitored from elsewhere. It is called a bug because of its diminutive size. To **debug** means to remove electronic bugs from a location. A **sweep** is a search for bugs. Embassies and CIA offices overseas must be swept regularly to debug them.

The Technical Security Division also is responsible for making sure that all of the CIA's security systems are state-of-the-art. They install the locks for buildings and safes, and the alarms.

McLean Says ...

To make sure that the buggers, if you'll pardon the expression, and the debuggers stay on the top of their game, they play games at CIA HQ. The buggers plant bugs and the debuggers try to find them. The two teams work independently of one another much of the time and are not quick to share their secrets with the other team, such is the competitive nature of the bug games. Another reason to have the games is to keep the debuggers busy. No non-CIA bug has ever been found inside CIA headquarters.

I've heard some tall tales of these games, most likely embellished. One relates to dozens of olives and onions being spread around the cafeteria to confound the debuggers.

Another tale concerns some pet toys that let out odd sounds designed to delight animals but drive sweepers bonkers. It took a while for the debuggers to figure out where the intermittent sounds came from. As has been said, the only difference between men and boys is the price of their toys.

Countering Drugs, Terror, and Nuclear Proliferation

Three unique centers exist within the Directorate of Administration:

♦ **The Counternarcotics Center** uses the same type of satellite surveillance used in times of war, to spot coca fields and smuggling ships.

Top Secret

Following the Lockerbie plane crash that killed 259 people in Scotland in 1988, it was the counterterrorism center that put together the U.S. investigation, and was responsible for linking the sabotage to high-ranking Libyan officials, including Qaddafi's brother-in-law!

♦ **The Counterterrorism Center** tracks terrorist activity throughout the world. It was started by William Casey during the 1980s and has an incredible technological ability. For example, using a satellite it can trace a terrorist's bank account and stop financial transactions.

♦ **The Center to Combat Proliferation** dedicates its activities to preventing the spread of nuclear weapons to nations that do not already possess them.

Administration also houses the Office of Logistics, which makes travel and shelter arrangements for agents no matter where they are in the world. It wouldn't do for our man in Berlin to sleep on a park bench.

Office of Financial Management

The Office of Financial Management, part of the DA, is in charge of cash flow for operations. They make sure that officers and agents cannot be traced through the source of their paycheck. They do this by laundering the money, just as the Mafia might do, funneling it through on-paper-only corporations, so that it doesn't appear to have originated with the agency.

Spooks in White

The doctors—that is, the physicians—at the CIA work in the Office of Medical Services, which is, of course, in charge of the health of CIA employees. Most CIA employees go to an OMS doctor. Employees may receive both physical and psychiatric treatment here.

The OMS doctors have been known to work as medical detectives with stories deserving of a weekly TV show. The spooks in white have been known to diagnose illnesses in foreign leaders from hair and feces samples provided by agents in the field. (Hey, the intelligence business isn't always pretty.)

School Days

The CIA's internal education system is also part of Administration. Someone has to teach people how to be spies, and the DA's Office of Training and Education has them. There is a training camp—spy school—in Virginia, where this office holds its courses.

McLean Says ...

The spy school at Camp Perry, also known locally and among spooks as "The Farm," was an open secret for years. Actually, I stumbled onto it by mistake. I was headed back to New Jersey during a two-week leave from the Army and was driving from Fayetteville, North Carolina, where Fort Bragg was located, up through the Virginia countryside. With military service winding down, I thought I should check out job prospects in and around Washington, D.C. Making a wrong turn, I was immediately stopped by strangely dressed guards, so I flashed my Army ID card and Security Badge. That made things worse.

Later, after a lot of explaining that I had flunked map reading 101, I was heading on to D.C. Seems there was some special project going on, or as the military liked to call them, maneuvers. Wasn't anything like I had ever seen at that point—odd uniforms, civilian clothes, nervous people and they were a bit loose with handguns. So much for the secrecy of The Farm.

The Office of Training and Education also publishes the CIA's internal organ, *Studies in Intelligence*, which keeps employees abreast of the latest developments in intelligence. There is also an annual unclassified edition of this journal as well.

The DA also operates the CIA's airlines, Air America. The Office of Personnel is the CIA's head hunting department. They recruit personnel, sometimes through recruiting campaigns on college campuses. The DA's history staff keeps the complete history of the CIA. When an officer retires, they are encouraged to give their memoirs to the history staff. And the Office of Communications is in charge of getting messages, coded and otherwise, to personnel around the globe. The DA is a busy place.

The Least You Need to Know

- The CIA is made up of four directorates and the office of the director.

- The four directorates are Operations, Administration, Science and Technology, and Intelligence.

- In general, operations gathers the intelligence, Intelligence interprets it, Administration manages the office, and Science and Technology provides the equipment.

- Some compartments of the CIA are not within a directorate, but directly beneath the office of the director.

Chapter 3

A Tour of CIA Headquarters

In This Chapter

◆ Finding Langley (good luck)

◆ What HQ looks like

◆ The CIA's private museum

◆ A high-tech intelligence library

Some folks find it humorous that there are road signs directing motorists to the CIA's supposedly secret headquarters in Virginia. You know:

CIA

Next Right

½ mile

Is It the CIA or Burma Shave?

In the early 1960s, Attorney General Robert Kennedy thought it was ridiculous, too.

So the signs came down for a while, but the cat was already out of the bag as far as the location of CIA headquarters was concerned. Commercial airline pilots had been known to point the complex out to their passengers:

"And on the right side you can see America's most secret compound, headquarters of the mysterious CIA. Flight attendants, please prepare for landing at Dulles."

It didn't make any difference if there were signs or not—a lot of people knew where the CIA was housed. Furthermore, without the signs, people who legitimately needed to find CIA headquarters sometimes struggled—so the signs went back up.

The CIA road signs frequently have to be replaced because sticky-fingered motorists want them for their garage walls.

McLean Says ...

KGB agents, as well as domestic organizations out to harm the CIA, used to stakeout CIA headquarters' front entrance. When cars went in they would write down the license plate numbers.

Then they'd call the Motor Vehicle Bureau and find out who owned those cars. A radical group exposed many individuals working for the CIA during the 1970s by learning their identities in this manner and publishing their names.

It's as easy as ever to copy the numbers off license plates, but identifying CIA personnel in this fashion is much more difficult these days because Motor Vehicle Bureaus have become a lot more tight-lipped. They won't give out the names of car owners who have particular license plate numbers—and you can bet that CIA officers are among those whose Motor Vehicle data is top secret.

So Where the Hell Is Langley?

Where is CIA headquarters?

Lots of people know the answer to that one, right? Langley, Virginia. It's common knowledge. So, here's a challenge. Go get a map and find Langley, Virginia, on it. You can't do it, can you? That's because Langley doesn't actually exist. Creepy, huh?

But, just because Langley isn't on the map doesn't mean that it was never on the map. If you find a map that is old enough, Langley should be there. It did exist, on the outskirts of Washington, but was absorbed by the town next to it in 1910.

McLean Says ...

Some friends and I were discussing the first World Trade Center bombing and wondering why the trials and information obtained hadn't alerted authorities to the September 11 potential. Fact is, that may be traced to the FBI's failure to translate all materials captured in the first Trade Center bombing.

According to reliable sources, the FBI only had one Arabic translator available at the time, and it would have been very costly—up to $250,000—to out-source translations of all the materials. That lack is also seen by veteran intelligence officers as a crippling deficiency in other areas: diplomatic, military, intelligence, and counterintelligence, which covers domestic situations.

The CIA's headquarters are located in suburban Washington, D.C., in McLean, Virginia. The complex, officially called The George Bush Center for Intelligence, is more popularly known as Langley, which was the name of the nineteenth century estate that once occupied the land.

Top Secret
Langley, Virginia, was originally an estate owned by members of Robert E. Lee's family.

Lovely Langley

CIA HQ is situated on the west bank of the Potomac River on approximately 225½ acres of land and looks a lot like a college campus. The two main buildings consist of an original cast concrete structure, which was built in the 1950s, and a newer glass and steel building built in the 1980s. There is even a 7,000-seat auditorium—the round structure looks like a huge globe from the outside, and is known as The Bubble. The HQ also has its own museum, of sorts (read on to find out more about the museum).

The original complex was built with $46 million allocated for that purpose by a bill signed by President Eisenhower in 1955. The current complex, if you wanted to purchase it outright, would cost about a half-billion dollars.

With 22,000 employees working there, CIA headquarters is large enough to have its own zip code: 20505.

McLean Says ...

If you ever get the chance to enter the CIA's lobby, you'll encounter the following biblical quote etched into the wall: "And ye shall know the truth and the truth shall make you free." John VIII-XXXII

We can't get into details about the security around CIA HQ, but—as you might imagine—it is extremely tight. It has thus far been impossible for unwanted personnel to get inside. Even a small army wouldn't get very far!

Here, There, and Everywhere

The CIA hasn't always had a huge complex seven miles from downtown D.C. When it first began, there was nothing centralized about the working conditions of the Central Intelligence Agency.

Tradecraft

A good spy doesn't believe everything he or she reads in the papers. Don't trust the media to give you a true picture of people and their culture. Reporters cover news but sometimes without in-depth knowledge or without checking all their facts.

Spookspeak

No, a **Black agent** isn't an African American Intel person. Actually it is the Israeli Mossad tradecraft word for one of its Arab agents.

Offices were all over Washington, one in this building, another in that. Temporary buildings, little more than shacks, put up in front of the Lincoln Memorial during World War II, provided CIA office space during the early days. There was a headquarters but it was in the Foggy Bottom section of Washington, where security was an issue, and it was too small. It was DCI Allen Dulles who suggested the move to the 'burbs. He wanted a site far enough from the city to easily maintain a secure perimeter yet within 10 miles of the White House.

For obvious reasons, the CIA doesn't disclose information about most of its facilities. However, we do know about a few gems, including a museum of sorts and the CIA's library. The Directorate of Science and Technology has research labs where all sorts of classified experiments are underway.

McLean Says ...

A basic rule is never to acknowledge another intelligence officer whom you may know, or with whom you may have worked, in any public gathering or place unless it is part of that specific assignment or otherwise authorized. You never know who may be watching you.

For example, one year I encountered a good friend with whom I had trained in Army Intelligence years before. We were both coming out of different elevators in an office building near the United Nations. I was delighted to see him and was about to stop him, shake hands, and invite him to have a cup of coffee. Fortunately, my training kicked in, and instead, I stopped to check my watch as he walked by. Our eyes met briefly and he immediately looked at the floor. I was not on any assignment, but as I later learned, he was.

Blasts from a Spooky Past

Let's start with the museum. It's called the National Historical Collection, and it's a dream-world for folks who like James Bondish gadgets, although much of the material there remains classified and the collection isn't for public viewing.

Among the items that you could see there—if they let you—are diminutive spy cameras from the early Cold War era. Weapons of all sorts dating back to the Civil War are on display, as are personal belongings of past DCIs and legendary officers.

Top Secret

Words and stars carved in the marble facade of the north wall of the foyer of the CIA Headquarters Building permanently immortalize those CIA officers who lost their lives in the service of their country. Some of the stars have no name next to them, as those employees remain, even in death, undercover. Also in the CIA headquarters main lobby, on the opposite wall, is a memorial dedicated to the Office of Strategic Services, the CIA's predecessor organization. (See Chapter 6 for more about the OSS.)

CIA Library

The CIA library houses the greatest single collection of information about intelligence in the world. The library—sorry, CIA personnel only—contains 125,000 books and subscribes to 1,700 periodicals. The Library has three main collections:

- Reference
- Circulating
- Historical Intelligence

Additions to these collections are selected according to current intelligence objectives and priorities. The reference collection contains core research tools, including encyclopedias, dictionaries, commercial directories, atlases, diplomatic lists, and foreign and domestic phone books. There is also a CD-ROM section and extensive database services in this collection.

Spookspeak

Bona fides means credentials or the results of interrogation used to establish the identity, trustfulness, and authenticity of a defector or potential agent. Persons must be thoroughly checked out to prove their honesty and worth, as well as the validity of their bio and credentials.

In the circulating collection there are monographs, newspapers, and journals; a digital library that allows researchers to come in, plug in, and work on their laptops. The library also participates in inter-library loans of circulating items with other domestic libraries.

The Historical Intelligence Collection—now 25,000 volumes large—is an open-source library dedicated to, as the agency librarians put it, "the collection, retention, and exploitation of material dealing with the intelligence profession."

So there you have it, a little tour of CIA HQ. In many ways, working there is similar to working at any corporate headquarters. The biggest difference comes when you go home and your mate asks: "How was work?"

All you can reply is: "Sorry, that's classified."

The Least You Need to Know

- CIA headquarters is a well-guarded complex 10 miles outside Washington, D.C.

- It is very difficult to find Langley, Virginia, since it technically no longer exists.

- CIA headquarters has the largest intelligence library in the world.

- In many ways, working at Langley is like working at any large corporate headquarters.

Chapter 4

Time to Meet the Family: The Intelligence Community

In This Chapter

- ◆ Team work
- ◆ Air, sea, and land intelligence
- ◆ Cabinet spooks
- ◆ Friends at the Pentagon

The Central Intelligence Agency doesn't stand alone as a U.S. intelligence-gathering organization. It is one member of the U.S. intelligence community, an assemblage of 13 organizations, the activities of which are all overseen by the Director of Central Intelligence. In this chapter, we will be looking at the other members of the U.S. intelligence community—what they do and what their relationship is with the CIA.

The Coven of Thirteen

The intelligence organizations discussed in this chapter that support political, economic, and military decision makers get their resources and funding from the National Foreign Intelligence Program (NFIP), which is developed by the DCI and submitted to Congress for approval annually. Other intelligence organizations, which are intended mainly to support tactical military forces, are funded by two programs within the Department of Defense: the Joint Military Intelligence Program and the Tactical Intelligence and Related Activities aggregate. These budgets are handled by the Deputy Security of Defense.

As you can probably imagine, the DCI can't personally oversee every action of the 13 intelligence community members. The Community Management Staff supports the DCI in his role as head of the intelligence community.

The 13 components of the U.S. Intelligence Community.

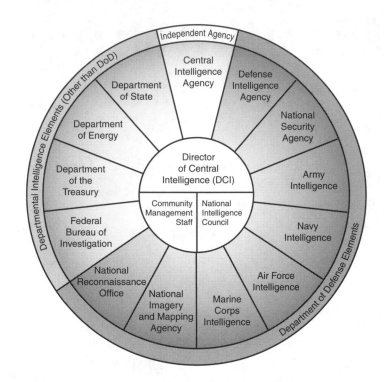

The Defense Intelligence Agency

One of the most important members of the U.S. intelligence community is the DIA, the Defense Intelligence Agency, which is a Department of Defense combat support agency with more than 7,000 military and civilian employees all around the world.

The DIA produces and manages a major portion of our country's foreign military intelligence. The DIA provides military intelligence to warfighters, defense policymakers, and force planners in the Department of Defense and the Intelligence Community, in support of U.S. military planning and operations and weapon systems acquisition.

Three-Star Director

The Director of the DIA is the principle adviser to the Secretary of Defense and the Chairman of the Joint Chiefs of Staff on matters of military intelligence. The DIA's director also coordinates activities of the defense intelligence community as the chairperson of the Military Intelligence Board, a decision making forum that formulates Defense intelligence policy and programming priorities. The DIA director is always a three-star military officer.

> ### McLean Says ...
>
> On assignment one evening I was driving my wife's diesel sedan, which was a four-cylinder chugchug vehicle. Comfortable, but no pick up and certainly no jack rabbit starts for getaway power. My partner and I were cruising back roads when I picked up headlights following. Automatically I speeded up and then slowed down. The car behind did, too. Obviously, they didn't want to pass. At nearly midnight, out in the boonies on assignment, I didn't like the thought of a tail.
>
> At the next curve, I turned and cutback. Passing the oncoming car after reversing direction, I hit the brights into their face. A driver and passenger were apparent. Turns out it was our backup team. The problem was, no one told us we had a backup that night!

The DIA's headquarters are at the Pentagon in Washington, D.C., with major operational activities at the Defense Intelligence Analysis Center (DIAC), Washington, D.C., the Armed Forces Medical Intelligence Center (AFMIC), Frederick, Maryland, and the Missile and Space Intelligence Center (MSIC), Huntsville, Alabama.

Join the DIA, and See the World

The DIA has a workforce skilled in military history and doctrine, economics, physics, chemistry, world history, political science, bio-sciences, and computer sciences. Their missions range from highly complex missile trajectory data to biographical information on foreign military leaders.

DIA employees have an opportunity to travel the world, and meet and work closely with other professionals from foreign countries. Employees are also offered education and training programs. DIA agents enjoy state-of-the-art computers and technical equipment.

The National Security Agency

The NSA is the United States' most secret, secret agency. (The old joke used to be that NSA stood for "No Such Agency.") It is also reputed to be the largest and the most powerful, with the largest budget. Trouble is, everything we know about it would fit on a four-page brochure.

Spookspeak

ADONIS isn't what you think, a handsome, almost god-like man. It is the National Security Agency codeword for a specific cryptograhic system.

According to James Bamford in his book *The Puzzle Palace: A Report on America's Most Secret Agency*, "At 12:01 on the morning of November 4, 1952, a new federal agency was born. Unlike other such bureaucratic births, however, this one arrived in silence. No news coverage, no Congressional debate, no press announcement, not even the whisper of a rumor … Equally invisible were the new agency's director, its numerous buildings, and its 10,000 employees."

Codemakers and Codebreakers

The NSA is the nation's cryptologic organization, that is, it employs the country's premier codemakers and codebreakers. It is the largest employer of mathematicians in the U.S. and perhaps the world.

The NSA coordinates, directs, and performs highly specialized activities to protect U.S. information systems and produce foreign intelligence information. Using state-of-the-art technology in both communications and date processing, the NSA is also one of the most important centers of foreign language analysis and research within the Government.

Top Secret

Think your electric bill is too high? NSA's yearly electrical bill is more than $21 million.

NSA research led to the development of the first large-scale computer and the first solid-state computer, predecessors to the modern computer. Also, NSA research into methods of information storage led to the development of the tape cassette. NSA also made ground-breaking developments in semiconductor technology and remains a world leader in many technological fields.

Spookspeak

SIGINT, or Signals Intelligence, is the science of intercepting coded messages and decoding them. SIGINT's modern era dates to World War II, when the United States broke the Japanese military code and learned of plans to invade Midway Island.

This intelligence allowed the U.S. to defeat Japan's superior fleet. The use of SIGINT is believed to have directly contributed to shortening the war by at least one year. Today, SIGINT continues to play an important role in maintaining the superpower status of the United States.

Design 'Я' Us

The NSA's mission is two-fold: 1) to design codes that will protect the integrity of U.S. information systems; 2) to search for weaknesses in adversaries' systems and codes.

The agency's school, the National Cryptologic School, helps keep NSA employees ahead of the rapidly changing world of technology. The school also serves as a training resource for the entire Department of Defense.

NSA sponsors employees for bachelor and graduate studies at the nation's top universities and colleges, and selected agency employees attend the various war colleges of the U.S. Armed Forces.

Tradecraft

The inventor of the first modern cipher machine—a machine that could quickly and randomly encipher (that is, encode) a message—was Edward H. Heburn.

Fort Meade Headquarters

Most NSA employees, both civilian and military, are headquartered at Fort Meade, Maryland, located between Baltimore and Washington, D.C.

Its workforce consists of analysts, engineers, physicists, mathematicians, linguists, computer scientists, researchers, as well as customer relations specialists, security officers, data flow experts, managers, administrative and clerical assistants. In terms of dollars spent, floor space occupied, and personnel employed, the NSA would rank in the top 10 percent of the Fortune 500 companies.

Top Secret

The NSA's headquarters in Fort Meade is the second largest building in the United States. Which building is number one? The Pentagon.

The NSA may have been born after World War II, but it can trace its roots all the way back to World War I when a group of *cryptographers* went to work for the government decrypting foreign coded messages.

By Sea: Naval Intelligence

The Office of Naval Investigation (ONI), which was recently reorganized, is composed of the director of Naval Intelligence and his staff, a chief of staff and an assistant of Naval Intelligence, all of whom oversee eight directorates.

By Land: Army Intelligence

It's no contest. Army Intelligence—which is *not* an oxymoron, contrary to the old joke—is the oldest member of the U.S. Intelligence Community, dating back to 1776 when Nathan Hale spied on the British for General George Washington. Since 1984, all Army intelligence production has been centralized under a single organization: the Army Intelligence Agency.

Spookspeak

Cryptographers are codebreakers.

G-Codes are Army classifications. G-1 is Personnel, G-2 is Intelligence, G-3 is Operations and G-4 is Supply and Logistics. The Air Force uses S-codes.

The Army created Combat Electronic Warfare and Intelligence Units during the 1980s in order to better coordinate electronic intelligence with battlefield tactics. The units were first used in the Gulf War.

Army Intelligence structure is designed—and its personnel are equipped, trained, and prepared—to provide military commanders with unique capabilities and a balanced flexible force that can be tailored to meet any contingency.

Semper Fi-Style: Marine Intelligence

Not to be left out of the intelligence loop by the Army and Navy, the U.S. Marine Corps has its own intelligence department as well. Marine Corps Intelligence Activity (MCIA), according to them, is a "vital part of the military intelligence 'corporate enterprise,' and functions in a collegial, effective manner with other service agencies and with the joint intelligence centers of the JCS [Joint Chiefs of Staff] and Unified Commands [which coordinates and adjusts the various U.S. military commands around the globe]."

MCIA provides services and specialized products to support the Commandant of the Marine Corps as a member of the Joint Chiefs of Staff, as well as to the Marine Corps Headquarters Staff. It not only helps determine what missions will need to be carried out to achieve a certain outcome, but will then train personnel to accomplish that mission, adapting the specific mission to where it will take place and who will be involved.

MCIA is headquartered out of several locations. It is a full partner with the Office of Naval Intelligence and Coast Guard Intelligence in the National Maritime Intelligence Center, and at Marine Corps Base Quantico, Virginia. These locations facilitate maximum effective use of infrastructure and resources, while ensuring that MCIA remains attentive to its primary customers within the Marine Corps.

MCIA produces a full range of products to satisfy customer needs in peace, pre-crisis, or contingency situations, and to support service obligations for doctrine development, force structure, training and education, and force modernization.

By Air: Air Force Intelligence

In addition to working in support of the operations of other members of the Intelligence Community, the U.S. Air Force also has its own organization assigned to intelligence: The Air Intelligence Agency (AIA).

The AIA is headquartered at Lackland Air Force Base in Texas. It has been in existence since October 1, 1993, and was reorganized on February 1, 2001 under the structure of the Air Combat Command and the Eighth Air Force.

With the realignment, the AIA commander serves as the Eighth Air Force deputy commander for information operations. The Eighth Air Force, with its bomber and information operations capabilities, is the Air Force's first operational force designed to achieve and maintain information superiority. The AIA commander also serves as commander of the Joint Information Operations Center, a subordinate unit of U.S. Space Command.

According to the AIA, their mission is to "gain, exploit, defend and attack information to ensure superiority in the air, space and information domains. The agency's people worldwide deliver flexible collection, tailored air and space intelligence, weapons monitoring and information warfare products and services." Information warfare involves attacking an enemy with information or by disrupting its information systems.

National Air Intelligence Center

The National Air Intelligence Center (NAIC), also part of the Air Force, is headquartered at Wright-Patterson Air Force Base, Ohio (near Dayton). It is the primary Department of Defense producer of foreign aerospace intelligence.

NAIC develops its products by analyzing all available data on foreign aerospace forces and weapons systems to determine performance characteristics, capabilities, vulnerabilities, and intentions.

As the Department of Defense experts on foreign aerospace system capabilities, the folks at the NAIC have been involved in the past in supporting American weapons treaty negotiations and verification. The NAIC got its organizational beginnings in the Air Force Systems Command's Foreign Technology Division, which got its start in 1961.

Secret Pictures and Maps

Another member of the Intelligence Community, the National Imagery and Mapping Agency (NIMA), was established October 1, 1996. The creation of this organization centralized government responsibility for imagery and mapping.

Spookspeak

Geospatial means consisting of both Earth and space.

Top Secret

NIMA workers are trained in the fields of cartography (map making), imagery analysis, marine analysis, the physical sciences, geodesy (determining the exact location of objects on the Earth's surface), computer and telecommunication engineering, and photogrammetry (measuring distance using aerial photography).

NIMA is headquartered in Bethesda, Maryland, but there are also facilities in northern Virginia, Washington, D.C., and St. Louis, Missouri. NIMA has smaller offices around the world.

NIMA says that its mission is to "provide timely, relevant, and accurate Geospatial Intelligence in support of national security."

A number of smaller organizations that used to stand on their own are now combined within NIMA. Brought together were Defense Mapping Agency (DMA), the Central Imagery Office (CIO), and the Defense Dissemination Program Office (DDPO) in their entirety; and the mission and functions of CIA's National Photographic Interpretation Center.

Also included in NIMA are imagery exploitation, dissemination and processing elements of the Defense Intelligence Agency, National Reconnaissance Office, and the Defense Airborne Reconnaissance Office.

Satellite Intelligence: National Reconnaissance Office

The mission of the National Reconnaissance Office is simple. It has been assigned to meet U.S. government needs through spaceborne reconnaissance. In other words, the NRO's job is to ensure that the United States has the technology and spaceborne assets needed to enable U.S. global information superiority. This is done through research, development, acquisition, and operation of the nation's intelligence satellites.

The NRO is an agency of the Department of Defense. It receives its funds through that portion of the National Foreign Intelligence Program (NFIP) known as the National Reconnaissance Program (NRP).

According to the Department of Defense,

> The NRO's assets collect intelligence to support such functions as indications and warning, monitoring of arms control agreements, military operations and exercises, and monitoring of natural disasters and other environmental issues. The Director of the NRO is appointed by the President and confirmed by the Congress as the Assistant Secretary of the Air Force for Space. The Secretary of Defense has the responsibility, which is exercised in concert with the Director of Central Intelligence, for the management and operation of the NRO. The DCI establishes the collection priorities and requirements for the collection of satellite data. The NRO is staffed by personnel from CIA, the military services, and civilian Department of Defense personnel.

> **Top Secret**
>
> For years the very existence of the NRO was classified. The public was not allowed to know it existed until September 18, 1992, when the DCI recommended that information about its existence be declassified.

Smart Money? Department of the Treasury

The Treasury Department's Office of Intelligence Support, founded in 1977, replaced the Office of National Security (ONS). ONS had been set up in 1961 to connect the Treasury Department with the National Security Council.

Because it is essential for economic policymakers to be fully informed, the Treasury Department has been represented on the National Foreign Intelligence Board since 1972. Today a special assistant to the Secretary of the Treasury is a senior intelligence officer of the Intelligence Community.

The Special Assistant's staff supports his roles as chief economic and financial adviser to the president, head of the second largest law enforcement department in the federal government, and the official responsible for the integrity of the country's currency.

The Special Assistant represents the Treasury Department and maintains continuous liaison with other elements of the Intelligence Community. He or she reviews all proposed support relationships between Community components and Treasury offices and bureaus.

The Office of Intelligence Support has three main functions:

◆ It alerts the Secretary and other officials to fast-breaking events, foreign and domestic.

◆ It provides intelligence reports and products to Treasury officials.

◆ It oversees the intelligence relationships of Treasury's offices and bureaus.

The Office also helps prepare the National Intelligence Estimates and other Community-wide intelligence products, developing and coordinating Treasury Department contributions.

Power Intelligence: Department of Energy

The Department of Energy has been represented in the Intelligence Community since July 1947. Department of Energy's foreign intelligence program's missions are to:

◆ Provide the department and other U.S. Government policymakers and decision-makers with timely, accurate, high-impact foreign intelligence analyses.

◆ Detect and defeat foreign intelligence services bent on acquiring sensitive information on the department's programs, facilities, technology, and personnel.

◆ Provide technical and analytical support to the DCI.

◆ Make the department's technical and analytical expertise available to other members of the Intelligence Community.

Their particular intelligence responsibilities include:

◆ Nuclear proliferation ◆ Fossil and nuclear energy

◆ Nuclear weapons technology ◆ Science and technology

Executive Order 12333 directs the department to "provide expert technical, analytical and research capability to the Intelligence Community; to formulate intelligence collection and analysis requirements where the expert capability of the department can contribute; to produce and disseminate foreign intelligence necessary for the Secretary of Energy's responsibilities; and to participate with the Department of State in overtly collecting information with respect to foreign energy matters."

State Secrets: The State Department

The Department of State's Bureau of Intelligence and Research (INR), founded in 1946, serves as that department's primary source for interpretive analysis of global developments.

INR is the focal point within the State Department for all policy issues and activities involving the Intelligence Community. The INR Assistant Secretary reports directly to the Secretary of State and serves as the Secretary's principal advisor for all intelligence issues.

INR reacts to policy priorities and gives early warning and analysis of events and trends that affect U.S. foreign policy and national security interests. INR does not have to answer to other sections of the State Department, and it is not formally connected to any other members of the Intelligence Community.

INR also coordinates with the national security community on visa denials, intelligence sharing, and requirements and evaluation for collection in all intelligence disciplines.

INR develops intelligence policy for the Department of State, ensuring that intelligence activities abroad are in harmony with U.S. policy and that collection resources and priorities are in accord with our diplomatic interests and requirements.

Finally ... the FBI

The Federal Bureau of Investigation is often thought of as the federal police, but they function much more like an intelligence agency than like a police department.

The agency now known as the FBI was founded in 1908, when Attorney General Charles J. Bonaparte appointed an unnamed force of Special Agents to be the investigative force of the Department of Justice. The Special Agent force was named the Bureau of Investigation in 1909, by order of Attorney General George W. Wickersham. Following a series of name changes, the FBI officially received its present title in 1935.

The FBI is in charge of investigating federal crimes (which consist predominantly of crimes that cross state lines and crimes against federal officials or on federal land).

When it comes to counterterrorism, the FBI's mission is to identify and neutralize the threat in the United States posed by terrorists and their supporters, whether nations, groups, or individuals.

Tradecraft

Not all intelligence agencies in the world are funded by a government. There are individuals and corporations rich enough to afford their own spies. Corporate espionage features all of the intrigue of the patriotic sort.

The techniques are the same. It is just that the clients are different. Corporate spies are apt to break U.S. laws, whereas CIA spies only break the laws of other countries, right?

So there they are: the 13 members of the U.S. intelligence community, the activities of which are overseen by the Director of Central Intelligence. They are complementary parts designed to provide the United States with a shield of intelligence.

The Least You Need to Know

- The CIA is one of 13 members of the U.S. Intelligence Community.
- The Director of Central Intelligence oversees not just the CIA but the entire Intelligence Community.
- Each branch of the military has an intelligence component.
- The DIA produces and manages a major portion of our country's foreign military intelligence.
- The FBI functions more like an intelligence agency than a police department.

Chapter 5

So You Want to Be a Spy?

In This Chapter

- ◆ Do your homework
- ◆ Learn a foreign language
- ◆ Check out these jobs
- ◆ Send your resumé today

Intelligence is one of the most challenging, interesting, and rewarding careers—for the right person, that is. Right might be defined as curious, inquisitive, intelligent, and with a deep love of country. Equally important, the right candidate must be able to work without outward praise or reward, because much of what a CIA Officer does must remain unsung.

Today, the need for professional, dedicated CIA Officers is greater than in decades. Our country faces an ongoing, hidden threat from terrorists and their allies that may, unfortunately, last as long as the Cold War did.

Although the CIA has been deluged with new applicants, it still needs highly qualified individuals. You'll find out whether the CIA might be right for you, and about the CIA's diverse opportunities and requirements, in this chapter.

The Basics

Before getting into the specifics of the job opportunities at the CIA and how to apply for them, let's get a few things out of the way. For the specialized jobs at the CIA (i.e., nonsecretarial, maintenance, etc), you must meet the following requirements:

- Be a U.S. citizen.

- Be no older than 35 years old.

- Have at least a four-year college degree with a grade point average of B or higher.

> **Top Secret**
>
> Since the terrorist attacks on the World Trade Center, applications for employment at the CIA have increased tenfold! That may diminish somewhat as the glow of patriotism drops off a bit. Whatever the case, good officers are needed to rebuild HUMINT, the critical Human Intelligence on the ground at the scenes of action, which was neglected in the past few decades.

The first two requirements are no-brainers—the CIA doesn't want to risk hiring people who might have allegiances to other countries, and they want their employees to be young enough to train and to commit their professional career to the agency. The CIA also wants their employees to be highly educated. Let's look a little more closely at just what kind of education the CIA likes its employees to have.

What's Your Major?

As long as you have a four-year degree, it doesn't really matter what your area of study is. The CIA picks the best-qualified people from nearly all fields. Of course, if you studied international relations and speak Farsi, Arabic, and Mandarin Chinese, it's a safe bet that you're in a better position to be hired than if you're a Victorian lit major who also speaks passable French.

> **McLean Says ...**
>
> We had joked as young intelligence officers in the challenging 1950s that there were two choices for language: Russian and Chinese. Optimists took one and pessimists studied the other. Trouble is, we couldn't decide which was which.

The moral: If you're still in college and you want to work for the CIA, tailor your studies to what the CIA is interested in (we'll get to that a bit later). However, it doesn't matter what you study if you don't have an outstanding academic record—the CIA likes to hire smart people, so concentrate on being near the top of your class in whatever field of study you choose.

Got Any Skeletons in Your Closet?

If you pass the academic muster and the CIA thinks you have the right stuff, they'll make what's called a "conditional offer of employment." In other words, they'll hire you on condition that you pass their thorough background check. According to the CIA, the purpose of the background investigation is to examine "your life's history, your character, trustworthiness, reliability and soundness of judgment. Also examined is one's freedom from conflicting allegiances, potential to be coerced and willingness and ability to abide by regulations governing the use, handling and the protection of sensitive information." Whew!

It makes sense that the CIA wants to hire only people they thoroughly trust—after all, their employees often know or have access to highly sensitive material. In other words, the nation's security is at stake.

Oh, and don't bother fudging that C you got in freshman biology—the agency uses a polygraph (i.e. lie detector) to, as they put it, "check the veracity of the information" they find in your background check. In other words, be prepared to answer questions about past and present drug use, your criminal history, and maybe a few more, shall we say, *personal* questions. By the time it's through, the agency will know more about you than your mother does.

Finally, you must pass a health exam to prove that you are in acceptable physical and mental health. It should go without saying that the CIA doesn't hire anyone who currently uses illicit drugs—it's one of the top reasons people are denied security clearance.

> **Top Secret**
>
> Even though they do thorough checks on all prospective employees, the CIA isn't recruiting saints! Officers' work is tough and dangerous, and the agency knows the best-qualified people aren't always going to have perfect records. A few missteps back in the early days of college aren't necessarily going to disqualify you.

Location, Location, Location

If you live on the West Coast and simply can't imagine residing more than 10 miles from the Pacific Ocean, then it's probably not worth your time applying to the CIA. All serious candidates must be willing to live in the Washington, D.C. area. There are, of course,

> **Tradecraft**
>
> Enter and exit a building to reverse directions. Just push the door open, walk inside the lobby, and then turn around and exit. Or better yet, go out a different door than you walked in. That helps throw off anyone following you and also gives you a chance to observe anyone whom you think might be.

assignments outside of Washington, but everyone starts there and most employees are expected to maintain a home there.

Something Else to Consider ...

Since the attacks of September 11, the CIA has been deluged with applications. Unfortunately, some of these applicants may simply have felt a knee-jerk impulse to be patriotic or applied because it was the "thing to do" at the time, not to mention that it sounds like a sexy career that's great to talk about at cocktail parties. (To set the record straight, CIA people don't talk about their work at cocktail parties—or anywhere else, for that matter. They use social time to build contacts and bridges and to cultivate sources and assets.)

> **Top Secret**
>
> CIA Officers and investigative reporters are a lot alike. Both share the same goals: getting secret information that they and their superiors can use. Whereas reporters get to see their names in print, CIA Officers must be satisfied with the knowledge of a job well done.

However, the CIA's fight against terrorism is an old one. It was going on long before September 11 brought it to everyone's attention, and it will continue long after Osama bin Laden has released his last amateur videotape.

So before you send in that application, make sure you're doing it for the right reasons: for love of country and because you think you have something to contribute to the CIA.

McLean Says ...

In years past there was a certain competition between the FBI and the company. Fact is, that sometimes led to withholding of information. That old problem has been resolved to a good degree. It must be totally resolved today, considering the war on terrorism. Our country can't afford to miss any bits and pieces of information that might help solve an intelligence puzzle.

Help Wanted

Now that you know the minimum requirements for being an agency man or woman, let's take a look at the kinds of positions the CIA is looking to fill.

The CIA breaks their jobs into five categories:

◆ **Clandestine service.** You guessed it—these are the spies of the CIA, the people who put their lives at risk to gather intelligence on foreign countries. The CIA says they are looking for people with "an adventurous spirit, a forceful personality, superior intellectual ability, toughness of mind, and a high degree of personal integrity, courage, and love of country. You will need to deal with fast-moving, ambiguous, and unstructured situations that will test your resourcefulness to the utmost."

Jobs in this category include Operations Officer, Staff Operations Officer, Collection Management Officer, and the Professional Trainee Program.

◆ **Analytical positions.** People in these positions turn raw data into finished intelligence. Think it sounds boring? Think again: This is the polished information that the president and other key senior policy makers read and rely on for the decisions they make.

Jobs in this category include economists, military, counterterrorism, and political analysts, and statisticians.

◆ **Scientists, engineers, and technologists.** Whereas people in these fields in the commercial workplace use their skills to create particular products and fill particular needs, the CIA says that working for them is a lot more like working in a University setting, where research is done more for the sake of research. And who knows, you just might be involved in developing some of the most highly advanced communications gathering devices ever made.

Jobs in this category include engineering and electronics specialists, systems engineers, network design and management, web, software, and applications developers, and information systems security.

◆ **Language positions.** The CIA is always looking for people with fluency in foreign languages and knowledge of particular areas around the world. People in language positions read, research, and translate material, providing the raw data for the analysts to work with. They also teach others those languages.

Jobs in this category include foreign language instructors, Middle Eastern language specialists, and open source officers (the people who read and watch all the foreign media and identify pertinent information).

◆ **Professional positions.** These are the folks who keep the agency operating on a day-to-day basis—they are the administrative professionals who support the agency's core functions, and there is an amazing variety of positions available in this area, from architects to paralegals to physicians' assistants to daycare providers.

Not everyone who works for the CIA is a staff employee. The agency also employs what are called contract agents. These people have a one- or two-year contract with the CIA to perform a specific task.

The CIA employs about 4,000 contract agents at any given time. Some of these are former full-time intelligence officers, others soldiers of fortune. All contract agents must sign a secrecy agreement and pass a thorough background check.

Okay, now that you know the general categories, let's take a look at a few of the positions the CIA is hiring for right now.

Wanted: Clandestine Service Collection Management Officers

If you worked as one of the CIA's Clandestine Service Collection Management Officers you would function as the liaison between operations officers in the field and those who are shaping foreign policy back in the United States.

Tradecraft

Carry a different jacket and tie in your attaché or business case to change appearances quickly in a restroom. Simply remove the jacket and tie you are wearing, put on the other, add a hat and return to the street. Even with the quick change, it pays to be alert for anyone following you.

You would guide the collection of and direct the dissemination of intelligence. You'll be required to know the needs of the U.S. policy maker and be able to clearly communicate those needs to officers in the field.

Because of the state of the world at the moment, the Company is particularly looking for candidates with backgrounds in Central Eurasian, East Asian, and Middle Eastern languages and cultures. You must have extensive knowledge of the areas in which you would be operating as well as extensive knowledge about the countries from which the CIA is attempting to acquire intelligence.

The starting salary is between $43,500 to $60,400, depending upon your background. Candidates must have a Bachelor's or Master's degree with a B average. Degrees in the following subjects are preferable:

- International business/finance/relations
- Economics

- ◆ Physical Science

- ◆ Nuclear/biological/chemical engineering

According to the CIA personnel department, a good candidate for this job would have the following qualities:

- ◆ Good oral expression

- ◆ Write clearly and accurately

- ◆ Well-developed interest in foreign affairs

- ◆ Impeccable personal integrity

- ◆ Strong interpersonal skills

- ◆ Ability to handle ambiguity

- ◆ Ability to take calculated risks

- ◆ Foreign language proficiency

- ◆ Work experience

> **Top Secret**
>
> The CIA still has a reputation as a white, male organization, but hiring statistics at the agency indicate that this is no longer the case. Forty-four percent or the people hired these days are women and 22 percent are a member of a minority.

Wanted: Economists

The DI needs regional and international economists, particularly specialists on the Middle East, Asia, and Africa, and international economists focusing on financial vulnerabilities, analysis, and illicit finance.

Agency economists monitor and assess foreign economic policy and determine how they affect U.S. security interests. They work with political leadership and military analysts in order to prepare briefings for U.S. policy makers.

In order to qualify for this position you must have a graduate degree in economics. However, economic graduate students may want to work in a CIA summer program while studying for their degree. To be considered, you must have a grade-point-average of 3.2 or higher.

You must have analytical, written, and oral communication skills. Obviously, the more knowledge—including knowledge of the language—you have of the areas in which you will be working, the better chance you will have of getting the job.

Wanted: Engineers and Scientists

Engineers or scientists working for the DI analyze foreign weapons development, weapons proliferation, information warfare, and emerging technologies.

You will be a professional intelligence officer, applying your knowledge to solve intelligence problems and brief U.S. policy makers. Creativity and initiative are very important. Candidates must have a B (3.0) average with a Bachelor's or Master's degree in one of the following fields:

- Aerospace Engineering
- Mechanical Engineering
- Electrical Engineering
- Computer Engineering
- Computer Science
- Nuclear Engineering
- Physics
- Mathematics
- Chemistry and Chemical Engineering
- Biology and Biotechnology

Graduate students and college undergraduates studying in one of the above fields may want to apply to be a CIA summer intern (more on this later in the chapter).

Wanted: Military Analysts

A DI military analyst must address foreign military developments at the program, operational, and strategic levels and produce written and oral analysis for key military and civilian policy makers worldwide.

Take this job and you'll be expected to collect, evaluate, integrate, and analyze information from classified and unclassified sources to determine the information's immediate and long-term implications for U.S. national security.

You must gauge the size of enemy forces, and create scenarios for dealing with crises. Naturally, a military expertise is expected. (Military experience as an officer in an operations or logistics command is most desired.) But, in addition to that, a successful

CIA military analyst will also be familiar with a region of the world such as China, the Middle East, Central Asia, or South Asia.

One of the most fascinating areas of Intel is Order of Battle, a military specialty. Basically, you must sort through photo interpreter reports, translated documents, captured prisoner interrogations, reports from patrols, forward observation posts, behind the lines spy reports and whatever else you can put together.

The job is to identify what enemy unit you are facing, their armament, state of readiness, combat efficiency, ammo and food supply and even identify the units from battalion, regimental and divisional size. If you can identify the commanders, so much the better. Sometimes you can determine if that commander is prone to defense or offense.

That type of background can be helpful as an analyst in foreign countries to determine the potential of that nation's fighting ability. Conversely, it may help spot weaknesses and officers or groups that might be recruited and led into revolt or similar uses against an adversary nation's leaders we hope to replace.

Candidates must have Master's degree with a 3.2 GPA in international security affairs or military history. A perfect candidate can speak Mandarin Chinese, Arabic, Farsi, Urdu, or Hindi.

Wanted: Statisticians

Formerly known as the "slide-rule set," the CIA statisticians are all on computers now, crunching the numbers and turning them into knowledge. CIA statisticians assess the threat from foreign weapon systems, and analyze foreign political and economic developments. They support international treaty negotiations.

Candidates must have a Master of Science or Ph.D. in statistics, applied mathematics, or operations research; excellent analytical and problem-solving skills; well-developed interpersonal and communications skills; ability to function well as part of a multidisciplinary team; knowledge of one or more of the standard statistical packages such as S-Plus; and consulting or industry experience would give them an advantage.

Wanted: Political Analysts

As we go to press, the CIA has a strong need for political analysts with an expertise in Asia, especially China, and the Middle East. If this is you, your job with the CIA would be to brief policy makers on the goals and motivations of foreign governments, factions, and leaders.

Assigned to a foreign government, you would examine their cultures, ideologies, society, values, resources, capabilities, how they think and make decisions, and their strengths and weaknesses.

Candidates must have a Master's degree (GPA 3.2 or higher) in an area of study that directly relates to their global region of expertise. They should also be able to speak at least one foreign language, applicable to their assignment.

Wanted: Operations Officers

As any CIA recruiter will tell you, becoming an operations officer is more than taking a job. It is more like becoming a job.

This is the Clandestine Service, the vital human element of intelligence collection. These people are the cutting edge of American intelligence, an elite corps gathering the vital information needed by our policy makers to make critical foreign policy decisions.

> **McLean Says ...**
>
> Years ago, two young State Department staff members were posted to the Embassy in Peru after graduating with high honors from their Ivy League University. They came from well-healed families, had earned high grades, and enjoyed the cocktail party circuit. Seems one State Department guy dared the other to dance with "that lady over there in the red dress and hat."
>
> A $5 bet was agreed. As the music began, the second staffer walked over and tapped the person in the red gown on the back and asked, "May I have this dance?"
>
> The person in red wheeled around, stared at the young American and hissed, "You American fool. I am the Papal Nuncio and the music is the beginning of the Peruvian anthem."

Wanted: Staff Operations Officers

If you want to enjoy the excitement of a CIA operation without ever leaving your Washington, D.C. office, then you want to be a CIA staff operations officer (SOO).

In support of your colleagues overseas, you will be expected to quickly meet their operational research and case management needs.

You will be expected to develop an expertise in the area of your assignment so as to better serve the operation. Candidates must write well and must have demonstrated resourcefulness in solving problems that occur in complex overseas environments.

You must have a Bachelor's degree with a B or better average. You will be an ever more attractive candidate if you have a graduate degree, foreign travel experience, foreign language proficiency, previous residency abroad, or military experience.

How to Apply

The CIA actually strongly prefers that you apply for positions online, and the agency makes it very easy to do so at their website: www.cia.gov/cia/employment. Of course, you can still apply the old-fashioned way, too, by sending your resumé with a cover letter explaining your qualifications to the following addresses.

For Clandestine Service Positions:

CST Division
P.O. Box 4605, Dept. Internet
Reston, VA 20195
Or you may fax the application to 703-613-7871

For all other positions:

Recruitment Center
Attn: (fill in position applying for)
P.O. Box 4090, Dept: Internet
Reston, VA 20195

Top Secret

The way to become an op officer is to take the CIA's Clandestine Service Trainee Program. You must have a strong academic background, strong writing skills, and strong interpersonal skills.

Candidates are expected to have an all-consuming curiosity about world affairs. Military experience and foreign language proficiency are major plusses. An exceptional candidate would have knowledge of Central Eurasian, East Asian, and Middle Eastern languages.

Starting salaries for operations officers are $43,500 to $60,400. And hey, you get to see the world.

Sorry, Your Report Card Is Classified

Since 1961, the CIA has had a student trainee program. It provides college students an opportunity to gain practical experience that complements their academic studies. Only the most highly motivated students need apply.

Fields of study for which the CIA offers a cooperative study program are engineering, computer science, mathematics, economics, physical science, nonromance languages, area studies, business administration, accounting, finance, and logistics.

> **Top Secret**
>
> CIA jobs do not pay as much as the same sorts of jobs in the private sector, but you get to serve your country.

Students receive an opportunity to participate in the CIA's substantive work and to meet intelligence pros. There is one hitch. Only students who are attending schools that participate in the program will be considered, so check with your college or university before you apply. Students must have a B or better average. The good news is that the program pays a salary that is competitive to similar positions offered in the private sector.

Graduate Studies Program

The graduate studies program is for post-graduate students who are studying international affairs, languages, economics, physical sciences, or engineering. In this program, you'll work side by side with professional intelligence analysts. Your work will be expected to be of top quality and may be distributed agency-wide.

Students who are accepted into the program receive tuition assistance, and approximately half of the students who partake in the program later return to the CIA for full-time employment. So, if you are looking to "get a foot in," this is the way to do it.

Applicants must have a B or better average. As is true with the student trainee program, applicants for the graduate studies program must be graduate students at schools that are participating members of the program—so check before you apply.

Internships

Neither the student trainee program nor the graduate studies program are internships. The CIA's intern program is a separate entity, although CIA internships also pay a competitive salary.

McLean Says ...

What do we look for in operations officers? We value integrity above all else. We look for individuals who are self-confident but not arrogant. Assertive but not overly aggressive. Sociable ... it is very much a people business. People who are endlessly curious about everything. People with mature judgment (loose guns on the deck need not apply). People with a sense of humor (if you can't laugh at yourself and the world sometimes, you have a problem). Those who are adaptable (people who can adjust to almost anything, think on their feet, deal with ambiguity, make swift and correct decisions). We look for people who have been places and done things with a spirit of adventure, but not adventurers off on a frolic. Amazingly, perhaps, we find these people. Most are motivated by patriotism and a desire to contribute to our country. The skills they bring include nearly every profession. There is a need for them all, but not all make it through the rites of passage to become intelligence officers.

The internship program gives students a chance to gain practical work experience that will complement their studies. You will work side by side with intelligence professionals and learn first-hand how the CIA gathers and analyzes intelligence.

Students must work either a combination semester and summer internship or two 90-day summer internships. They receive many of the same benefits as permanent employees. Applicants must have a B or better average and are subjected to the same background and polygraph checks as full-time CIA employees.

Rejection Hurts

It can take between two months and a year to go through the entire hiring process—we told you those background checks are thorough! But as you can imagine, only a small percentage of those who apply actually get hired by the agency.

Ever hear the saying "Don't call us, we'll call you"? Well, that applies to the CIA. Agency personnel will only be in touch if they are interested in finding out more about you. Furthermore, if you do make it past the first round or even further into the interview process but are eventually rejected, don't expect the CIA to give you an explanation. They *never* explain why an applicant is denied employment. That's classified information.

Top Secret

Don't be discouraged if you're turned down for a CIA job. The FBI needs good people, too, especially people with language skills. So does the Immigration Service and the Customs Service. You can find out more about intelligence job opportunities on various U.S. government agency websites.

The Least You Need to Know

- Most CIA employees must be U.S. citizens, take a polygraph, and pass an extensive security check.

- It may take the CIA up to a year to check a prospect's background.

- With applications mounting, it is more important than ever that candidates study hard and do well in school.

- International and scientific knowledge is a big plus, as is military experience.

Part 2

Fathers of Intelligence

Who's your daddy? In the case of the CIA, Daddy was the Office of Strategic Services (OSS), which was created during WWII to keep tabs on our enemies. Over the years, the agency was also shaped by its colorful directors, whom we profile in Chapter 7.

While we're at it, we take a peek at some key foreign intelligence agencies and preview some new and not-so-new gadgets and gizmos.

Chapter 6

Born of the OSS

In This Chapter

- ◆ Intelligence deficiencies
- ◆ Donovan's deal
- ◆ Post-war reorganization
- ◆ Cold warriors

The CIA was not created from scratch, but rather evolved from a previous series of organizations. The grandfather of the CIA was the Office of Strategic Services, better known as the OSS. Because of World War II and the emergence of the era of global warfare, the United States needed an organization to oversee the gathering, processing, and disseminating of wartime intelligence.

FDR's Concern

The idea for the Office of Strategic Services came even before the Japanese attack on Pearl Harbor in 1941, when President Franklin D. Roosevelt became concerned with deficiencies in the United States' ability to gather intelligence.

FDR asked a talented lawyer from New York, William J. Donovan, to write up a proposal for a foreign intelligence service. Donovan's report became the basis of the OSS, which was established in June 1942, with Donovan in charge. He was to become legendary.

Spookspeak

The **Eleventh Commandment** is especially important to all spooks. Basically it advises: "Thou shalt not get caught!" A most important commandment indeed.

The OSS was mandated to collect and analyze strategic information required by the Joint Chiefs of Staff and to conduct special operations not assigned to other agencies. For the remainder of the war, intelligence supplied by the OSS played an important role in guiding various military campaigns.

Tradecraft

If you think you're being followed, stop to window-shop. Use the window reflection to look for anyone who stops behind you to look in your direction, or otherwise just stops to look around. Move to the next window, stop and window-shop again. Check to see if anyone who might be following has also stopped. If so, it's time to lose the dog.

Wild Bill

Born New Year's Day 1883 in Buffalo, New York, General William "Wild Bill" Donovan became known as the "Father of American Intelligence." Under his direction, the Office of Strategic Services collected foreign intelligence and conducted covert action in Europe, the Middle East, and Asia.

Donovan wanted to be a lawyer so he went to Columbia University. He earned his Bachelor's degree in 1905 and graduated from Columbia Law School in 1907. After school he returned to Buffalo to start up a law practice—but he soon became restless.

Donovan once wrote, "I wanted more excitement and the chance to serve my country. In 1912 I formed my own cavalry troop and fought in Mexican border skirmishes.

Spookspeak

Most spy enthusiasts know 007, the code number for James Bond. What does **109** signify? It was the World War II code number for "Wild Bill" Donovan.

When World War I came, I was there with the US Army's 165th Infantry in France. I was wounded three times during that war and was awarded many medals, including the Medal of Honor, for my service. I was a colonel when discharged …. What with being a lawyer, a diplomat, public official, and army officer, I'd say that I've had a pretty full life …" Donovan died in 1959.

OSS at Work

The OSS's first job of the war was to infiltrate North Africa and gather intelligence that would aid a future allied invasion there. The OSS used its established bases in North Africa as launching points for trips into Nazi-occupied Europe. Both southern France and Italy were scouted by OSS agents in advance of allied invasions.

One of the OSS's most famous missions came in conjunction with British and Free French intelligence. In the days after D-Day and the allied invasion at Normandy, France, teams of three, called *Jedburgh teams*, were dropped behind enemy lines in France to help allied troops who were advancing in that direction. These teams were not only able to get useful intelligence to the people who needed it, but were soldiers as well, frequently being forced to battle German troops as they went about their tasks.

> **Spookspeak**
>
> The **Jedburgh teams** were known at times as Donovan's Private Army.

Following the allied invasion of western Europe, OSS bases sprung up in Bern, Istanbul, Madrid, Stockholm, and Lisbon. Allen Dulles, the future Director of Central Intelligence, headed the OSS's Switzerland base.

From that location, Dulles not only recruited the agents needed to arrange the Nazi surrender during the summer of 1945, he also foresaw the upcoming Cold War against the Soviet Union and formed Operation Paper Clip. This program recruited many German agents of the German intelligence agency, called *Abwehr*, to come to the United States and continue their anti-Communist programs. Also recruited were space scientists whose research, formerly used to build rockets that could bomb England, would now be used to launch American astronauts into space.

> **Top Secret**
>
> The OSS was never put fully in charge of all foreign intelligence. The FBI was in charge of foreign intelligence in Latin America during the duration of the OSS's existence.
>
> Other men who worked for the OSS include Arthur M. Schlesinger, Jr., and future Supreme Court Justice Arthur Goldberg. TV chef Julia Child served with the OSS in Washington and in Beijing.

The OSS was also busy in Burma, where it was helping the allied effort to kick the Japanese off the Asian continent. Donovan himself went deep into Burma, 150 miles behind enemy lines, during the OSS campaign in that region.

For the most part, however, the OSS did not participate in the war against the Japanese. General Douglas MacArthur, who commanded allied forces in the South

Pacific, didn't believe in the OSS, so they weren't allowed in his region. When the OSS was dissolved following the war, two powerful men were not exactly heartbroken. One was MacArthur and the other was FBI director J. Edgar Hoover, who believed that the OSS unnecessarily stepped on the FBI's jurisdiction.

By the end of the war there were 9,028 employees in the OSS.

McLean Says ...

I always thought that the KGB had an easier time procuring useful overt, or open, intelligence than the CIA. The United States gave intelligence away. Did you know that KGB agents would arrive in U.S. airports and wait patiently for the latest copy of *Aviation Week* magazine to be put on the newsstand. They bought a copy, then flew by Aeroflot to Moscow, translating on the way. That's just one classic example of how America's "open media" made gathering useful intelligence easy for the Russians. How hard did the KGB have to work to get their hands on schematic drawings of the latest U.S. hardware? Not very hard. *Jane's*, a publisher of books about military hardware, was publishing the stuff. Fact is, *Jane's* is a source for much good information that all Intelligence Services find helpful.

October, 1945: OSS Abolished

The OSS had been set up exclusively as a war effort, so when World War II came to an end, it was quickly abolished. By October 1945, the war having ended less than two months before, the OSS was no more, and the functions were taken over by the War and State Departments.

However, the need for determining national intelligence objectives and correlating all government intelligence remained, even in peacetime. President Truman believed so strongly in the importance of intelligence that he said if such an organization had existed as part of the U.S. government before the war, it would have been "difficult, if not impossible" for the Japanese to successfully attack Pearl Harbor. As soon as the OSS was dissolved, plans began to create an organization to replace it.

Spookspeak

Joe, just good old Joe. That basic American name was the jargon used by the OSS during World War II for an agent.

Central Intelligence Group 1946

On January 22, 1946, Truman founded the Central Intelligence Group to take the place of the OSS. The CIG operated under the aegis of the National Security Agency during its short existence. The CIG lasted only a year and a half. The president replaced it with a new organization: the Central Intelligence Agency.

National Security Act of 1947: The CIA Is Born

The CIA—as well as the National Security Council and other intelligence-oriented organizations—was born on July 26, 1947, with the signing, by President Truman, of the National Security Act.

The Act enabled a coordinated definition of intelligence needs and allowed the president, as the chair of the National Security Council, to oversee the entire intelligence-gathering process and sort out any difficulties between members of the U.S. intelligence community.

The Intelligence Advisory Committee

On January 19, 1950, an Intelligence Advisory Committee was born to lend further organization and control over the multi-faceted U.S. intelligence community.

According to the act that created it, the committee was to consist of "the Director of Central Intelligence, who shall be Chairman thereof, the Director, Federal Bureau of Investigation, and the respective intelligence chiefs from the Departments of State, Army, Navy, and Air Force, and from the Joint Chiefs of Staff (JCS), and the Atomic Energy Commission, or their representatives, shall be established to advise the Director of Central Intelligence."

The legislation continues: "The Director of Central Intelligence will invite the chief, or his representative, of any other intelligence Agency having functions related to the national security to sit with the Intelligence Advisory Committee whenever matters within the purview of his Agency are to be discussed."

The Directorate of Intelligence, 1952

During the first years of the CIA, the production of finished intelligence was managed by the CIA's Office of Research and Reports. But, in 1952, DCI Walter Bedell Smith created the Directorate of Intelligence, which further streamlined the process of creating finished intelligence.

Loftus Becker, an attorney who had served as military adviser at the Nuremberg War Trials, became the first Deputy Director for Intelligence. Also in 1952, President Truman ordered that all presidential candidates be given intelligence briefings. The reason was to prevent candidates from inadvertently exposing clandestine programs while criticizing an incumbent. In other words, the candidates needed to be briefed so that they would know what *not* to say.

The House Permanent Select Committee on Intelligence

From the very beginning of the CIA, there was a framework by which the people would have some control over what the agency did. The people elected the Congress, and the Congress a permanent committee designed to see that the U.S. intelligence community worked as efficiently as it could given its budget and that it followed the rules that had been set up for it.

> **Top Secret**
>
> For more about the Permanent Select Committee on Intelligence, check out their website at www.intelligence.house.gov.

According to the current chairman of the House Permanent Select Committee on Intelligence, Porter J. Goss:

Intelligence capabilities are critical to the security of the United States. Through intelligence, we can find out what is happening throughout the world, beyond what other countries or entities present for public consumption. Such information can be used to ward off crises by allowing time to avert crises rather than just react to them. More importantly, intelligence is often the only way to find out the plans and intentions of countries, organizations or individuals who intend to do us harm or negatively affect our interests. There is no doubt that intelligence is and must be our first line of defense. Although it is important to have a robust intelligence capability, it is also important to have an effective oversight process to ensure that intelligence resources are not misused and that intelligence activities are conducted lawfully. Intelligence operations and law enforcement activities are governed by laws which are not in all cases the same. Ensuring that these laws are followed is a key component of our oversight responsibilities and was the primary reason for the creation of the congressional intelligence committees. Because of the sensitivities of intelligence operations and resources, the intelligence budget is classified. These same sensitivities require that the budget receive an extra amount of congressional scrutiny, and there is a legal requirement that intelligence funding not only be appropriated, but authorized as well.

McLean Says ...

During the Nixon era troubles, government officials were worried about protesters at the Pentagon. I was asked to see how easy it might be to penetrate that military complex. I took the subway to the Pentagon, went into a rest room and put on a blue doctor's smock, added an official looking name tag, donned a stethoscope, and put my jacket and tie into a black doctor's bag. Then, I went to the subway entrance to the Pentagon in a brisk walk and asked the security guard, with some urgency in my voice, how I could get to a numbered room. "I'm Dr. Plant," I said, pointing to my name tag.

Without hesitation, or checking for any other credentials, the guard let me though, pointed down a corridor, told me to proceed and the Marine guard inside could direct me. I thanked him and hurried in and down the corridor. The military guard was even more courteous and helpful. He directed me to the right elevator and told me which way to turn and walk when I got to the second floor.

Once I had found the room, I left a mark on the door and then proceeded to the main exit, said hello to the reception people and left. Appearances and a good act can often breach even what should have been a highly secure situation.

Ivy League Recruiting Ground

During the first years of the CIA, many officers were recruited out of the *Ivy League*. But you no longer have to go to an Ivy League school in order to qualify to work in the CIA—and actually, you non-Ivy Leaguers have always been part of the agency.

For many years now the CIA has tried to rid itself of its "Northeastern Intelligencia" reputation. Officers today are just as likely to be recruited from colleges in middle America, or religious colleges such as Fordham University, as from the Ivy League.

Spookspeak

Ivy League schools include Harvard, Yale, Princeton, Dartmouth, Columbia, Cornell, Penn, and Brown.

The Least You Need to Know

◆ During World War II, the OSS was mandated to collect and analyze strategic information required by the Joint Chiefs of Staff and to conduct special operations not assigned to other agencies.

◆ After the war the OSS was replaced by the Central Intelligence Group and then the CIA.

◆ The American people, through their elected officials, have some control over the CIA through the House Permanent Select Committee on Intelligence.

◆ The agency is trying to lose its "Ivy League Only" reputation.

The Men Who Have Stood at the Helm

In This Chapter

- ◆ What it takes to be DCI
- ◆ Dulles' heyday
- ◆ When Helms was at the helm
- ◆ From Souers to Tenet

The position of Director of Central Intelligence has existed since 1947 when Congress created it. As noted in Chapter 2, the DCI oversees both the Central Intelligence Agency and the U.S. Intelligence Community.

The DCI is appointed by the president, subject to the approval of the U.S. Senate. The president alone can fire a DCI. Because the position is whatever the standing president wants it to be, DCIs have varied greatly in significance and duties over the years.

Whereas some DCIs have been master spies whose entire careers have been dedicated to spookdom, others have been purely political appointments, with Democrats appointing Democrats and Republicans appointing Republicans.

Some DCIs worked intimately with the presidents who appointed them, becoming something akin to another member of the president's cabinet. Others were virtual strangers, whose interchanges with their president were limited to memoranda.

Rear Admiral William H. Souers: January 23, 1946–June 1946

Souers was appointed by President Harry S Truman as the first Director of Central Intelligence on January 23, 1946, one day after Truman signed the presidential directive that gave birth to the Central Intelligence Group.

Souers, born in 1892, was a 1914 graduate of the University of Miami of Ohio. He was a businessman who had great success with his investments. Souers was appointed a lieutenant commander, an intelligence officer, in the Naval Reserve in April 1929 and, as far as we know, was not called into active duty until 1940.

During the first years of World War II, Souers worked in district intelligence offices in Great Lakes, Illinois; Charleston, South Carolina; and San Juan, Puerto Rico. He must have done some good things while he was there because he received a major promotion in July 1944, when he was named assistant chief of naval intelligence in charge of plans and the deputy chief of naval intelligence in Washington, D.C. He was promoted to rear admiral in 1945 and served on a committee representing the secretary of the Navy, determining the feasibility of forming a central intelligence organization. President Truman liked Souers proposal so much that he put him in charge of the Central Intelligence Group's formation, and named him its first director.

Considering that President Truman had an almost sixth sense for picking good people for important jobs, we can assume that Souers had the credentials to achieve what the President wanted done and the perseverance to get it done.

Tradecraft

Cabs can be helpful in breaking a tail. Flag a cab, get in and go a few blocks. Get the cab to circle several blocks while you pretend to look for a building you are trying to find. That explains why you would be constantly looking on either side and behind the cab. If you spot a tail, use your training to lose them.

After getting the CIG up and running, Souers retired briefly to private life before returning to government work at the request of the Atomic Energy Commission, for whom he conducted a study to determine the security requirements of preserving the secret of The Bomb.

In September 1947, Truman appointed Souers the first executive secretary of the National Security Council, and Souers remained in that position until 1950. He retired from the Naval Reserve in 1953 and spent much of the 1950s speaking out against McCarthyism and its indiscriminate anticommunism, a symptom of paranoia, he felt, more destructive than communism itself.

General Hoyt S. Vandenberg: June 1946–April 1947

Vandenberg was born in 1899 and graduated from the U.S. Military Academy in 1923. At the start of the World War II, he was the assistant chief of staff of the U.S. Army Air Forces.

From 1943 to 1946, he was deputy chief of the Air Staff. In that capacity he became the senior air member of the U.S. Military Mission to Moscow in 1946. He was named DCI that year by President Truman.

Vandenberg was the nephew of Senator Arthur Vandenberg, the Republican president pro tem of the Senate during the late 1940s.

It was during Vandenberg's tenure as DCI that Central Intelligence was given the responsibility of gathering intelligence in Latin America, which before that had been the responsibility of the FBI.

When the U.S. Air Force was formed as its own branch of the service in October 1947, Vandenberg was named Vice Chief of Staff with a rank of full general. In the Washington, D.C., scheme of things, this looks like a demotion; but Gen. Vandenberg was a key figure in establishing the U.S. Air Force as a separate service. His was a labor of love, and he was uniquely qualified to the job. From May 1948 until June 1953, Vandenberg served as Chief of Staff of the Air Force. He died in 1954.

Rear Admiral Roscoe H. Hillenkoetter: May 1, 1947–October 7, 1950

Born in 1897, Hillenkoetter was a graduate of the Naval Academy. He served as assistant naval attaché at the U.S. Embassy in Paris from 1933–35 and 1938–40, until the start of the Nazi occupation of that city.

Commander Hillenkoetter was the executive officer of the battleship *West Virginia* at the start of World War II and was present during the Japanese attack on Pearl Harbor on December 7, 1941.

In 1942, he directed the Intelligence Center Pacific Ocean Area (ICPOA) in Hawaii. While there, he became the Navy's top code-breaker. He became the commander of a destroyer tender during 1943–44. (A tender is a ship employed to provide provisions for other ships or a warship that provides logistical support.)

After the war, Hillenkoetter was named the commanding officer of the battleship *Missouri* before returning to Paris as the naval attaché; he held that position when President Truman named him the director of the Central Intelligence Group.

Ordered to prevent a Communist victory in elections in Italy, Hillenkoetter ordered clandestine financial and public-relations help to the pro-U.S. candidates, who ended up winning the election.

During the summer of 1950, when North Korea invaded South Korea, Hillenkoetter admitted that the CIA had known about troop buildups at the border yet had not anticipated the invasion. Taking the blame for the intelligence lapse, Hillenkoetter was fired as DCI by Truman. He died in 1982.

Lt. Gen. Walter Bedell Smith: October 1950–February 1953

Smith, born in 1895, served as chief of staff to General of the Army Dwight D. Eisenhower, the Supreme Allied Commander in Europe, during World War II. Eisenhower called him "the general manager of the war." Following World War II, Smith was named by President Harry S Truman to be the U.S. ambassador to the Soviet Union. In 1949 he became the Commanding General of the First Army and was stationed in New York City.

> **Top Secret**
>
> Does the CIA have its own X-Files? Maybe. Walter Bedell Smith thought that these UFO's could have national security implications and ordered a study to be done on their existence. The results? Sorry, still classified.

Smith left the CIA and retired from active duty in the army in 1953. He became the Under-secretary of State for a year before retiring to a writing career during which he published books such as *Eisenhower's Six Great Decisions* (1956) and *My Three Years in Moscow* (1949). Smith died in 1961.

Allen W. Dulles: February 1953–November 1961

Born in 1893, Dulles was the nephew of a secretary of state and the grandson of another. It was hoped by the family that Allen would become the family's third secretary of state, but, despite his many accomplishments, this was never to be. There was a third secretary of state in the family, but it turned out to be Allen's brother, John Foster Dulles.

> **Top Secret**
>
> In November 1942, Dulles opened the OSS office in Bern, Switzerland. He was designated Agent 110 and referred to in OSS communications as Mr. Bull.

His first government job was at the U.S. Embassy to the Austro-Hungarian Empire, but after the United States entered World War I, he was moved to Bern, Switzerland. Following the war, he resigned from the state department and went to work on Wall Street. Dulles was a master spy with the OSS during World War II.

After World War II, Dulles practiced law. He first went to work for the CIA in January 1951. Eight months later he was named the agency's deputy director. President Eisenhower appointed Dulles DCI in 1953. As DCI, Dulles ordered his agents to

carry out clandestine operations through-
out South America and the Middle East.
It was during his tenure that the U-2 spy
plane was developed and he was responsi-
ble for the digging of the Berlin tunnel
(see Chapter 10). He also plotted to kill
Fidel Castro, the revolutionary leader of
Cuba who had declared his allegiance to the
Communists. According to Dulles' Deputy
Director of Central Intelligence, Richard
Bissell, the CIA-sponsored attempts on the life of Castro were so secret that only
Dulles received reports about them. He was fired by JFK after the Bay of Pigs fiasco
and later became a member of the Warren Commission (see Chapter 13 for more on
the CIA's role in the Bay of Pigs).

Tradecraft

According to General Dwight
D. Eisenhower's chief of intelligence during World War II,
General Kenneth Strong, "Allen
Dulles was undoubtedly the
greatest United States professional
intelligence officer of his time."

One of Dulles's most influential programs at the end of World War II was Operation
Paperclip, which recruited members of Germany's intelligence and science community
into the American fold. The move had two positive benefits: it recruited a lot of knowledge, and it prevented the Soviets from recruiting the same. (Of course, having the same
idea, they recruited their own Germans.) Some people have argued that Operation
Paperclip gave certain U.S. organizations—NASA and the CIA, in particular—a fas-
cist mindset, but others believe that the early CIA was actually on the liberal end of
the political spectrum during the Cold War.

John A. McCone: November 1961–April 1965

John McCone was born in 1902. He graduated from the University of California at
Berkeley in 1922 with a degree in Engineering. After school he worked as an engi-
neer, and then later as a corporate executive.

McCone's business career was interrupted with increasing frequency by government
appointments. Among the positions he held before becoming DCI are: member,
President's Air Policy Committee, 1947–48; Deputy Secretary of Defense, 1948;
Under Secretary of the Air Force, 1950–51; and chairman of the Atomic Energy
Commission, 1958–60.

When President Kennedy fired Allen Dulles, he appointed McCone as his replacement in November 1961, and it was McCone who was DCI during the October 1962
Cuban Missile Crisis. During that crisis he was among the select group who met with
President Kennedy daily. His advice to JFK was to not invade Cuba. McCone's other
major known accomplishment as DCI was in developing the CIA's role in Vietnam.

The CIA did not warm up to McCone when he was first appointed DCI. He replaced Allen Dulles, who was beloved by many, and he had no previous intelligence experience. He had never been in the military, although, as a civilian, he had worked in the Pentagon. Many CIA employees were also suspicious of the fact that McCone was a friend of both President Kennedy and Attorney General Robert Kennedy. Because of the timing of the hiring it was feared that McCone's appointment was a public relations move designed to save face following the Bay of Pigs.

After McCone's stint as DCI, he served as a U.S. representative at The Vatican. He died in 1991.

Vice Admiral William F. "Red" Raborn, Jr.: April 1965–June 1966

Born in 1905 in Texas, Admiral Raborn is known as a DCI with one of the shortest tenures. He held the position for only 14 months. He graduated from the Naval Academy in 1928 and became an ordnance specialist and naval aviator.

From 1955 to 1962 he managed the *Polaris* missile program, which were the first missiles to be launched from submarines. Promoted to Vice Admiral, Raborn served from 1962 to 1963 as Deputy Chief of Naval Operations.

Raborn was appointed DCI by President Lyndon B. Johnson, who was also from Texas. Raborn's was the second consecutive unpopular DCI appointment at the agency, where the spooks wanted their director to be promoted from within. Following Raborn's stint as DCI, he returned to private business. He died in 1990.

Richard McGarrah Helms: June 1966–February 1973

With Richard Helms' appointment as DCI in June 1966, the employees of the CIA got what they wanted. For the first time since Allen Dulles's tenure, the top man at the CIA was himself a spymaster.

Some of the biggest abuses in the CIA charter occurred during Helms' watch. Delving into what should have been the FBI's territory, in 1967, Helms established the Special Operations Group, which was put in charge of an internal security function—that is, keeping track of Americans who were against U.S. participation in the war in Vietnam. The Special Operations Group had files on 7,200 U.S. citizens.

> **McLean Says ...**
>
> The CIA knew the KGB had set up a fair number (estimates range from 100 to several hundred) of Sleepers before the Vietnam War. These were women who had been carefully trained, indoctrinated, and motivated to marry U.S. officers at the end of World War II, move to the United States, and 'go to sleep'—not just with their husbands but for the KGB. They would then be contacted periodically and "activated" as needed.
>
> Some people argue that the presence of these sleepers justified the CIA spying on the American people.

Helms was fired as DCI by President Nixon during the aftermath of the Watergate scandal. Nixon wanted Helms to say that the investigation into the Watergate burglary should be called off because it might accidentally expose CIA methods. Helms refused to lie for Nixon (there is no evidence that the CIA was involved with Watergate) and lost his job.

Helms had a history of not caving in to pressures from the White House. Early in his tenure as DCI, Helms had said no to President Johnson when LBJ asked that the CIA confirm the "Domino Theory," which stated that Communism needed to be nipped in the bud in southeast Asia or else many other countries would, one by one, fall to communism. CIA studies, on the other hand, indicated that this probably would not be the case and that the domino theory was not a good reason to maintain a U.S. presence in Vietnam.

James R. Schlesinger: February 1973–July 1973

Born in 1929, Schlesinger earned his Bachelors, Masters, and Doctorate at Harvard. He was director of strategic studies at the Rand Corporation from 1963 to 1969. He was chairman of the Atomic Energy Commission from 1971 to 1973.

He held that position when President Nixon appointed him DCI. Although he was not DCI for long, he orchestrated sweeping changes. He fired about 5 percent of CIA personnel and installed a new rule that forced officers to retire after 20 years of service.

William E. Colby: September 1973–January 1976

Following several months in which Lt. Gen. Vernon A. Walters was the acting DCI, William Colby was given the job. Born in 1920, Colby graduated from Princeton in 1941. He joined the army and volunteered for the OSS. As a spy he parachuted into German-occupied France in 1944 and German-occupied Norway in 1945.

After the war, Colby went to law school at Columbia and, for a time, was the legal partner in private practice of OSS founder William Donovan. Colby joined the CIA after the outbreak of the war in Korea. He served at the U.S. Embassy in Stockholm, then in Rome, and from 1959 to 1962 he was the station chief at the U.S. Embassy in Saigon.

Colby returned to Vietnam in 1968 to run the CIA's Operation Phoenix, a program that located and identified, for the South Vietnamese Army, Vietnamese who were supportive of the Viet Cong. (For more about Operation Phoenix, see Chapter 12.)

After his stint as DCI, Colby practiced law and worked as an international consultant.

In a bizarre turn, Colby appeared in a 1992 television advertisement calling for the military budget to be cut in half so that that money could be spent on education and health care.

Colby had an unusual death. During May of 1996, Colby, 76 years old, called his wife from his Maryland home saying that he didn't feel well, but that he was going to take the canoe out anyway. He took the canoe out onto the Wicomico River. The next day his canoe was found but there was no sign of him. His body was found a week later on a grassy riverbank.

George H.W. Bush: January 1976–January 1977

George Herbert Walker Bush, the 41st U.S. president and father of the 43rd president, once wrote: "During my career, I have had the rare opportunity to serve on both sides of the coin in the intelligence cycle—producer and consumer. As the Director of Central Intelligence, I advised the President and the National Security Council on foreign intelligence matters, and I have been recipient of that intelligence as President of the United States!"

He was born in Milton, Massachusetts, and joined the Navy and became a Naval aviator during World War II.

"It was tough and risky business flying off aircraft carriers during the war. I think it strengthened my ability to meet the challenges that lay ahead," President Bush once recalled. Bush was awarded the Distinguished Flying Cross and three Air Medals, and was discharged with the rank of lieutenant (junior grade). He attended Yale University, graduating in 1948, and went on to start an oil company, Zapata Petroleum Corporation. He was director and later president of the Zapata Off Shore Corporation.

Bush was the Director of Central Intelligence from January 1976 to January 1977, when he was replaced by the new president, Jimmy Carter. He was the vice-president of the United States under Ronald Reagan from 1980 to 1988. He was president from 1988 to 1992 and his son became president in 2000.

Admiral Stansfield Turner: March 1977–January 1981

For a couple of months Enno Henry Knoche was the acting DCI, until the appointment of Stansfield Turner. Born in 1923, Turner graduated from the Naval Academy in 1946. As a graduate student he attended Oxford University in England on a Rhodes Scholarship. He earned his Master's degree at Oxford in 1950.

After 24 years in the Navy, he was promoted to rear admiral in 1970. He became a full admiral in 1975 when he became NATO's Commander in Chief Allied Forces Southern Europe. President Carter appointed Turner DCI because they had been classmates at Annapolis, although they apparently were not friends while there.

As DCI, Turner supported prioritizing satellite intelligence while de-emphasizing human intelligence. Because he was an admiral, he tended to give orders according to personal whim, which caused great resentment in the CIA. Turner, for example, prohibited drinking at lunch. Many CIA officers heard that and thought, "This guy has to go." But he didn't. He stayed DCI for almost four years.

William J. Casey: January 1981–January 1987

During the last years of World War II, Casey was the chief of Special Intelligence for the OSS in Europe. During the 1970s he became chairman of the Securities and Exchange Commission. In 1980 Casey was campaign manager for Ronald Reagan's first successful run for the White House. He was appointed by Reagan as DCI in 1981.

The top CIA scandal to come out of Casey's regime was the Iran-Contra scandal, in which the U.S. traded weapons to Iran in exchange for American hostages they held. It turned out that the CIA had little if anything to do with the operation, and were as

Tradecraft

Casey was somewhat uncooperative during the Iran-Contra hearings. The DCI could enunciate quite clearly when he wanted to, but when he was called upon to testify before a government hearing under oath, he used an old trick of his and mumbled like James Dean and Bob Dylan put together, so much so that court reporters sometimes found it impossible to transcribe his testimony.

much in the dark as everyone else. The whole incident was an undeserved embarrassment for the agency. According to James McCullough in *Studies in Intelligence*, "Bill Casey … does not deserve to have his memory stained by false charges of involvement in a conspiracy to conceal the facts of the Iran affair. It just did not happen that way."

It was Casey who established the CIA's counterterrorism center—which, of course, has been plenty busy so far in the twenty-first century. The center had instant success, helping to catch a terrorist in Lebanon. Casey remained in charge until a stroke sidelined him in 1986. Robert M. Gates, a future DCI, was acting director from 1986 to 1987.

William Hedgcock Webster: May 1987–August 1991

Webster has the distinction of being the only man to be both DCI and Director of the FBI (1978–1987). Born in 1924, Webster earned a Bachelor's degree from Amherst and a law degree from Washington University Law School in St. Louis.

During World War II, Webster served in the Navy. He rose to lieutenant and stayed in the service until after the end of the Korean War. After returning to the U.S., he practiced law in St. Louis. In 1960 he was appointed U.S. Attorney for the Eastern District of Missouri.

Top Secret

During the Gulf War, DCI William H. Webster had four regular telephones in his office, plus 15 hotlines which gave him direct access to his senior officials.

Webster was appointed to a federal judgeship by President Nixon in 1971, and was appointed to head the FBI by President Carter in 1978. As DCI, he said that his biggest goals were to improve counterintelligence and to make U.S. Embassies around the world more secure. During his time as the head of U.S. intelligence, he told those he dealt with that he was most comfortable being referred to as "Judge."

Webster resigned as DCI after he was criticized by members of Congress and President Bush's administration for failing to predict Iraq's invasion of Kuwait in 1990. He resigned on May 8, 1991, but at President Bush's request, remained on the job until the end of that August. He was one of the tough old boys, and a man of great personal integrity. He did what he did well, and bowed out gracefully. Some Spooks believe he gave ground too easily.

It was only during Webster's tenure as DCI that the CIA stopped being a mostly white and male organization. According to the FBI's public affairs office, the number of female special agents working for the CIA during the time Webster was DCI rose from 147 to 787. Black and Hispanic employment more than doubled.

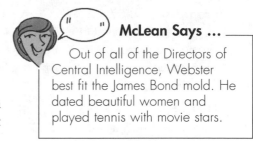

McLean Says ...

Out of all of the Directors of Central Intelligence, Webster best fit the James Bond mold. He dated beautiful women and played tennis with movie stars.

Robert M. Gates: November 1991–January 1993

The acting DCI from September to November 1991 was Richard J. Kerr. He was replaced by Robert M. Gates, who was born in 1943. From Wichita, Kansas, Gates graduated from the College of William and Mary.

Gates had a Master's degree in Eastern European history from Indiana University and a Doctorate in Russian history and language from Georgetown University when he joined the CIA as an assistant national intelligence officer for strategic programs in 1966. From 1974 to 1979, Gates worked for the National Security Council. Returning to the CIA, he worked briefly as national intelligence officer for the Soviet Union and as Chair of the National Intelligence Council before being appointed in 1982 as Deputy Director of Intelligence, or DDI.

During Gates's time as DCI, he moved the CIA away from the Cold War, its *raison d'etre* for so many years. A new emphasis was put on preventing the proliferation of nuclear weapons, counterterrorism, and counternarcotics. He also became the first DCI to enter the Kremlin, when he went to Russia in 1992 for a meeting with Russian President Boris Yeltsin.

When Bill Clinton became President in 1993, Gates retired from the CIA.

R. James Woolsey: February 1993–May 1994

Woolsey, born in 1941, was a graduate of Stanford University. After receiving his Bachelor's degree he traveled to England where he studied at Oxford under a Rhodes Scholarship.

He earned his law degree at Yale Law School and served in the U.S. Army from 1968 to 1970, prime Vietnam years. At that time he served on the staff of the National Security Council, and, as a lawyer, worked on strategic arms limitation issues.

From 1970 to 1973 Woolsey served as the general counsel to the Senate Committee on Armed Services. He was Under-Secretary of the Navy from 1978 to 1979. After a short time running his own private law practice, he returned during the 1980s as a representative of the U.S. government talking with NATO and Soviet officials about arms limitations.

He had once again returned to his private law practice when President Clinton appointed him DCI in 1993. Clinton wanted Woolsey to accomplish several major tasks. It was a Cold War organization and the Cold War was over. Clinton wanted to pull the CIA into the future. He also wanted an increased number of women and minorities hired.

However, Woolsey was in charge of intelligence in 1994 when it was discovered that Aldrich H. Ames had been a Soviet mole operating within the agency. When Woolsey failed to harshly punish the CIA officials who had been in charge of Ames, he was fired.

John M. Deutch: May 1994–December 1996

Deutch, a former MIT chemistry professor, was among the least popular of the DCIs with agency personnel. His job was to pull the CIA past the horror of Ames' discovery. With Deutch's appointment, the job of DCI was once again raised to cabinet-level. So Deutch was the first DCI since Casey to be considered a member of the President's cabinet.

Deutch is the only DCI to have been born outside of the United States. He was born into a Jewish family in Belgium in 1938. He and his family fled the Nazis and came to the U.S. when he was still a baby. They moved into a suburb of Washington, D.C.

Deutch was a very smart guy. He simultaneously earned a chemical engineering degree at the Massachusetts Institute of Technology (MIT) and a history degree from Amherst.

Under President Carter, Deutch was an undersecretary in charge of nuclear weapon production programs for the new Department of Energy. Under the first President Bush, he was a member of the president's Foreign Intelligence Advisory Board.

Although Deutch was not DCI for long, he had his share of controversy. When a silly rumor started that the CIA was pushing crack cocaine in Los Angeles, Deutch, instead of ignoring it with the understanding that rational people wouldn't believe it anyway, actually made a speech in Los Angeles to deny the rumor, an act which only lent the rumor credence to some.

George J. Tenet: January 1997–

The current DCI, George Tenet, was born in New York City in 1953. Tenet received a Bachelor's degree in 1976 from the School of Foreign Service at Georgetown University and a Master's degree from the School of International Affairs at Columbia University in 1978. He began government work at age 29 working on the staff of Pennsylvania Senator John Heinz. In 1985, Tenet began work on the staff of the Senate Intelligence Committee, and, in 1989, he became that committee's staff director.

Tenet was only 44 years old when he was appointed DCI, which makes him the youngest ever. It has been said that he quietly let the CIA know that there would be a return to CIA tradition when, on his first day on the job, he moved the portrait of Richard Helms from the hallways and put it up in his private office.

When President George W. Bush took office, Tenet was the only survivor from the Clinton Administration to remain on the president's national security team. Following September 11, Tenet refused to allow the CIA to be a scapegoat for that security disaster. And, to his credit, under his tenure, the CIA has continued to rebuild its paramilitary forces—all but extinct in the years after Operation Phoenix—so that CIA officers were ready to hit the ground in Afghanistan immediately.

Which brings us to the present. So, as you can see, there is no "mold" out of which DCIs fall. The men who have directed our Central Intelligence have come from many different walks of life, and with various levels of experience when it comes to intelligence-gathering. Yet they were all men of distinction in their many fields.

The Least You Need to Know

♦ Souers was appointed by President Harry S Truman as the first Director of Central Intelligence on January 23, 1946.

♦ DCI Allen Dulles was a master spy with the OSS during World War II.

♦ With Richard Helms appointment, for the first time since Allen Dulles's tenure, the top man at the CIA was himself a spymaster.

♦ Tenet was only 44 years old when he was appointed DCI, which makes him the youngest ever.

Brothers in Espionage: Foreign Intelligence Agencies

In This Chapter

◆ The lowdown on British Intelligence

◆ Making sense of Mossad

◆ CIA's Soviet Counterpart—and more

Now we are going to turn the magnifying glass around. Instead of looking inward, at the U.S. intelligence community, we're going to look outward, at a sampling of the major foreign intelligence agencies around the world.

Let's start with the most famous intel agency in the world, thanks to a suave spook named 007. (The 007 designation was the invention of James Bond's creator Ian Fleming, and many of the more dramatic aspects of Bond's character are either fictional inventions or extreme exaggerations— caricatures, if you will—of real life spookdom.)

Where James Bond Would Have Worked (Had He Been Real, That Is)

As in the United States, the gathering of domestic and foreign intelligence is handled separately in the United Kingdom. Just as the United States has the CIA and the FBI, Great Britain has MI5 (Military Intelligence 5) and MI6. Although the lines of distinction are not identical, MI5 is basically equivalent to our FBI, while MI6 more closely resembles the CIA.

The Security Service—better known as MI5—is the United Kingdom's security intelligence agency. Its stated purpose is "to protect national security from threats such as terrorism, espionage and the proliferation of weapons of mass destruction, to safeguard the economic well-being of the UK against foreign threats, and to support the law enforcement agencies in preventing and detecting serious crime."

MI5 was born in March 1909, when Prime Minister Herbert H. Asquith instructed the Committee of Imperial Defence to consider the dangers from German espionage to British naval ports. On October 1, following the Committee's recommendation, Captain Vernon Kell of the South Staffordshire Regiment and Captain Mansfield Cumming of the Royal Navy jointly established the Secret Service Bureau. MI5 was originally known as MO5, or Military Office 5; when it became part of the newly created Military Intelligence directorate, it retained its "5" and was known as MI5. MI6 had its origins around the same time and was originally known as the British Secret Intelligence Service.

> **Top Secret**
>
> One former MI5 officer who went on to write great spy books is David Cornwell, better known to the world by his *nom de plume*, John Le Carré.

To fulfill the Admiralty's requirement—the Admiralty being the British equivalent to our Navy Department—for information about Germany's new navy, Kell and Cumming decided to divide their work. Thereafter, Kell was responsible for counterespionage within the British Isles (MI5) while Cumming was responsible for gathering intelligence overseas as head of MI6, or the Secret Intelligence Service.

Real Life "M" and "Q"

One thing about the Ian Fleming's James Bond novels that did reflect reality was that the leaders of British Intelligence organizations tended to be known only by one initial, while their true identities remained secret. The men in charge were not known as "M" or "Q", as in the books, but rather as "K"—for Kell—and "C"—for Cumming.

Another element of the James Bond books, of course, is that the heroic spy is invulnerable. Unfortunately, in real life spies die just as easily as everyone else. (That's what makes them heroes!) During the mid-1950s, with the Cold War giving the world the shivers, MI6 sent an ex-Navy diver-turned-spy named Lionel Crabb on a secret mission to Portsmouth Harbor, to examine the underwater hull of a new Soviet cruiser. Crabb never returned from his assignment, and later a headless corpse was found floating in the harbor, presumably the all-too-mortal British spy.

> **Spookspeak**
>
> **A Force** is another neat Intel term. It refers to or may be considered the nickname for the British MI6 organization that conducted sophisticated deception operations during World War II.

A Closer Look at MI5 and MI6

MI5 has six divisions: Administration, Counterespionage, Security, Military Liaison, Aliens, Overseas Control. These days, MI5 is preoccupied with counterterrorism, with the bombing campaign of the Irish Republican Army being their primary concern. MI6—the organization that James Bond would have worked for, had he been real—is active in the war against Al Qaeda and global terrorism.

The U.S. and British intelligence agencies have worked together for a long time. Because of England's location, the spy organizations there are better positioned to spy on Europe than their American counterparts. This is equally true when it comes to their signals intelligence (SIGINT). Although the British Intelligence services have been suffering from budget cuts, they remain key partners to the CIA.

As with the CIA, there was a time when British Intelligence was just about an all-male club. Those days are gone, however. In fact, the head (the director-general) of MI5 is a woman: Dame Stella Rimington was promoted out of MI5's countersubversion division department to lead the agency.

> **Top Secret**
>
> At MI6, headquarters is referred to as "Y." Overseas stations are called "YP." Y is divided into 10 divisions, each given a Roman numeral: I) Political; II) Military; III) Naval; IV) Air; V) Counterespionage; VI) Industrial; VII) Financial; VIII) Communications; IX) Cipher; X) Press.

Don't Mess with Mossad

If you're a young nation surrounded by enemies who openly call for your destruction, your intelligence agency had better be good. Very good. *Mossad*, Israel's intelligence agency, meets that criteria.

The agency was established by then Prime Minister David Ben Gurion on April 1, 1951, three years after Israel was formed. Mossad is responsible for Israel's human intelligence collection, covert action, and counterterrorism. Though the founders of Mossad were Nazi-hunters, Mossad's focus has always been on Arab nations and anti-Israeli organizations throughout the world.

Mossad also is responsible for the clandestine movement of Jewish refugees out of Syria, Iran, and Ethiopia. Mossad agents are active in the former communist countries, in the West, and at the United Nations. Its HQ is in Tel Aviv.

Mossad employs an estimated 1,500 to 2,000 personnel. The identity of the director of Mossad was traditionally a state secret, but that changed in March 1996 when the Government announced the appointment of Major General Danny Yatom as the replacement for Shabtai Shavit, who resigned in early 1996.

Intelligence, according to Israeli government, "constitutes the first line of defense" against enemies that have besieged the Israeli state since the country's creation.

Spying on Mossad

It is believed that Mossad has a total of eight departments, though details remain obscure. One thing that spooks respect about Mossad: they sure can keep things secret. At least six of those departments are known:

♦ **Collections**. Mossad's largest division. Equivalent to the CIA Directorate of Operations. Responsible for all espionage activities, with case officers stationed at various "desks" around the world.

♦ **Political Action and Liaison**. In charge of cooperative efforts with the intelligence services of other nations as well as contacts with unfriendly nations.

♦ **Special Operations**. This division is sometimes called Metsada. This is Mossad's assassination and sabotage division. We can say no more. (Okay, okay, here's a little more: You may have seen some news reports during the past year or so about assassinations of alleged terrorists in Israel or Palestine territories.)

Metsada was most likely responsible for these assassinations, and more will undoubtedly make the news as the escalating problems in the Middle East erupt from time to time.)

◆ **Lahamah Psichlogit.** The most difficult of the divisions to pronounce, this is the division in charge of psychological warfare. They disseminate propaganda and disinformation, and play other games of psychological deception.

◆ **Research.** Prepares the daily situation briefs and handles the day-to-day chores of intelligence gathering. A huge section of the Research division is dedicated to tracking nuclear proliferation.

◆ **Technology.** In charge of researching the latest pertinent technology and implementing it to the advantage of Israel.

Mossad's job is to gather intelligence from outside Israel. They do this by planting spies, either Mossad or locals who have been recruited as agents, in Arab countries.

In addition to the accumulation of intelligence, Mossad also has counterterrorism and covert action capabilities. It is known that Mossad is structured similar to the CIA rather than British intelligence.

McLean Says ...

During the hours following the September 11 attacks there was a frenzy of activity in intelligence agencies around the world to determine who was behind the attacks. In Washington, there was a deep suspicion that America's old nemesis, Iraq, along with Osama bin Laden and Al Qaeda, might have had something to do with it. When the CIA asked Mossad for their input, however, Mossad said that their analysis revealed that bin Laden had acted alone and that Iraq had had nothing to do with it.

Mossad's thinking was that, because the United States is monitoring all Iraqi communications, Al Qaeda would not have wanted to work with them for fear that the element of surprise would have been blown. It's great that Mossad has such confidence in the CIA's intelligence gathering abilities, but there's a dangerous arrogance to this analysis. If Saddam Hussein wanted to get a message to Osama bin Laden without the United States knowing about it, he would have found a way. There is evidence, for example, that one of the September 11 hijackers met with a senior Iraqi intelligence officer.

Operation Thunderbolt: Entebbe

The Mossad's most famous success came in 1976, and it occurred 2,000 miles from Israel. Palestinian terrorists had hijacked an Air France passenger jet and had flown it to Entebbe, Uganda, where they were holding its 97 passengers hostage.

In what Mossad referred to as Operation Thunderbolt, the agency quickly gathered information that would help in their plan to overtake the hijacked plan. As it turned out, the airport had been built with Israeli support, so data on the airport was easy to come by.

Using information provided by Mossad, Israeli special forces raided the airport and rescued all but one of the hostages, who was killed. Six terrorists and 20 Ugandan soldiers were also killed in the fighting. The commanding officer of the Israeli attack force was that group's only fatality.

> ### McLean Says ...
>
> Pakistan's formidable intelligence service is called the Inter-Services Intelligence Agency (ISI). It is a military agency, although it is semi-autonomous.
>
> Latest indications are that several of the top ISI officials have anti-American feelings and ties to Islamic militants. In America and Great Britain and other European Allies, the government intelligence organizations are tools of the political leadership. We tend to think that is proper and normal. However, in many other countries—including Pakistan, if intelligence reports are accurate—the Intel organizations may have control over their own destiny and, at times, can be adversaries to their nation's political leadership. Given the tense relations between Pakistan and India, checks and balances are more important than ever. One rogue agent with too much power and not enough restraint could cost millions of lives in that hot spot.

The Powerful KGB

The KGB was the Soviet Government's Committee of State Security. It was commonly thought of as the Soviet counterpart to the CIA, but the KGB was a larger organization with a wider scope of duties and responsibilities than any single U.S. agency.

> ### Spookspeak
>
> **KGB** is the Russian abbreviation for *Komitet Gosudarstvenny Bezopasnosti,* which translates to the Committee of State Security. It was the Soviet Secret Service.

The KGB was the Soviet counterpart to not only the CIA, but the NSA, Secret Service, many functions of the FBI, Customs Service, and Armed Forces counterintelligence agencies. As the French so perfectly express it: *Trés formidable!*

Sizing Up the KGB

The KGB was organized into 17 "chief directorates" of which the first, the Foreign Directorate, was the most notorious. The Foreign Directorate was in charge of Soviet espionage. It was responsible for the collection of all nonmilitary—and much military—foreign intelligence, foreign counterintelligence, recruitment of foreigners, foreign propaganda, and disinformation. Another directorate dealt with nonmilitary counterintelligence. A third dealt with military counterintelligence.

The others directorates were Transportation; Ideological (monitored and repressed all real, or imagined, dissidents in the USSR including activists involved in political, religious, environmental, human rights, and other causes); Economic Security (which guarded against illegal trading); Surveillance; Anti-Terrorism; Communication; Guards; Archives, Electronic Surveillance, Bunkers (for nuclear weapons); Communications Security; Communication Troops; Border Guards; and Information Analysis. It is difficult to say with any precision how large the KGB was. Estimates from 1990 said that the KGB had 500,000 employees, not counting 240,000 border guards. That's a lot of spics!

> **Top Secret**
>
> One of the biggest successes the KGB had during the Cold War was the recruitment of a former U.S. Navy Warrant Officer as an agent. The traitor was John A. Walker. He gave away the codes used in Navy communications.

Russia's FSK and SVR

Since the collapse of the Soviet Union during the early-1990s, the internal security and counterintelligence organization in Russia has become known as the FSK. It was created by Russian President Boris Yeltsin in December 1991 to replace at least part of the KGB. Their stated enemies are organized crime and fascists. It has been estimated that the FSK currently has 75,000 employees, both military and civilian.

Russia's foreign intelligence agency is known as the SVR and it was formed by Boris Yeltsin at the same time as the FSK. The third organization necessary to completely replace the huge KGB was called the SBP, which is in charge of presidential protection.

Détente Breeds Influx

There's no question that during the height of the Cold War the KGB and the CIA infiltrated each other's systems. And although some might think that the KGB infiltration into U.S. systems would have slackened off with the era of détente, or lessening of tension, in the 1970s, the precise opposite was true. The thawing of diplomatic relations permitted an influx of KGB agents into the United States and other Western countries.

They posed as Soviet and East European diplomatic, cultural, and commercial officials. It's been estimated that a quarter of the Soviet citizens inside the United States during the 1970s and 1980s were involved in intelligence gathering. In Third World countries, that number increased to more than half. Soviet citizens with no background in intelligence were aware that, if they intended to travel abroad, chances were good that they would be receiving an assignment from the KGB.

> **Top Secret**
>
> The KGB had little trouble recruiting officers, especially for overseas work. KGB employees were paid very well by Russian standards. They received a military rank and got to live in another country.

The KGB recruited graduates at the top of their classes at the best Soviet schools for espionage work. Before they were put into the field, they had to attend a two-year postgraduate training course at its Higher Intelligence School located near Moscow. The curriculum included the use of ciphers, arms and sabotage training, history and economics according to Marxist-Leninist theory, law, and foreign languages.

Taking a Nap for the Russians

KGB Sleepers were a unique phenomena and an ongoing problem for the United States during the Cold War.

At the end of World War II, the Soviets rolled across Germany and into Berlin, as part of the U.S., British, and Soviet agreement. Berlin was divided, and the Soviets got control of what became East Germany. Within East Germany there were many former Communist Youths, who during the Nazi era had been oppressed by the Nazi Youths and were eager to get even with their Nazi Youth tormentors. The Soviets cleverly took advantage of that situation (as did the United States, in other ways). They recruited many, provided them with schooling, programming, and indoctrination, and brought many of these young people on board as spy tools for the USSR. Once carefully trained, female former Communist Youths were instructed to find, date, and marry American and British Officers. Perhaps as many as several thousand of these women married American officers from the Army, Air Force, Navy, and Marines. Then, they went to sleep.

> **Spookspeak**
>
> **Naked** isn't nice in polite society. In the intel business it describes something far more dangerous, an agent working entirely on his or her own without any support from the intelligence organization that hires the agent. Nasty, risky stuff.

The assignment was to marry and sleep with the American officers, be good wives, and support their husbands' careers. That way they would have access to Officers Clubs, PX and Commissaries for shopping, live in military housing on military bases, and otherwise blend in to America's military establishment. Neat idea, and it worked, too. Although a certain number of these women became Americanized when they were back in the United States, others retained their loyalty to Russia. They were assets in place, waiting to be set in motion and their talents used. More important, they were in the right places to be especially useful to the Soviets.

> **McLean Says ...**
>
> In February 2002, former KGB archivist Vasili Mitrokhin released a 178-page paper quoting KGB messages and files describing the Soviet Union's nasty campaign of bribery, sabotage, assassination and deception in Afghanistan between 1978 and 1983.

Single Female Soviet Spy Seeking American Military Man

Consider one case. An attractive German woman enjoyed dancing. She met a young Naval officer who was stationed in West Germany. He loved dancing, too. They dated. They married. Eventually, he was rotated back to the United States. One duty was Norfolk Navy Yards in Virginia, a prime spot for his wife to observe what happened at that major Navy port. Then, back overseas to Italy. Next, back to the United States as a ranking Officer at the Brunswick Naval Air Station in Maine. Good deal for the KGB.

Brunswick was the home of the Navy Aircraft that flew submarine search missions along the entire Eastern Coast of the United States (subs, of course, can be seen from the air). The wife played bridge and attended parties at the Officers Club. She charmed the other ladies and officers with her obvious wit and dancing ability. She even won some contests. In the process, she picked up details about America's submarine watchers, including: how many flights, when, where, and on which routes. She most likely even had the names of the Navy pilots.

Somehow, someone who had seen her in Germany years before developed suspicions. He alerted the CIA. Facts were dug up. Photos were taken at Officer Club parties and compared with some that were in West German intel files. Pieces of a puzzle were put together. Letters were obtained and handwriting compared.

> **Spookspeak**
>
> **Ladies** has a different meaning in intel jargon. It refers to female operatives who attempt to compromise people by seduction of one level or another, depending on need.

Solid investigation and some luck led to a revelation: She was indeed a KGB Sleeper. That was verified by the West Germans who followed her when she visited a sick "relative" in Germany. That relative was verified as KGB.

From that point, the FBI was given the files. Since then, they have identified at least two other KGB Sleepers.

Keeping the World Informed

Although we only touched on a few of the world's major intelligence agencies in this chapter, several other countries have specialized intelligence organizations, including Italy, Bulgaria, Poland, China, Japan, and Canada. Check out Appendix F for a list of intel agencies around the world.

The Least You Need to Know

- The Security Service—better known as MI5—is the United Kingdom's security intelligence agency.

- Mossad is responsible for human intelligence collection, covert action, and counterterrorism for the nation of Israel.

- The KGB was the Soviet counterpart to the CIA, the NSA, Secret Service, many functions of the FBI, Customs Service, and Armed Forces counterintelligence agencies.

- KGB Sleepers were a unique phenomena and ongoing problem for the United States during the Cold War.

Gadgets and Gizmos

In This Chapter

- ◆ Mind-boggling equipment
- ◆ Secret messages
- ◆ Concealed weapons
- ◆ Deadly toys

Every year the manufacturers of spy gadgets and gizmos, always on the cutting edge of technology, have a convention in the Parisian suburb of Le Bourget. Prospective buyers get to see what's new and exciting. Among the items on exhibit in 2002 were exploding robots and remote-controlled spy planes. Some of the high-tech vendors sip champagne as they look out at the spectators from between rows of state-of-the-art guns. It's a wild scene.

As advanced and powerful as the weapons and gadgets on display at the annual trade fair are, you can bet that the CIA and other U.S. intelligence agencies have even more advanced and powerful tools at their disposal. And with the advent of the war on terrorism, the toys that our CIA ops get to use in the field have only gotten better.

Unfortunately, because of the classified nature of most of the equipment, we can't go into much detail about them in this chapter. We will, however, sketch some highlights about the kind of gadgets and gizmos under development or available right now. Then, we'll take a look at some pretty neat spy tools of the past, some of which might still be in use today … who knows?

> **Top Secret**
>
> CIA officers, diplomats, world leaders and others who might be considered high-risk for kidnapping may soon be implanted with an ID chip and personal GPS (Global Positioning System) device, so they can always be located.

We Are the Jetsons!

Some of the weapons that are either being used right now in the war on terrorism or will be available soon include the following:

- Stun guns that heat flesh with a microwave.
- Satellite surveillance that sees through camouflage.
- Rifles that lob laser-guided grenades.
- Squadrons of unmanned *MAVs*, deployed like flocks of birds, to peek over hilltops or sniff for biochemical agents.

Some inventions are researched and developed for the CIA by independent contractors; however, for security reasons, most gadgets are created in-house by the researchers in the Directorate of Science and Technology.

> **Spookspeak**
>
> **MAV** means Micro Air Vehicles. They are flying robots. Groups of them can fly in formation, radio-controlled from the ground.

Child's Toy or Modern Spy Tool?

For years invisible ink was an invaluable tool in intelligence work. Some historians say that it was used as far back as 230 B.C.E. We know that invisible ink was used by Queen Elizabeth I's spies.

> **Tradecraft**
>
> Rice water makes a great invisible ink. The words become visible when the paper is treated with iodine.

How It Works

Invisible ink is a clear fluid of some sort that is used like ink to write a message. Because the "ink" is clear, the message is invisible. Later, the recipient of the message, by using some process—most commonly by applying heat—makes the clear fluid show up so the message can be read.

Lemon juice, for example, can be made visible by holding a flame under the paper—not too close, of course. The lemon juice will turn brown before the paper burns, making the once invisible message visible.

Inky Secrets Still Classified

The United States has used invisible ink in the past, during World War I.

Want to know what the United States used as invisible ink during the war? Sorry, can't tell you. Classified. Lawyers and non-profit groups are trying to get the CIA to cough up those secrets.

The lawyers say there is no reason to keep the info secret because the science of invisible ink is arcane. The CIA's response is that they aren't using invisible ink now, but they might want to again someday and, if they do, they want their technique to be secret. End of story.

Or maybe not the end, if recent Russian accusations are true. The Soviet FSB, one of the agencies that has replaced the KGB, recently accused the CIA of using invisible ink to send messages to a Russian scientist they say the CIA had recruited.

> **Top Secret**
>
> According to "C", as the British Intelligence Chief during World War I was referred to, the best invisible ink is semen. Now that's a piece of trivia worth knowing!

Tradecraft

During World War II, British spies were known to carry their invisible ink in miniscule rubber bags, which were concealed inside a hollow tooth.

Tradecraft

During World War II, entertainer Josephine Baker breezed past starstruck security guards. Little did they know that Baker was smuggling secret information for the French Resistance, which was written in invisible ink on her sheet music.

German Ink

Although the public doesn't know what invisible ink technique the CIA would use if they used one, they've long known about the aniline pens used by German agents during World War II.

Aniline pens used aniline, an oily liquid that responds to heat much like lemon juice, as ink. The big difference between aniline "ink" and lemon juice is that aniline reacts to the heat from specially prepared matches. The chemical had previously been used in the making of drugs and dyes.

Concealed Weapons

You're probably familiar with many of the gadgets used by James Bond, such as the ejector seat in his Aston-Martin and the jet backpack that turned him into a human helicopter. Well, the CIA has some gadgets of its own.

However, in real life, the gadgets and gizmos tend to be less ostentatious. This isn't show business after all. Many of the items are designed to be concealed on one's person.

There are specialized weapons—such as those designed to get past any security system and items that aid in the concealing of messages during a search

Here's a quick look at some ingenious concealed weapons of the past:

The Shoe Knife

The shoe knife is a blade that could be concealed in sheaths inside a shoe's cushion insoles. The blade is shaped to follow the shape of the foot, making the blade easier to conceal and the shoe more comfortable to wear. The double-edged blade is serrated along one portion.

> **McLean Says ...**
>
> Life as a spy can get real spooky at times. Sometimes it also gets hilarious and lets you laugh at yourself, once you stop shaking from fear. I was working a project in New York City, near the UN, late one night. Several watering holes were the favorite after hour spots for various younger members of delegations who had access to valuable information. At times I would sit at the bar and chat a bit, but mostly listen, express sympathy for bad day stories, and otherwise be Joe Friendly. After a few hours of listening in, I decided to catch the late train for home.
>
> Walking to the station, I heard footsteps following me. Trying to be nonchalant, I continued walking at a normal pace. The footsteps continued. Was it a mugger? A thief? I increased my pace, and so did the footsteps. I slowed down, ready to swing to take on an adversary, but the footsteps also slowed. Obviously, I was being followed, but my pursuer was keeping his distance. It was too dark to see the person or persons in store windows by getting their reflections. There were no other people on the side street and no cabs or cars coming past with lights to help. Without any weapon, I felt somewhat helpless. Coming toward a corner, I decided to move ahead quickly, turn the corner and be prepared to face what followed. I did. It did. Then it whinnied.
>
> An un-mounted police horse had followed me for an entire block. No officer in sight. The reins hung loose, so the horse must have pulled away from where the police officer had tied it while going inside for a quick pick-me-up. What a relief. I began to laugh. Then another thought hit me. What would happen if I got arrested for stealing a horse? I could see the headlines, "Intelligence Officer Arrested for Stealing Police Horse." I quickly tied the reins to a parking meter and ran to catch my train.

Some spies chose to wear a blade in both shoes. It was difficult to wear a shoe blade on one foot and a normal shoe on the other because the difference in weight caused a change in gait. To counter-balance the blade in one shoe, some officers carried gold in the other.

The gold not only served to balance the gait—it also provided an emergency source of funds. Other agents might have hidden their gold in their belt buckle, and a hollowed belt buckle just for that purpose was also available.

The Trick Comb

It looks like a normal comb, made out of opaque nylon plastic in a variety of colors. However, it has two hidden compartments that are exposed when you draw back on the two housings that slide along rails on the main part of the comb body.

Officers could store ammunition for a .22 calibre weapon, suicide capsules, or a small saw blade in the compartments. Some combs came with one large compartment, instead of two smaller compartments, so operatives could carry a dagger in their comb.

Spy Suppositories

Not everybody's favorite subject, but a good spy must be willing to use his or her entire body, from top to bottom—with an emphasis on the bottom. Spies have been known to carry a multitude of objects in *suppository* form.

Everything from daggers, files (for escapes), tiny guns, and wire cutters can be carried around inside special CIA waterproof suppositories.

Spookspeak

A **suppository** is a tablet that is inserted inside the anus and held inside by the sphincter. All but the most invasive body searches will miss an object carried in this fashion.

Mini Guns

The CIA prefers .22 caliber weapons. Beyond that, though, there are no limitations. CIA guns come in any size and shape, and often look like anything other than a gun.

The Stinger .22 caliber gun looks like a tube of toothpaste, and is reloadable. Designed by the CIA, the toothpaste gun was manufactured by the Military Armaments Corporation and was sold with the brandname "Single-Shot Survival Weapon."

Another favorite CIA weapon was a gun that looks like a filter cigarette (I believe it only comes in one brand, European). It came loaded and could be fired only once. The weapon fires a 40-grain .22-caliber bullet. Twist the filter to cock the gun and push the filter to fire.

Very similar to the cigarette gun, but designed for spies who don't smoke—and there are more of them every day—is the pencil gun. The pencil gun comes in a variety of lengths. The length of the gun's barrel varies as well—it's available with barrles $1^3/4$, 3, $4^3/4$, or 5 inches in length. Here are some of the cigarette guns' other specifications:

- **Overall length:** $2^3/4$ inches
- **Barrel length:** $1^1/4$ inches
- **Muzzle velocity:** 759 feet per second
- **Powder charge:** 50 mg.

A bullet fired from the cigarette gun will penetrate a piece of soft pine almost two inches.

Lock Picks

Sometimes the equipment carried by an intelligence operative resembles that carried by the petty crook—and, of course, there are times when the two careers are not that different. A spy merely breaks the laws of one country with the permission of another.

CIA agents could equip themselves with a Lock-Pick Knife. Instead of the typical series of whittling blades and maybe a bottle opener, when you fold this baby open and you have yourself an assortment of lock-picks, all designed to open a different type of lock—without a key, of course.

The Utility Belt

You've read the Batman comic book or seen the movies, right? When Batman gets into trouble he always has the item he needs inside his trusty utility belt. Well, CIA operatives had their own version of the Bat-belt, in the form of a hollow belt buckle.

It was up to the spy to decide what to put inside of it, but he or she had plenty of options, including a variety of saws for escaping from a prison cell.

Lapel Daggers

One of the oldest concealed weapons in the CIA catalog are Lapel Daggers, which, of course, are short, double-edged blades that are hidden inside the lapels of one's coat or jacket.

The Lapel Daggers have been around since at least the earliest days of the OSS, and some say they were based on Scottish weapons that were carefully concealed beneath one's kilt.

The Blister Maker

The blister maker looks like a felt-tipped pen, but enemies that officers wrote on with this pen and had something on their skin the next morning that they wouldn't have been able to wash off: blisters.

The weapon is less than three inches long and could easily have been concealed by CIA operatives. The stuff that came out of the pen looked like clear oil and didn't give the victim an immediate indication that anything was wrong.

So, if somebody asks you if it's true that the CIA ever used chemical weapons, remember the blister maker. It might not be the sort of chemical weapon the person had in mind, but there's no doubt that it fits the bill.

Itch Machines

CIA operatives could order something called an "Itch-Floc Disseminator," which is a long metal tube that comes in 8, 10 and 12-inch lengths. Inside the tube was a compressed gas that, if released, formed a cloud that would make anyone it touched itch.

Indoors where there wasn't any wind, the cloud of itchy stuff could spread to cover an area 400 square feet in size. The itching material caused no serious damage, but could create quite a diversion.

Those are just a smattering of CIA arts and crafts that were used in the field.

McLean Says ...

I noticed something one day in Kennebunkport when President Bush was shopping at the Dock Square Pharmacy: A casual, nicely dressed man couldn't seem to get a piece of gum out of its package. That caught my eye, so I watched him for a few minutes. Finally it dawned on me that he wasn't interested in a stick of gum. The package was his disguised radio. He was a Secret Serviced agent keeping in touch with the other agents on the President's detail.

A History of Gadgets

In February 2002, in Simi Valley, California, a number of CIA gadgets were put on public display for the first time. The show, which was held at the Ronald Reagan Presidential Library, included items that are usually on display at the CIA's Langley headquarters.

Tradecraft

Lloyd Salvetti, of the CIA's Center for the Study of Intelligence, explained why it was important to put the items on public display: "Questions have been asked about why we invest so much money in the intelligence community. We thought we should team with the President's Library to get out our message about why we exist."

Top Secret

One of the most popular, and tiniest, displays in Simi Valley was the world's very first microdot, a document shrunken down to a tiny point. It dated back to 1852.

The show presented a history of spy gadgets, including some stuff that dated back as far as the American Revolution. There were a series of spy cameras, one from World War I that was designed to be mounted onto a carrier pigeon, an 1885 camera that could be concealed on one's person, and a Cold War camera that fit inside the back of a person's glove.

The show featured spy gadgets both from real life and from famous fictional spies. A deadly poison-pellet umbrella from a James Bond movie, Dr. Evil's ring, and Maxwell Smart's shoe phone were popular exhibits. There were even KGB items.

A large wooden seal of the United States was also on display. The seal had been a present from Moscow to the U.S. Embassy in Moscow, and had hung for many years over the ambassador's desk—until the listening device inside it was finally discovered.

It is great fun to watch this stuff being used in James Bond movies, and it's tempting to think of spy equipment as "toys." But it's also important to remember that these toys are often used in a deadly game.

The Least You Need to Know

◆ Since September 11, the manufacturers of spy equipment have had to increase their output to keep up with the demand.

◆ The CIA says it doesn't use invisible ink anymore, but the agency is keeping its invisible ink techniques secret anyway, just in case.

◆ Spy "toys" are serious business and can often be deadly.

Part 3

The CIA on the Front Lines of the Cold War

Truth *is* stranger than fiction, at least when it comes to the CIA's role in the Cold War. In an era when the United States and the Soviet Union were sometimes only minutes away from nuclear war, the CIA fought off the communist menace around the globe by digging tunnels, planting bugs, overseeing invasions of foreign countries, arranging for assassinations of foreign leaders, drugging U.S. citizens, and fighting secret wars—all in the name of liberty.

While some of these activities are less than admirable, others saved hundreds if not thousands of lives and helped to bring an end to an unforgettable era.

Berlin: The Wall

In This Chapter

- ◆ Recollecting the Cold War
- ◆ Digging tunnels
- ◆ Listening in
- ◆ The wall comes crashing down

Although the United States joined forces with the Soviet Union during World War II (1939–1945) to defeat the Axis powers of Germany, Italy, and Japan, a new kind of war was developing between the two allies before the last shots of WWII were fired: the Cold War. A war in which no battles ever officially took place between the two superpowers, the Cold War represented a war of ideologies. The United States believed strongly in a democratic society that relied on capitalism to drive the economy, whereas the Soviet Union held fast to the tenets of communism, in which the government seized ownership of all the businesses and aspired to an equal distribution of wealth amongst all people.

The Cold War evolved into a kind of turf war, in which both nations worked furiously to gather allies all over the world. It was "fought" in those countries that the two superpowers were trying to woo, including states in Eastern Europe, Central and South America, Southeast Asia, and Africa.

A war, even a war of ideologies, needs soldiers, and the men and women who worked for the CIA often served on the front lines … and behind them!

The Cold War's Foot Soldiers

The agency gathered intelligence on the goings-on in countries already under Soviet sway and kept tabs on other countries that U.S. policy makers feared might be susceptible to communist influence.

On the Front Lines of the Cold War: Berlin

When World War II ended in 1945, the victorious Allies—the United States, Britain, France, and the Soviet Union—divided Germany into four sectors. Each country controlled one sector. The United States, France, and Great Britain joined their sectors into a single country, known as The Federal Republic of Germany, or West Germany. The Soviet sector became the communist state of East Germany, formally known as the German Democratic Republic. To prevent a mass exodus of people from east to west, the borders were sealed off by the Soviet Union and its East European allies, forming the barrier that Winston Churchill was the first to call the Iron Curtain.

> **Top Secret**
>
> Journalist Walter Lippmann was the first to describe the relationship between the Soviet Union and the United States as a Cold War.

Berlin Also Divided

Even though Berlin lay deep within the Soviet sector of Germany, the Allies thought it best to divide this metropolis as well. Therefore Berlin was also divided into four sectors. Again the U.S., British, and French Sectors combined to form West Berlin. The Soviet sector became the East German capital, East Berlin.

People who lived in West Berlin were allowed to travel through East Germany to get to West Germany, either by road or rail, but their papers had to be in order and they had to pass through East German checkpoints.

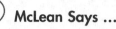 **McLean Says ...**

I had finished a project in Caracas, Venezuela and was at the airport waiting for a flight back to the U.S. Everything was fine.

Suddenly a businessman, Jon, who lived in my home town in New Jersey saw me and began walking rapidly across the airport lobby, calling my name and waving at me. I quickly looked away from him. He came closer, still waving and calling my name to get my attention. As he came near, I frowned, and shook my head: "No señor, no dinaro, no money, no Englese," and gestured for him to go away.

Jon stopped and just stared at me in disbelief. "No money, no dinaro," I repeated. His blush from embarrassment was obvious as the turned away. I just stood and looked after him. He turned, looked at me again and kept walking away. Looking around me I noted that several people were looking at me. With a deliberate shrug, I pointed my finger at my head and made a gesture: "Americans!" I said and shook my head to let them know I thought the American was crazy. A few smiled and nodded and continued on their way. I looked around and then decided to visit the rest room until departure time.

Several weeks later Jon joined me on the Erie Lakawanna commuter train from our little town in New Jersey to New York. He confessed that he had made a fool of himself in Caracas because, as he explained, "I saw a guy there that could be your twin. No kidding, a dead ringer for you. I went to say 'Hi' and he thought I was trying to get money from him. Boy, was that humiliating."

"Where's Caracas, is that in Peru?" I asked. "Oh, no, it is in Venezuela, and I'm sure glad I'll never be there again after that stupid move," he replied.

Point: Think fast and stay loose. In this situation, Lady Luck was on my side. If he had spoken Spanish, I would have had real trouble because my Spanish is basic at best.

To keep the people of East Berlin from leaving to West Berlin, beginning in August 1961 the East German government erected a wall—they called it "the anti-fascist protection wall"—to separate the sections of the city. Anyone attempting to escape over the wall risked being killed, with his or her body left hanging on the wall for a while to discourage others from attempting the same thing.

The wall was an average of four meters high, topped with concrete tubing and barbed wire. The wall was also multi-layered, so if those trying to leave East Berlin managed to get past one barrier, another barrier would stand between them and freedom. In addition to the main wall, there were often barbed wire fences

> **Top Secret**
>
> During the wall's 28 years, more than 5,000 people tried to escape. One hundred people were killed in the process.

and deep trenches that would have to be negotiated before the Iron Curtain would part. There was also a patrol track with a corridor for watch dogs, watch towers, and bunkers.

Citizens of West Berlin expressed their outrage with the wall by covering their side with graffiti.

McLean Says ...

The CIA had its first major intelligence victory of the Cold War in 1952 when Lieutenant Colonel Peter Popov of Soviet military intelligence volunteered to supply info to the United States. Popov's info turned out to be very valuable. He gave away the IDs of several Soviet intelligence officers and turned over a precious copy of the Soviet army field manual.

The Tunnel at No. 60 Wernerstrasse

When completed, the wall was 166 kilometers long. Germans trapped behind the wall dug several escape tunnels underneath of it, part of an extraordinary resistance movement.

The largest tunnel under the wall was in the basement of a house at No. 60 Wernerstrasse. Twenty-nine people successfully passed from East Berlin to West Berlin at this location. When the East Germans became hip to the fact that houses near the wall (on their side, of course) were being used to camouflage tunnels, all structures within a certain distance of the barrier were torn down. This demolition began on September 20, 1961.

Top Secret

For obvious reasons, the CIA was never able to maintain very many agents inside the Soviet Union during the Cold War. But some of those that were developed by CIA officers were invaluable to national security—not to mention the Pentagon's budget.

One agent was a Soviet scientist named Adolf G. Tolkachev, who was involved in the development of the Soviet submarine program. The information he provided allowed the United States to tailor its anti-sub forces specifically to the Soviet subs.

The U.S. anti-sub program had been developing equipment that turned out to be unnecessary, so Tolkachev's info ended up saving the Pentagon many millions of dollars.

Hotbed of Intelligence Activity

During the time the Berlin Wall was in existence, it was a hotbed of intelligence activity. The United States and its allies, particularly Great Britain, wanted to know everything that was going on in East Berlin.

The agency paid some people to sneak into East Berlin every day, buy a newspaper while they were there, and then sneak back. Not only did the CIA want the newspaper—for the gathering of overt intelligence—but it also wanted to gauge how difficult it was to get across the wall at different spots at any given time. It wasn't the Great Wall of China, but it was dangerous.

A Different Kind of Tunnel

The CIA wanted more than just overt intelligence from newspapers, and the agency wasn't going to let a little thing like a heavily guarded and mined wall keep them from accessing covert East German intelligence. In 1953, the United States' ability to listen in on East German communications with the Soviet Union took a great leap with the construction of the Berlin Tunnel, a 600-yard-long tunnel underneath the Berlin Wall.

Because Europe's communications systems had been wired before the Cold War, most communications between the rest of the world and Moscow were wired through Berlin, which—being the largest city on the continent—was used as a hub. That meant, to put it simply, it was very difficult for the Soviets to keep their phone conversations private.

They were highly susceptible to phone taps. The phone lines were both above ground on poles and underground. The CIA decided in 1952 to target those underground cables for tapping. Place a tap on an underground wire and the chances of it being discovered are practically nil.

Proper approval had to be gotten before such a tap could be put in place. The plan was drawn up by DCI Allen Dulles and approved by President Harry S. Truman in January 1954. The first job was to find out which cables carried the phone calls from the Kremlin.

A CIA agent whose cover was as a worker in an East Berlin post office managed to get his hands on this critical information. The all-important cables, as it turned out, went through the Altglienicke district section.

> **Tradecraft**
>
> Gather several types of hats. Try them on while looking in a mirror. Notice the difference just a hat can make. Then, switch hats and jackets and types of coats. Hats can be part of a simple light disguise system. Keep several handy.

> **Top Secret**
>
> The Berlin Tunnel was 6 feet tall and 15 feet under the ground. Through it were run 432 separate telephone wires.

The United States publicly announced that it was going to build an Air Force radar site and a warehouse in the Altglienicke district. But this story was a cover. In reality, a hole was being dug just to tap into the phone cables under the ground there. In February 1954, one month after the president's approval, work began. The tunnel, with its phone wires in place, was completed by February 1955.

A Mole in the Tunnel

The CIA was convinced that everything was going perfectly. Little did they know that they had been victimized by a mole, a KGB spy among them, who had told everything immediately. Indeed, the Russians had known all about the Berlin tunnel even before Truman had signed off on it.

The information leaked on October 22, 1953 when U.S. intelligence officers briefed members of British intelligence, including a KGB mole named George Blake. Blake reported the tunnel to his case officer, Sergei Kondrashev, during a London meeting soon thereafter.

According to the Russians, the information provided by their mole could not be fully exploited. To drastically change the phone system would not only be extremely difficult, since so much of it existed on the other side of the Iron Curtain, but to obviously change their communication habits might jeopardize their mole, from whom they expected further revelations.

In fact, neither Soviet military intelligence nor East German authorities were ever informed of the Berlin Tunnel's existence. It took the Russians some time to locate the tunnel, which they did by late 1955. In 1956, they came up with a plan to shut down the tap without outing Blake. They decided to "accidentally" find the tunnel.

On April 21 and 22, 1956, a Soviet signal corps team dug and found the tunnel. Unfortunately for the Soviets, the commencement of the digging had been spotted by CIA observers, and by the time the Russians "accidentally" found the tunnel, everything inside had been cleared out. The Soviets found only a microphone, which recorded their approach.

> **Top Secret**
>
> Legendary Cold Warrior William King Harvey (1915–76) was responsible for the building of the Berlin tunnel, a.k.a. Harvey's Hole.

Although the Russians today claim that they didn't take advantage of their knowledge of the tunnel, we can safely assume the information was put to some good use, even if it was to use phone conversations to disseminate disinformation.

Built For Eavesdropping

The tunnel enabled CIA wiretappers to eavesdrop on communications between the East Germans and the Soviets, and it has been called the CIA's most ambitious project of the 1950s. To protect their mole, the KGB allowed much good intelligence to slip out. The complete *Order of Battle* of the Soviet military in East Germany was learned because of the phone taps inside the Berlin Tunnel.

> **Spookspeak**
>
> **Order of Battle** is information regarding the strength and organization of a military force. This includes the name of the units, unit commanders, manpower estimates, types of armaments, the units' mobility, and the capability of the enemy force.

Attack of the Woodpeckers

In 1989, as the Soviet Union began to fall apart at the seams, wall "woodpeckers" started to use hammers and chisels to knock out pieces of the wall. Shortly thereafter, a massive emigration of East Berliners to West Berlin began. On November 10, 1989 and later on December 22, 1989 checkpoints were opened for pedestrians at Potsdamer Platz and the Brandenberg Gate.

Finally on July 1, 1990 East and West Germany were united. They assumed West Germany's old name, The Federal Republic of Germany. The West, with the help of the CIA, had won the Cold War.

The Least You Need to Know

- When Europe was divided up after World War II, the Soviet Union was given East Germany, while the remaining allies, (the United States, England, and France) shared occupation of West Germany.

- The capital city of Berlin was also divided, and a wall was built to keep those on the communist side from leaving.

- Tunnels were built under the wall and agents routinely crossed into the Communist sector of the city to see and hear what was going on.

- During the time the Berlin Wall was in existence, it was a hotbed of intelligence activity.

Cold Wars and Covert Actions: The CIA on the Frontline

In This Chapter

- ◆ Drastic measures in dire times
- ◆ The many kinds of covert action
- ◆ Dead dictators

It would be a mistake to portray the CIA's activities during the Cold War as exclusively in the domain of intelligence gathering. It also performed functions in the interests of the U.S. government that didn't have anything to do with gathering intelligence. The fear of communist expansion was a great one, after all: By the middle of the twentieth century the Soviets controlled much of Eastern Europe, and had very close ties with Fidel Castro in Cuba (only 90 miles off the coast of Florida). A Communist party had violently taken control of China, sending the old government into exile and exerting a strong communist influence over the rest of Asia. Many in the United States believed that the American way of life—including their liberty—was at stake.

Sometimes the United States policy makers felt it was necessary to take direct, albeit secret, actions to influence politics in countries it felt were susceptible to communism.

Creating Change ... Quietly

These non-intelligence-gathering activities are called *covert actions*. According to the CIA, a covert action is a "special activity abroad in support of foreign policy where the role of the U.S. Government is neither apparent nor publicly acknowledged."

Covert actions can take many forms—ranging from simple propaganda campaigns (involving the distribution of leaflets) to paramilitary campaigns that involve the use of heavy artillery. The following are three basic kinds of covert actions:

Spookspeak

A **covert action** is a special activity abroad in support of U.S. foreign policy, where the role of the U.S. government is neither apparent nor publicly acknowledged.

Spookspeak

Black propaganda conceals its origins. **White propaganda** makes the person or group responsible for the information known.

◆ **Propaganda** Action intended to undermine beliefs and values of people or to convert them to another belief system. Such campaigns can involve radio broadcasts, distribution of leaflets, and even paying journalists and academics to include information in their reports that they might otherwise not include.

◆ **Political actions** Action intended to change the power structure or policies of a foreign country. Can include involvement in foreign elections by offering financial support to favorable electoral candidates or providing support to friendly governments to help keep them in power.

◆ **Paramilitary operations** Actions undertaken by military forces separate from the regular armed forces of a nation. They are often used in an effort to camouflage the true source of the operation.

Top Secret

The Freedom of Information Act (FOIA) gives U.S. citizens the right to access government documents—including CIA documents—as long as the documents pass a certain classification criteria. A document that might expose an agent or a CIA method would not be released.

Many documents have been partially released—that is, with a portion of the text redacted. Because so many documents are repeatedly requested through the FOIA, the CIA has created a website that will, in theory, save them a lot of paperwork.

The website (www.foia.cia.gov/default.asp) is called the "Electronic Reading Room." The site is fully searchable and has an advanced interface, which allows limiting by date. A list of Frequently Requested Records is also available.

When the Prez Says ...

To even start the planning of a covert action, the CIA must get a written order from the President of the United States. The National Security Council is usually responsible for recommending that the President make any such request. According to the CIA, covert actions are considered as options when U.S. foreign policy objectives might not be "fully realized by normal diplomatic means and when [open] military action is deemed to be too extreme an option."

Once tasked with a covert action, the Director of Central Intelligence must notify the intelligence oversight committees of the Congress.

During the late 1980s, DCI William Webster revamped the Covert Action Review Group, which was in charge of examining and approving proposals for covert action from the president and the National Security Council. The Group, Webster decided, didn't work as it was because it never turned any proposals down, instead functioning merely as a rubber-stamp. Since Webster's tenure, the Group now looks at proposed covert actions with a more critical eye, examining the purpose, feasibility, and potential *blowback* of a plan.

> **McLean Says ...**
>
> One operative was known for her attractive jewelry. She favored large opal stones. Except they weren't real—they were hollow replicas. Hidden materials could be removed quickly in a restroom transfer, or an extra ring given to a contact person or agent.

> **Spookspeak**
>
> **Blowback** is potential bad publicity that might result if a CIA operation is exposed to the public.

Notable Successes

Only about half of the CIA's covert actions have ever become public, and even that number is considered way too high for most CIA officers. During the Cold War, in particular, the CIA engaged in covert actions in dozens of countries throughout the world. As with any government operation or program, some of those activities were smashing successes, whereas others didn't achieve their stated goals. A few of the CIA's successes include the following:

◆ In 1948, Christian Democrats were elected in Italy instead of the communists. The CIA's program gave an average of $30 million annually to anti-communist candidates in Italy.

◆ In 1950, Huk guerrillas attempted a coup in the Philippines, but legendary CIA operative Major General Edward Lansdale came to the rescue. He built up an anti-Huk powerbase using, among other techniques, psychological warfare. Lansdale ordered the anti-Huk forces to 1) spread rumors that a vampire was loose killing Huk guerrillas, and 2) put puncture wounds in the necks of any Huk guerrillas they happened to kill, thus lending credence to the vampire story.

◆ In 1953, the shah, recently overthrown in Iran, was put back in power after the CIA overthrew Dr. Mohammed Mossadegh, a left-wing revolutionary. This successful joint CIA/United Kingdom op was called Operation Ajax.

Top Secret

A proprietary is a company that, in whole or in part, exists as a front for CIA activities. We can't vouch for the accuracy of these reports, and of course, all companies deny it, but the following companies have been called CIA proprietaries in published reports:

◆ A.P.I. Distributors, Inc.

◆ Actus Technology

◆ Aero Associates

◆ Air America

◆ American Council of Churches

◆ Civilian Military Assistance

◆ Evergreen International

◆ Fiduciary Trust

◆ Gibralter Steamship Corp

◆ Howard Hughes Medical

◆ Inter-Probe, Inc.

◆ Massachusetts Institute of Technology

◆ Pacific Corporation

◆ Radio Free Europe

Keeping Communism at Bay in Latin America

A surprising number of covert actions carried out by the CIA took place in Latin America. The region had been considered important to United States national security for over a century. President James Monroe, in his famous 1823 Monroe Doctrine, stated that the United States would not sit by while European nations involved themselves in the free nations of the North and South Americas.

When the United States started sensing—whether real or imagined—communist power plays in its neighbors south of the border, the CIA wasted no time in taking action, and that action was often covert. Its actions in Cuba are described in Chapter 13. Some other Latin American covert activities include:

◆ An unsuccessful attempt to overthrow the Costa Rican government of Jose Figueres in 1953.

◆ A successful attempt to overthrow the Ecuadorian government of Jose Velasco Ibarra in 1961.

◆ Involvement in labor campaigns and other forms of propaganda to overthrow Brazilian government of Joao Goulart in the early 1960s.

◆ Assistance to the Bolivian government in capturing Ernesto "Che" Guevara.

Taking Pieces Off the Board

In addition to learning about the secrets of all the pieces on the political chessboard (intelligence gathering) or even moving pieces around on the chess board (most forms of covert action), at one time the CIA actually sought to take pieces off the board altogether—assassination.

McLean Says ...

My friend Kathy recalls how useful plain brown envelopes can be. She often had to deliver large amounts of cash to Cuban anti-Castro groups in Florida that America was funding. She would count the $50,000 and tuck it into a large brown envelope. Then she drove to the prearranged shopping center parking lot to meet her contact from the Cuban exile group. There she simply left the envelope on the seat and walked away where she could watch the car until the contact picked up the envelope. Sometimes they simply met and she gave the contact the plain brown package.

"What bothered me was when the money was in $20 bills. That took a much longer time to count," she recalls with a chuckle.

Death of Trujillo

Generalissimo Rafael Leonidas Trujillo had been the brutal dictator of the Dominican Republic for 31 years when he was assassinated by gunfire on May 30, 1961.

It has been said that CIA operatives in the Dominican Republic supplied the assassins with high-quality rifles. Trujillo was shot by rifle fire—just as U.S. President John F. Kennedy would be two years later—while riding down an open stretch of road in a limousine. The CIA, it is said, also promised the enemies of Trujillo that they would lend support once a new government was installed to replace Trujillo's. The coup was a failure however, and Trujillo's government was not replaced with a democracy. Instead, Trujillo's son took command and things continued much as they had been.

Many people feel that the CIA "hit" Trujillo, and there is evidence that the agency wanted to, but in the end the CIA probably just gave support to Trujillo's enemies and allowed politics to take their course.

President Allende?

In 1970, CIA Officer David Atlee Phillips was called to Washington to lead a special task force assigned to prevent the election of left-leaning Salvadore Allende as President of Chile. Although $8 million was put into forming a military coup that would prevent Allende from assuming power, the plot didn't work.

> **Tradecraft**
>
> You can't talk about the CIA in Latin America without mentioning legendary Cold Warrior David Atlee Phillips, who spent 25 years undercover for the CIA. He had been involved in clandestine operations in Guatemala, Cuba, Mexico, and Chile from the 1950s to the early 1970s.
>
> Phillips was on the scene when the agency, under orders from President Eisenhower, toppled the government of Jacono Arbenz Guzman in Guatemala in 1954. He was in Washington in 1960 when the CIA planned to get Cuba back from Castro. He served as Station Chief in the Dominican Republic and in Rio de Janeiro.
>
> His last assignment was as head of the Western Hemisphere Division, during which, he said, he ordered agents from Chile to distance themselves from the people then plotting to overthrow Allende, a Marxist.

Allende didn't stay in power for very long, however. He was killed in a military takeover in 1973. Phillips said when he resigned that the CIA played no role in Allende's demise.

Patrice Lumumba

In 1961 a similar scenario had played out in the Congo, which until 1960 had been a colony of Belgium. The United States didn't like the people in control there, especially Patrice Lumumba, the dictator, because they were communists.

DCI Allen Dulles wrote in the late 1950s: "In high quarters here, it is the clear-cut conclusion that if [Lumumba] continues to hold high office, the inevitable result will [have] disastrous consequences … for the interests of the free world generally. Consequently, we conclude that his removal must be an urgent and prime objective."

McLean Says …

It has always struck me as funny that there is a university in Moscow named after Patrice Lumumba. It is appropriate, I feel, that the university's most famous graduate was "Carlos the Jackyl" (real name Ilich Ramirez Sanchez), who became one of the world's deadliest terorists before his capture in 1994. Carlos was a freelance terrorist who had done nasty jobs for Mohamar Qaddaffi of Libya, Saddam Hussein of Iraq, President Assad of Syria, Fidel Castro of Cuba, George Habash and the Popular Front for the Liberation of Palestine (PFLP), the Italian Red Brigade, Columbia's M-19 Movement, the Baader-Meinholf Gang, and any number of other "Communist and Socialist" employers.

A CIA agent by the name of Sidney Gottlieb claims that he was sent to the Congo in 1960 with a vial of poison which he had been assigned to pour onto Lumumba's toothbrush. Gottlieb never got to the leader's toothbrush, however, and Lumumba lived another year.

Historians are still unclear as to who was behind Lumumba's death, but latest writings tend to give the CIA a clean bill of health, while pointing a guilty finger at Belgium.

Did the CIA Do It?

Lumumba, like Trujillo and Allende, went from being an enemy of the CIA to being dead, with an unknown number of degrees of separation in between. The CIA charter did not specifically prohibit the assassination of foreign leaders until 1976—and it's safe to say that *something* made President Gerald Ford think that such a rule was necessary.

Covert Actions Today?

Dollars to doughnuts the CIA is engaging in covert actions in the war against terrorism. Unfortunately, we'll have to wait several years before we find out about those secret operations—if we ever do …

The Least You Need to Know

◆ Covert actions are activities designed to change the leader, government or political party in a foreign country.

◆ Italy, the Philippines, Iran, and several Latin American countries are among the locations where the CIA pulled off successful covert actions.

◆ There was a time when foreign leaders who were enemies of the United States didn't live long.

◆ Since 1976, it has been against CIA rules to assassinate foreign leaders.

Other Wars: Vietnam and the Gulf

In This Chapter

- ◆ ID'ing VC supporters
- ◆ Reports from Nam
- ◆ Mind of a madman
- ◆ Sounds of silence (sounds like victory)

Since the CIA's inception, there hasn't been a conflict involving U.S. troops in which the agency hasn't played a part.

In this chapter, we are going to discuss two such wars: the controversial war in Vietnam, and the Gulf War, fought when Saddam Hussein's Iraqi troops invaded Kuwait.

Vietnam: A Quick Review

The United States military became involved in Vietnam to help South Vietnamese forces fight communist North Vietnamese guerillas in an effort to prevent the entire country from falling under communist rule. It was a protracted effort, lasting for years and costing over 2 million lives—58,000 of them American.

Gulf of Tonkin

Throughout the United States' participation in the Vietnam War, the CIA worked behind the scenes in support of those anti-communist efforts. In fact, the official entrance of the U.S. into the war in Vietnam, the Tonkin Resolution, stemmed from an incident that was itself wrapped around a CIA mission.

It was August of 1964 and the CIA was gathering electronic intelligence from a Navy destroyer off the coast of North Vietnam in the Gulf of Tonkin. In addition to gathering intelligence, the operation also called for hit-and-run attacks against North Vietnamese shore installations using speedboats driven by South Vietnamese or soldiers of fortune.

The North Vietnamese reacted to the hit-and-run attacks by running a torpedo across the bow of the destroyer, and this act of retaliation caused the U.S. Congress to pass the Gulf of Tonkin resolution, which gave the Pentagon the legal right to make war against North Vietnam.

700 CIA Employees in Nam

During the peak of the U.S. involvement in the war in Vietnam, more than 500,000 American soldiers were in Southeast Asia. But the number of CIA officers working in the area never got much higher than 700—which is still a tremendously large number by CIA standards.

The U.S. embassy in Saigon, the capital of South Vietnam, was practically taken over by CIA personnel during the late 1960s. A full three floors of the building were needed to house the CIA. Of course, the sign on the door did not say, "CIA." It said, "Office of the Special Assistant to the Ambassador." The head of the Office of the Special Assistant was William Colby, who was in reality in charge of the CIA's efforts in Vietnam and who would later become DCI.

Operation Phoenix

What might be the CIA's most all-time controversial operation took place in Vietnam. Operation Phoenix was a program run by the CIA that was designed to identify and neutralize civilians in South Vietnam who were supporting the North Vietnamese army (also called Vietcong or VC). Once the supporters were identified, the information was passed along to the South Vietnamese.

The theory was that the Vietcong could be destroyed from within if their local leaders and supporters were identified and arrested. The VC would be broken up by local police much like an organized crime family would be in the United States.

There was no indication that the CIA was behind Operation Phoenix. Anyone following Phoenix agents back to their controllers would learn that the operation was being run by something called "Civil Operations/Revolutionary Development Systems." By using loosely supervised agents to do the dirty work in Operation Phoenix, the CIA did not maintain the kind of control over things as they should have.

Many local Vietcong leaders were identified and rendered powerless by Operation Phoenix, but the Vietnamese agents being used by the CIA to rat out the VC leaders were also smart enough to know that their information was not going to be double-checked. Therefore, enemies of the informants—even if they weren't Vietcong—were put on the arrest list alongside genuine Vietcong leaders, and everyone on the list was treated the same. Some people on the list were arrested and interrogated; others were promptly killed.

What started out as a perfectly sound plan turned into a major black eye for the company a few years later, when it was discovered that the CIA was involved with the operation.

> **Tradecraft**
>
> Years ago, and probably still today, used cars destined for resale in Cuba and South American countries were useful to smuggle weapons and ammunition and other supplies to CIA agents. By identifying the car containing special materials, agents can pick up a load of needed supplies, especially for clandestine purposes.

> **McLean Says ...**
>
> By international agreement, diplomatic pouches are not subject to search. Consequently, they are very useful for transporting secret documents as well as other special spy tools. One friend recalls that she even neatly wrapped automatic handguns and trusted them to Diplomatic Staff members in their pouches. Although State Department officials tend to frown on use of their special status to smuggle weapons, when there is a will there is a way. Double-duty diplomatic pouches will continue to be a safe transport system.

Operation Phoenix earned a reputation as a prelude to a bloodbath. It has been a called an assassination program targeting civilians—but that was certainly not its intent from the CIA's point of view. In fact, many within the organization are still troubled by what the South Vietnamese Government did and how badly it damaged the CIA's reputation.

The CIA's "Secret War"

The CIA did more than assist the United States and South Vietnamese in the fight against communism in Southeast Asia; it also waged its own war—in the form of a paramilitary covert action—in neighboring Laos. Even before the United States engaged in military action in Vietnam, the CIA had planes and officers stationed in Laos to help the keep communism at bay.

By the time the Vietnam War was in full swing, the CIA oversaw the creation of an army consisting of tens of thousands of locals and mercenaries to help defend Laos against the North Vietnamese, whom the United States feared were trying to take control of the country. The CIA trained the soldiers, supplied them with arms, paid them, and directed their actions. The agency also provided its secret warriors with air support through its own airline, called Air America.

The CIA's "secret war," as it has been called, was in violation of an international agreement; however, it was undertaken with the knowledge and support of the Administrations at the time. It was the largest paramilitary action ever undertaken by the CIA.

Nam Report: Behind the Lines

Fighting the communist guerillas in the jungles and mountains of Southeast Asia made a lot of people nervous, and rightly so. It was a dangerous job, and many people lost their lives or were captured by the enemy and became prisoners of war.

Tradecraft

Trying to see things at night can be difficult. One tip to see better is not to stare at any given spot. It is much better to scan an area. Let your eyes move back and forth. That helps you to pick up motion better or objects that are not moving. Try it out.

Many CIA personnel were "sneak and peeks," doing reconnaissance, rescue, and other covert actions behind—sometimes as far as 100 miles—enemy lines. Although never officially verified, there were CIA operatives working with Army Intelligence and Reconnaissance patrols far behind lines. Some were just reconnaissance patrols; others were intended to capture documents, prisoners for interrogation, and some were designed to find Vietcong leaders and eliminate them.

It was never an easy job, but having the following gear made the job a little easier:

- **Cammy stick**   Camouflage greasepaint in applicator tubes, which was applied in alternating shades to resemble shadows.

- **Signal mirrors**   To give helicopters a "shiner" to locate the operative.

- **Pocket-sized emergency flare packets**   Flares as small as a pencil screwed into spring-loaded trigger mechanism to fire, useful as an emergency signal to choppers.

- **Colored smoke grenades**   For verification between team and pilot upon pickup.

- **Starlight scopes and binoculars**   Draw light from the moon and stars to highlight the field of vision but don't give off tell-tale red dot to enemy.

- **LRRP packets**   One dehydrated, noiseless meal in each canvas packet.

- **Plastic canteens**   Noiseless water containers.

- **Heat tablets**   Drop in hole and light for warmth and heating water.

- **Camouflaged poncho liners**   For warmth and sleeping.

Some personal weaponry included:

- **M-16**   Light and fast-firing full-automatic that fired bullets equivalent to a .22, but they had questionable knockdown power and a propensity to jam.

- **M-79**   Light and easy to carry grenade launcher that fired one round at a time.

- **M-60**   A machine gun with great firepower, but too long and heavy to carry on silent missions. Good for ambushes near firebases, etc.

- **M-50**   .50 caliber machine gun that requires a tripod and an open field of fire, as well as a trigger man and loader to feed the belts. With bullets as big as a finger, it was great for protecting firebase against mortar attacks, sapper attacks, etc. Capable of knocking down a helicopter.

- **Claymore mines**   C4 explosive lined with rows of steel balls for maximum damage.

- **Survival knives**   For utility, digging, and stabbing.

- **Commando knives**   Sharper, balanced double-edged. For throwing, slicing, and stabbing.

- **Fragmentation grenade**   A grenade with a four-second fuse; serious concussion power and fragments.

- **White phosphorus grenade**   Sends forth plume of white smoke and burns with intense heat.

- **Concussion grenade**   Good for clearing tunnels.

- **C4 plastic explosive**   Use with blasting cap for explosive purposes or light with a match to burn for heat.

Finally, some weapons of choice available only to Special Ops teams:

- **Captured AK47-Russian/Chinese made machine gun**   Better knockdown power than the M-16.

- **WWII Grease gun**   Slow and deliberate fire and great knockdown power, but hard to obtain.

- **12-gauge shotguns**   Good for dense foliage, close-up encounters.

> **Tradecraft**
>
> To avoid being seen from another building or the street, always stay back from the window itself and keep the room's lights off. You don't want to be backlit or obvious when you are doing surveillance of the street or other buildings.

> **Spookspeak**
>
> *S-2* designates an intelligence officer for the United States Army at a Battalion or Regimental level. At Division level and higher it is called *G-2*

The intelligence discovered on these dangerous reconnaissance missions was relayed via radio to headquarters, who would then pass the information to *S-2* for strategizing and planning troop movements at the battalion level. A secondary mission was to initiate contact with the enemy on the way out, after the reconnaissance mission was completed. The goal of these missions was to inflict maximum casualties, unnerve the enemy with infiltration and damage, and gather more intelligence by capturing POW's or rucksacks which contained papers on enemy troop movements, etc.

Even though the U.S. military and the CIA worked very hard to win the war in Vietnam, the lack of support at home and the growing casualties on the frontlines finally persuaded the United States policy makers to pull out by March 1973. Not long after, on April 30, 1975, South Vietnam surrendered to the north, and the Socialist Republic of Vietnam was formed.

McLean Says ...

At the time of the Vietnam war, I was stationed in Ethiopia—an area of great strategic importance to the United States during the Cold War—and teaching at a university there. The university was a hotbed of anti-American and Marxist activities, with students storming classes being taught by Americans and threatening them. I was approached by some students, who planned to stage a debate on the Vietnam War, and asked if I would take the American side. I told the students that I was an opponent of the war, but would do my best not to disappoint them. During the debate, I argued that North Vietnam was in violation of international law, and that the United States had come to the aid of South Vietnam under a valid regional defense treaty that was in accord with the United Nations Charter. Further, I said, the Vietcong were nothing more than an instrument of North Vietnamese aggression.

I have to admit that as the debate wore on, I definitely got the upper hand. By the end, my opponent was deflated and I received a standing ovation. I never told the students that my own reservations about American military involvement in Vietnam had nothing to do with my antipathy towards communism. What I believed then, as I do now, was best stated by former Secretary of Defense Casper Wineberger: "We must never put our armed forces in harms way without a strategy to win."

The Gulf War

The CIA played a very important role when it came to the liberation of Kuwait in 1991. During the Gulf War, President Bush made the great majority of his decisions—predicting Saddam Hussein's next move, executing Operation Desert Storm—based on reports from the CIA.

At the end of May 1990, Iraqi leader Saddam Hussein put the world on notice that trouble was on the way when he alleged that Kuwait and the United Arab Emirates were overproducing oil and said that such practices amounted to "economic warfare" against Iraq. Then, during the middle of July, Saddam accused Kuwait of stealing oil from Rumaylah oil field on the Iraq-Kuwait border and warned that they would use military action if it happened again.

Tradecraft

Learn to keep your head still when scanning a scene. Moving your head from side to side is a giveaway that you are carefully looking for or watching something. Just move your eyes from side to side. You get to see what you wish to see without becoming an obvious observer.

By July 22, the Iraqi army was beginning a military buildup along the Kuwaiti border. On August 2, Iraq invaded Kuwait. The army immediately seized Kuwait's oil field. The leader of Kuwait, the emir, fled his country. Iraqi troops continued to mass along the Iraq-Kuwait border. Before the day was out, the United Nations had condemned Iraq's aggression. Four days later, on August 6, President George H.W. Bush announced a trade embargo on Iraq. On August 8, Saddam Hussein announced that Kuwait had been annexed. In other words, as far as Hussein was concerned, he now considered Kuwait to be part of Iraq.

Meanwhile, Saudi Arabia, afraid that an attack from Iraq might come in their direction, asked the United States for military protection. On August 9, the first U.S. military forces began to arrive in Saudi Arabia. The buildup was steady, and on January 17, 1991, Operation Desert Storm, the liberation of Kuwait, began.

Even before the United States fired the first missile at Iraq, the CIA had filed more than 500 intelligence reports to President Bush.

Monday Morning Quarterbacks Say ...

Many people criticized the CIA for failing to predict Iraq's invasion of Kuwait. (Actually, CIA analysts did correctly predict that the invasion would take place in the next 24 hours on the day of the invasion; of course, that didn't give President Bush a lot of time to react.) However, Hussein had close personal security—only family members or long time friends were allowed in the inner circle. Placing an agent inside that ring of steel was next to impossible. Still, the CIA delivered a lot of useful information that helped the United States.

Top Secret

Some spies are moms. One mother spy knew the value of playing the part of just a "dumb woman" while in China. She playfully doted on her children. She would get them to stand in front of buildings, wave at her, pose different ways. As nearby guards smiled, she snapped pictures of planes, trains, warehouses, office buildings, and other places needed for intelligence purposes.

It turns out that Saddam Hussein was sending mixed signals, making it very difficult for the agency to figure out exactly what was going on. For example, he sent a message to President Bush saying that he did not intend to invade Kuwait. The message arrived at just about the time he invaded Kuwait.

McLean Says ...

I kept a small .22 caliber automatic as my backup weapon in my ankle holster. One day, that backup weapon came in very handy. At a prearranged meeting of two different Arabic groups, guards at the door of the hotel suite disarmed all attending. I gladly turned in my 9mm automatic when asked to do so. About an hour into the meeting the rival parties became angry, then incensed, and finally outraged. Things got very tense. Fortunately, nobody in the room was armed ... except for me.

I casually reached down to scratch my leg and came up with my trusty .22. That was sufficient to calm the meeting back down. At its conclusion both sides thanked me for my thoughtfulness.

Not all CIA analysis was late, however. The CIA said all along that trying to get Saddam Hussein out of Kuwait could not be accomplished in a timely fashion with economic sanctions alone. Such a tactic could take years before getting the desired results, intelligence reports indicated. Then-DCI William Webster correctly predicted in December 1990 that Saddam Hussein would only respond to one thing: brute force.

Tradecraft

If you knock out an opponent's sight quickly, they are vulnerable and the rest is easy. Go for the eyes with the stuff in your glass, mace or pepper spray, or your fingers. Don't waste time. If your life is threatened, there are no rules ... except to survive.

Probing Saddam's Psyche

Psychiatric experts at the Directorate of Intelligence analyzed Saddam's personality in the hopes of better anticipating his actions. They correctly predicted, for example, that Kuwaiti oil wells would be set on fire as the Iraqi troops withdrew, and that an oil spill would be released to foul the Gulf waters.

By having insights into a leader's personality, it is often possible to predict courses of action, however bizarre they may seem, that might be expected. In the case of the fires, it was vital to have specialists immediately available to put out the fires.

Experts also warned against judging Saddam as insane just because his actions didn't make

Top Secret

At times it seemed like the agency shrinks knew Saddam better than Saddam did. They correctly predicted that he would set ablaze oil wells and spill oil into the water when he retreated out of Kuwait. How do they say it in those golf commercials? "These guys are good!"

sense in American terms. In his own culture, what he was doing seemed justified. That underscores the need to have intelligence specialists who understand other cultures and can think as an adversary of that country might think.

Space Spies

As soon as the crisis in the gulf blossomed, four of the CIA's spy satellites—KH-11s and KH-12s—were moved so they could watch Saddam Hussein. With satellites parked directly over Iraq, the United States could observe troop movements and assess troop morale (numbers of desertions could be counted). For the first time a military force was being guided by real-time images taken from outer space. (For much more about the CIA's space-spying program, see Chapter 15.)

> **Top Secret**
>
> A satellite called Lacrosse took "pictures" of Iraq with radar, so it didn't make any difference if it was cloudy or at night.

Ears in the Sky, Too

The CIA could do more than look down at Saddam Hussein from space. It could listen in to his communications, as well. Using satellites named Magnum and Vortex, the agency could eavesdrop on Iraqi communications from hundreds of miles up in the sky.

According to Walter S. Mossberg in the *Wall Street Journal* (March 18, 1991): "Spy satellite photos, intercepted Iraqi military communications, and other data gave U.S. generals a capability their predecessors could only dream about—the ability to track just about every military action Iraq took."

Directorate of Operations: On the Job

More than 200 operations officers overseas were reassigned to the gulf. Agents overseas were hard at work as well. A propaganda-pumping broadcast center was set up, broadcasting with a strong signal constant urges to the Iraqis to surrender. The same propaganda program dropped leaflets with similar messages onto Iraqi soldiers.

The Directorate of Operations' National Collection Division used American businessmen as agents and obtained invaluable blueprints for enemy weapons depots and factories. These made great targets for state-of-the-art "smart" bombs.

> **Tradecraft**
>
> Always know protocol as best you can! President Clinton didn't get briefed right before his meeting with the Japanese Prime Minister a few years ago. They sat together at the White House with TV cameras carrying their amicable meeting across America and back to Japan. Without thinking, or perhaps because he didn't know better, President Clinton crossed his legs and pointed the sole of his shoe at the Japanese Prime Minister. It was in full living color for the world, and all in Japan, to see. In many countries, Japan included, pointing the bottom of your dirty foot at a person is considered a serious insult.

The intelligence reports regarding Iraqi military installations were being supplemented by similar information coming out of former Soviet-bloc nations that only a few years before would not have been cooperating with the United States.

The Silence of Success

The agency's Counterterrorism Center was also hard at work. It examined terrorist threats and analyzed terrorist acts in the days before and during the war, and thus kept a few terrorist acts from happening, which is about as specific as we can get about that.

Unfortunately, Americans rarely get to hear of CIA successes. But we all sleep better when they do happen and prevent attacks that could have occurred without good intelligence at work.

The Least You Need to Know

- During the age of the CIA's existence, there hasn't been a conflict that required U.S. troops in which the CIA has not played an important part.
- The CIA ran major operations in Vietnam and Southeast Asia, including a "Secret War" in Laos.
- The CIA played an important role in the Gulf war that led to the liberation of Kuwait in 1991.
- The CIA used hi-tech tools to watch and listen to Iraqi military moves.

Bay of Pigs and Cuban Missiles

In This Chapter

◆ A Castro-ectomy

◆ Training exiles

◆ Blood on the beach

◆ Brink of oblivion

The CIA has done a lot of great things to protect the United States from potential and real threats, putting its men and women in life-threatening danger in the process. However, the agency hasn't always been perfect. In this chapter, you'll learn about one of the CIA's less-than-stellar operations in Cuba, plus an important intelligence success in the island country only 90 miles off the coast of Florida.

Why Care About Cuba?

After the Spanish-American War of 1898, when the United States helped Cuba win independence from Spain, the United States enjoyed a special relationship with the island nation. Cuba, although officially an independent country, engaged in treaties with the United States that allowed the U.S. government to be involved in Cuban politics and to buy land from the country to establish a naval base at Guantanamo Bay. U.S. businesses exported goods to Cuba and even established operations there, and the United States became a major importer of Cuban sugar and other goods like fruit, rum, and cigars.

Warm relations came to an end, however, on New Year's Eve of 1958, when a former law student and staunch nationalist staged a successful coup. Within a few days, the former leader of Cuba, Fulgencia Batista, had fled to the Dominican Republic, and the country's new leader, Fidel Castro, had settled into power in Havana.

Figuring Out Fidel

The United States was uncertain about Castro's intentions at first, but it didn't take long for policy makers to realize they had a problem in their midst: Castro seized all American-owned property—including businesses—on the island. Not long afterwards, Cuba signed a trade agreement with the Soviet Union.

Fearing the threat of communism so close to U.S. borders, President Eisenhower wasted no time in deciding that Castro had to go.

What to Do About Castro?

Eisenhower and his advisors knew that if the U.S. Army invaded Cuba and threw Castro out, they were risking the start of a nuclear war, since Cuba had the full military backing of the Soviet Union. The casualties of such a war would guarantee that there would be no winners.

Instead of an overt U.S. military campaign, plans began under President Eisenhower for a covert action—a CIA invasion of the island, an invasion that perhaps the United States could undertake without looking like it had done it. Before the plan could come to fruition, Eisenhower's second term expired, and the Fidel problem was left for the youngest president in the nation's history, John F. Kennedy, to handle.

Needed: A Few Good Men

Because the invasion couldn't involve the U.S. military, the CIA needed to find another source of soldiers. The CIA used Cuban exiles, those who had fled the communist government and very much wanted to get their homeland back.

The exiles, called the Exile Brigade, were trained by the CIA and were supplied weapons and other supplies of war by the American military.

The new soldiers—1,200 of them in all—who had been trained rather quickly to fight, went to Cuba by boat. They hit the beach at the Playa Giron, the Bay of Pigs. The plan assumed that, once the Cuban people heard of the attack, they would rise up in revolt. Soon Castro would be out of power, they thought. The plan also assumed the United States would provide air support to the Exile Brigade once they landed in Cuba.

It didn't work out that way.

Air Support? What Air Support?

The invasion was a miserable failure. When the exiles landed they were given no air support. As it turned out, Eisenhower had promised them air support, but Kennedy decided against providing it—he believed that such a move might start World War III. However, no one bothered to inform the Exile Brigade of the change in plans.

During the short battle at the Bay of Pigs many died. The freedom fighters who weren't killed by Cuba's army were captured. No Cubans rose up in revolt in response to the invasion.

The invasion was poorly planned and carried out on every level.

Wasn't Us ... Well, Maybe It Was

At first the embarrassed CIA said that it had nothing to do with the invasion, that it had been entirely planned and carried out by the Cuban exiles. But the truth quickly came out. President Kennedy went on TV and took full responsibility for the invasion.

The captured Cubans weren't released until a few days before Christmas 1962, over a year and a half after their capture, when President Kennedy made a deal with Castro: The United States gave Cuba food and medicine and, in exchange, the Cuban exiles were allowed to return to the United States.

Top Secret
Many of the Cuban freedom fighters blamed President Kennedy for the failure of the invasion, feeling that the president had gone back on his word.

What Went Wrong

One of the many reasons that the Bay of Pigs operation was a failure was that, within the company, the left hand did not know what the right hand was doing. Obviously, the analysts in the Directorate of Intelligence had not been consulted. If the DI had

Tradecraft

Even during the past decade and today, despite the poverty of many, Castro has remained in place. His position and power were secure at the time of the Bay of Pigs, and the planners should have checked on their "spontaneous uprising" view then. That was one of the key failures of the invasion.

been informed of the plans, they would have been told the Directorate of Operations not to attempt such an invasion. The notion that the people of Cuba would turn on Castro once the battle started was a foolish one. There was ample evidence to prove that point, even then.

Castro has retained power for so long because he continued to have substantial support among the Cuban people. The improved health, education and other social programs he has provided the poor has made Castro a hero to many there.

Insisting on Deniability

Another problem with the plan is that the CIA wanted *deniability*.

That is, if things didn't go well on the beach, the invasion would look like it was purely a group of self-trained exiles invading in a patriotic attempt to get their island back. In other words, it was supposed to look like the United States didn't have anything to do with it.

Spookspeak

Deniability (also called "plausible denial") means, in case an operation is uncovered, the CIA can deny it had anything to do with it.

However, with all the media stories about activities of Cuban exiles organizing and training in the swamps of Florida, it was rather obvious something was up. To have such "exercises" continuing meant the United States was involved, or at the least, the exiles had the blessing of the United States.

A successful invasion of this size cannot come with deniability. Because of this fact, the Bay of Pigs was the first, last, and only time the CIA was given complete autonomy over a military operation of this scope.

Top Secret

At the time, Castro had his own spies operating in Florida among the refugee and exile groups. He wasn't and isn't a stupid person. He kept his long distance eyes and ears open.

It is ironic that the concept of deniability was a major flaw in this plan, because deniability was one of the reasons that President Harry Truman formed the CIA to begin with. Presidents had felt free to use the CIA to execute covert actions to effect military results without having to get Congress to declare war and without having to admit U.S. involvement.

After the Bay of Pigs disaster, President John Kennedy asked for the resignations of three CIA men, the DCI Allen Dulles, the Deputy DCI Charles P. Cabell, whose brother was the mayor of Dallas, and Richard M. Bissell, Jr., who had been called the "Father of the U-2 Program."

Five Wacky Ways to Harm Castro

One of the revelations to come out of the *Rockefeller Commission hearings* was that during the early 1960s the CIA had repeatedly plotted to kill Communist Cuban leader Fidel Castro. But they tried to be cute about it. Cute seldom works!

"Cute" ideas included a plan to …

- Put poison on the coral where Castro liked to deep-sea dive.

- Use agents who also worked for the Mafia, put a botulism tablet in his food, smuggled into his room by a mistress who had it hidden in a cold cream jar.

This last plan failed because the pill dissolved in the cold cream. Castro, it seems, did not have that much to worry about. It isn't that much of a shock that he is still alive today.

> **Spookspeak**
>
> The **Rockefeller Commission** was formed in 1975 to investigate claims that the CIA was illegally undertaking domestic investigations. For more on the Rockefeller Commission, named after Vice-President Nelson Rockefeller, who was its chairman, see Chapter 16.

> **Tradecraft**
>
> As you know, on November 22, 1963, President John F. Kennedy was assassinated in Dallas. The cause of death was a bullet through the head. The act was barbaric; unfortunately, however, it worked. Compare that messy but effective assassination style to the plans the CIA came up with to kill or discredit Castro. I'd like to think that the CIA invented these schemes for public consumption to keep actual techniques secret. Maybe Rube Goldberg was in charge, because some of these stories are bizarre.

Here, then, are other schemes against Castro. Some of these, you'll note, are surprisingly humane, designed to harm Castro's reputation and popularity as much as to cause him physical harm:

◆ Contaminate his cigars so that he would be intellectually incapacitated.

◆ Dose Castro with LSD just before he gave a speech on the radio.

◆ Put thallium salts in his shoes so that he would lose his hair, including his trade-mark beard.

Never Again? Maybe

Today, it is against the law for the CIA to assassinate a foreign leader. As noted in Chapter 11, assassination was first banned by President Gerald Ford in 1976. President Ronald Reagan later closed a loophole in the law by forbidding conspiracy to assassinate as well.

However, the war on terrorism has made some think that the rule may have to be rescinded.

Cuban Missile Crisis

The same agency that had looked less than on-the-ball during the planning and execution of the Bay of Pigs invasion and the attempts to assassinate Castro now showed the world that it was the eyes and ears of the Free World.

In October, 1962, the world came closer than it ever had before or since to nuclear war—and the CIA played a key role in the crisis.

Khrushchev Tries to Even Things

In 1962, the Soviet Union trailed the United States in the arms race. Soviet missiles could only be launched against Europe. U.S. "Jupiter" missiles, on the other hand, were in Turkey ready to fire—and they could strike anywhere in the Soviet Union. In late April 1962, Soviet Premier Nikita Khrushchev decided to even things up by placing *intermediate-range missiles* in Cuba.

> **Spookspeak**
>
> **Intermediate-range missiles** would not have been able to reach the United States from Russia and therefore needed to be based more closely to the United States to be used as an anti-American weapon.

This deployment in Cuba would double the Soviet strategic—that is, anti-U.S.—arsenal and provide a real deterrent to a potential United States attack against the Soviet Union.

Castro thought that the installation of the missiles on his island was a good idea. He had been looking for a way to defend Cuba from United States attack. Ever since the Bay of Pigs, he had felt that a second strike from the north was inevitable.

Ex-Comm's Seven-Day Huddle

One of the CIA's U-2 spy planes—the same kind of plane that had taken photos over the Soviet Union until one piloted by Francis Gary Powers was shot down (see Chapter 15)—took photos of inner Cuba showing that Russian nuclear missiles were being installed.

The missiles had been in Cuba since July when they began arriving by Soviet and eastern Bloc merchant ships. At the time, however, world events had taken the focus off of Cuba—more attention was being given to events in Berlin and in Vietnam. A military intelligence officer from the Defense Intelligence Agency first realized that the images in the new U-2 photos greatly resembled images seen in the Soviet Union that turned out to be strategic missile positions.

The crisis began on October 15, when the CIA photos of the Soviet missile sites under construction in Cuba reached President John F. Kennedy. While examining the photos, JFK huddled among a dozen of his most trusted advisers, a group he called Ex-Comm.

The 12 men debated for a solid week about what to do about the missiles in Cuba.

On October 22, President Kennedy went on live National TV and said, "Within the past week, unmistakable evidence has established the fact that a series of offensive missile sites is now in preparation on that imprisoned island. The purpose of those bases can be none other than to provide a nuclear strike capability against the Western Hemisphere."

Kennedy decided to impose a naval quarantine around Cuba. This would immediately stop new weapons from coming onto the island. The action, in retrospect, was a wise choice by JFK. The easiest and initial response would have been to invade Cuba, a strategy which, in the long run, could have cost more American lives than it was worth.

During the crisis, the United States armed forces were at their highest state of readiness ever, and Soviet field commanders in Cuba were prepared to use battlefield nuclear weapons to defend the island if it was invaded.

Top Secret
Soviet General and Army Chief of Operations, Anatoly Gribkov, later said, "Nuclear catastrophe was hanging by a thread … and we weren't counting days or hours, but minutes."

The Stare Down

Reconnaissance flights over Cuba were run every two hours, so that movements on the ground could be carefully watched. This obviously was risky, but it also provided real time intelligence for the decision makers.

The Russians at first refused to move the missiles, but diplomacy finally won out. Tensions began to ease on October 28, when Khrushchev announced that he would dismantle the installations and return the missiles to the Soviet Union, expressing his trust that the United States would not invade Cuba—and we haven't. The United States also agreed to remove its nuclear missiles from Turkey.

An Ace in the Hole

Unbeknownst to the public at the time, the CIA had an ace in the hole during the crisis. A member of Soviet Military Intelligence (GRU), named Colonel Oleg Penkovsky, was actually a mole reporting to the CIA. Because of Penkovsky, the CIA knew that the USSR was not nearly as prepared as it claimed to undertake a nuclear war with the United States. Score one for the CIA!

The Least You Need to Know

- ◆ The CIA operation to oust Castro with a Cuban-exile invasion at the Bay of Pigs was ill-conceived.

- ◆ Things might have gone better at the Bay of Pigs if the operation had not called for deniability.

- ◆ The U-2 spy plane discovered Soviet missiles in Cuba in October 1962.

- ◆ The world hovered on the brink of nuclear war before the Russians agreed to remove the missiles.

14

Mind Control Experiments

In This Chapter

- ◆ Fears of Soviet brainwashing
- ◆ Human guinea pigs
- ◆ Project Bluebird and Artichoke
- ◆ MK/ULTRA

The Cold War produced a lot of heady espionage games. There was even a time when some spooks thought that the secret to creating the perfect agent was mind control.

In the following sections you'll probably be amazed, astounded, and perhaps repulsed. As you read on, try to remember the era in which the experiments took place: Word had filtered across the land—true or false is immaterial at this point—that America was far behind the North Koreans and Russians in being able to control the minds of humans.

Keeping Up with the Joneses, er, Khrushchevs

Brain washing was on the minds of people during the Cold War. During the Korean War, U.S. prisoners of war had been used to make pro-communist propaganda statements. These prisoners returned from the war complaining that they could not help making the statements, that they had been drugged and had made the statements against their will. They had been "brainwashed," they said.

> **Spookspeak** _____
>
> **Mind control** for the CIA involved the attempt to use hypnotism and drugs to create an agent who could perform a mission and then not recall it afterward: A Manchurian Candidate. (The term "Manchurian Candidate" comes from the title of a novel by Richard Condon about an American prisoner who is programmed to become an assassin through brainwashing while in a Manchurian prison.) That agent, if caught, could never talk, never reveal his or her sources. A post-hypnotic block would be put in place to keep interrogators from getting to the portion of the agent's brain that functions during missions. It was known that the Soviets were conducting experiments along these lines at the time as well.

Thinking that an adversary could control minds and some sort of Oriental mystic could be capable of altering human behavior, even logical thinking leaders began to worry. The "what if" of brainwashing and mind control became an intensely discussed and researched topic behind closed and barred doors. Freedom of Information requests over the years finally pried some facts loose; however, the CIA destroyed the files of at least one of the major programs—or so reports have claimed—so we will probably never know the full extent of them.

> **Top Secret**
>
> The Army had its own mind control projects, along with some quiet "volunteer" programs that lured young officers into "worthwhile" projects for the good of our country.

Minding the CIA

The idea of mind control—sometimes called "brain-washing"—had been researched by the OSS since World War II. When Donovan formed the CIA, he placed those in charge of the OSS mind-control research very high in the bureaucratic pyramid.

> **Tradecraft** _____
>
> In 1942, when speaking to a select group of personnel attached to the U.S. War Department, Dr. George Estabrooks, the chairman of the Department of Psychology at Colgate University, boasted: "I can hypnotize a man—without his knowledge or consent—into committing treason against the United States. Two hundred trained foreign operators, working in the United States, could develop a uniquely dangerous army of hypnotically controlled Sixth Columnists."

Under a series of cryptic names, the CIA researched every known type of mind-control technology. Researched were:

- hypnotism

- electroshock

- drugs

- sleep deprivation

- reward and punishment

According to a 1957 CIA report, "Certainly research leading to a better understanding of the workings of the human mind is an essential element of intelligence and anything that contributes to the prediction of human behavior [and] makes possible its direction or control is of inestimable value."

Look Into My Eyes, You are Getting Sleepy ... Sleeeepy

The CIA's program of research into the possible intelligence value of hypnosis was called Bluebird; it was started in 1950. The director of the program was a fellow named Morse Allen, whose expertise in hypnotism was limited to a course he took from a stage hypnotist.

Allen believed that there was little use in experimenting on volunteers. He believed that the only valuable research would come from hypnotizing and experimenting on subjects who had no knowledge of the experiment.

He usually chose women from the CIA's secretarial pool as human guinea pigs. After hypnotizing his subjects, he would make them perform a wide variety of actions. He found he could make subjects steal secret files and deliver them to a complete stranger without them later remembering it. Obviously, many people thought this was immoral.

In 1950 Allen wrote, "We shall continually strive to attain more knowledge and better techniques. In the meantime, my general feeling is that because we have accomplished things which seem almost impossible, the authorities concerned almost believe that nothing is impossible. As you know, there are definite limitations, especially since we are so greatly handicapped by popular and official prejudice against some of our methods."

> **Tradecraft** _____
>
> Try this spy guy trick just for fun, to prove that more people than you would believe are willing to follow the leader as obedient sheep, if the leader takes command in a positive way. Ask several friends to join you in a town that has busy crossroads with traffic lights. Wait at the corner for a few changes of lights and until some other people you don't know come walking up to the red stop light.
>
> Wait until it turns green. Just before it does, step off the curb, walk a few steps into the street, being careful no cars are coming and, when the light turns green or sign says walk, turn, hold up you hand and loudly say, "Stop!" Watch what happens! It may surprise you how many blindly follow your order.

Peeling Away the Layers of Project Artichoke

In 1951, Project Bluebird was renamed project Artichoke. Project Artichoke basically carried on the same research that had been going on with Bluebird, only now the project was being sponsored by more members of the U.S. intelligence community. For Artichoke, the CIA joined forces with the intelligence divisions of the Army, Navy, Air Force, and FBI to perform hypnosis and interrogation experiments. The FBI backed out however, believing that the public would never approve of such research.

The other intelligence agencies all agreed to go ahead with the experiments. In one case, they attempted to create an agent who, if captured, would remember nothing of his or her mission.

MK/ULTRA

Richard Helms, who was then director of Clandestine Operations, was responsible for creating the CIA's most advanced look into mind control yet: project MK/ULTRA. This project was separate from Project Artichoke and was run by the CIA alone.

A New Concept for Reprogramming People

The roots of MK/ULTRA are said to be found in a speech that was given by Dr. Ewen Cameron, a Canadian psychiatrist who directed medical care at the McGill University mental facility, in February, 1953. In that speech, given in Little Rock, Arkansas, Cameron boasted he had a new concept for reprogramming people.

Dr. Cameron said, "We have explored this procedure in one case, using sleeplessness, disinhibiting agents, and hypnosis." Cameron also said that a brain could be reprogrammed by erasing it with electroshock treatments, then recording new information onto it using a repeated taped message.

Top Secret
It is believed that all records of activities related of Project MK/ULTRA were destroyed in 1973, per DCI Richard Helms' order.

Word Reaches Dulles

Word of Dr. Cameron's speech reached Allen Dulles, who was DCI at the time. On April 10, 1953, Dulles spoke at a Princeton University alumni convention and talked of the "battle for men's minds" that was going on in the Soviet Union. Dulles put forth the notion that, because the Russians were experimenting with mind control, we were forced to do so also, so that we could defend ourselves against it.

Dulles' speech was so powerful that Congress approved a multi-million dollar mind-control research program. The program proceeded under top secret conditions, although it is known that Dr. Cameron was brought on board by Dr. Sidney Gottlieb, the chemist who was put in charge of the program.

Dr. Gottlieb was particularly interested in developing substances that would cause subjects to think illogically or be publicly impulsive. Such states, it was believed, could later be used to discredit a witness, for example. Other research involved induced amnesia.

Gottlieb worked on the project in conjunction with the CIA's Technical Services Staff (TSS). The TSS did more than build gadgets and gizmos for CIA intrigue—it had a chemical division as well which, among other things, was busy developing mind-warping drugs.

Gottlieb's favorite of these newly developed drugs was called lysergic acid diethylamide—better known as LSD.

The studies of the effects of LSD on the human brain were conducted with the assistance of University of Illinois Medical School, a National Institute of Mental Health research center, and Columbia University and Mt. Sinai Hospital in New York City.

Spookspeak

The MK in MK/ULTRA meant, in code, that it was a TSS operation. The ULTRA was chosen at random. The program had nothing to do with the decoding operation of World War II that shared the same name.

Some of the human guinea pigs used for the experiments were volunteers, one of whom was kept on LSD for 77 consecutive days! Others subjects, however, were not volunteers. Since the researchers wanted to test the effects of being on LSD unexpectedly, some unwitting human guinea pigs were used. Many of the unwitting subjects were prostitutes and their johns, who were dosed with the drug and then filmed. It turned out that most subjects became very frightened and often developed mental difficulties because of the trauma.

MK/ULTRA's low point came on September 28, 1953, when an Army civilian scientist who had been given LSD without his knowledge committed suicide. Later it turned out that the man had suicidal tendencies and should not have been included in the sample.

These experiments took place predominantly in New York and San Francisco between 1953 and 1966, meaning that most of them pre-dated the LSD fad of the mid 1960s by several years.

Top Secret

Dr. Jose Delgado, a mind-control researcher working for the Navy, was interested in electronic stimulation of the brain. By implanting a small probe into the brain called a stimoceiver, Delgado discovered that he could wield enormous power over his subject. The stimoceiver operated by FM radio waves and was able to electronically orchestrate a wide range of human emotions, including rage, lust, and fatigue.

In 1966, Delgado announced that his findings, which were funded by the Office of Naval Intelligence, supported "the distasteful conclusion that motion, emotion and behavior can be directed by electrical forces." He added that "humans can be controlled like robots by push buttons." Delgado said he looked forward to a future when society could be "psychocivilized."

The Strange Story of Dr. West

Another of the doctors who used LSD on human guinea pigs during the 1950s was Dr. Louis Jolyan West, but this is not the only reason to put Dr. West in the Hall of Shame. Sadly and strangely, Dr. West once killed an elephant by giving it an overdose of LSD. Dr. West was referred to by former U.S. Naval Institute Intelligence Briefing Team member, the late Milton William "Bill" Cooper, as one of "the government's premiere experts in mind control."

Tradecraft

In 1964, the Warren Commission, investigating the assassination of President John F. Kennedy, asked Richard Helms of the CIA to brief them on the Soviet Union's mind-control capabilities. Helms responded with a memo that read: "Soviet Research and development in the Field of Direction and Control of Human behavior."

1. There are two major methods of altering or controlling human behavior, and the Soviets are interested in both. The first is psychological; the second, pharmacological. The two may be used as individual methods or for mutual reinforcement. For long-term control of large numbers of people, the former method is more promising than the latter. In dealing with individuals, the U.S. experience suggests the pharmacological approach would be the only effective method …

2. Soviet research on the pharmacological agents producing behavioral effects has consistently lagged about five years behind Western research …

3. The psychological aspects of behavior control would include not only conditioning by repetition and training, but such things as hypnosis, deprivation, isolation, manipulation of guilt feelings, subtle or overt threats …"

Dr. West was also the psychiatrist who treated Jack Ruby after he was arrested for shooting the accused assassin of President John F. Kennedy, Lee Harvey Oswald. Dr. West concluded that Ruby was in a "paranoid state, manifested by delusions, visual and auditory hallucinations and suicidal impulses."

Ruby's number one delusion was his belief that Dallas had been transformed by Nazis into a giant concentration camp where Jews were being systematically exterminated. Dr. West prescribed medication.

The Least You Need to Know

◆ The CIA researched mind control techniques to keep up with the Soviets.

◆ The CIA's most notorious mind-control program was code named MK/ULTRA.

◆ LSD, sleep deprivation, and hypnosis were all methods used to control people's minds, with inconsistent results.

Spying from Above

In This Chapter

♦ U-2: The plane, not the group

♦ The development of the Blackbird

♦ Are robotic planes the future?

♦ Satellite surveillance

The Cold War intensified during the 1950s. The Korean War, along with communist aggression in Hungary and several other countries, convinced Western leaders that the communist bloc posed a serious threat to international security.

The West needed to keep a wary eye on the communist states in order to defend against their next move. The Soviets, Chinese, and North Koreans effectively closed their borders to travel from the West.

Tourists Make Lousy Spies

Communist counterintelligence agents rounded up many of the Western intelligence agents and drove the remainder underground. Information was in short supply. The CIA attempted some desperate measures.

They approached every American who was traveling to the Soviet Union—and there weren't many of them back then—and asked them to look for missile sites during their visit. Not a single visitor stumbled upon any missile sites.

Only Way: From the Air

The CIA even dropped paratroopers behind the Iron Curtain in hopes of learning something, but this, too, was ineffective. It became clear that the only way to get intelligence was from the air.

The United States determined that it needed reconnaissance planes to fly over the communist bloc nations and determine the extent and location of their defenses, troop movements, industrial might, and thousands of other details.

"Weather" Balloons

The first attempts by the CIA to photograph the Soviet Union from the air came from unmanned balloons—their cover story was that they were weather balloons—which the United States floated over the USSR and China with cameras mounted on them. The balloons floated at 50,000 feet.

> **Tradecraft**
>
> Sometimes balloons do pay off. Back in the Civil War, artillery spotters rode in balloons and were able to see behind enemy lines. They could see where artillery was and so direct counterfire against it. The spotters also could see where enemy cavalry was assembling before attacks. They were the first air spy methods.

The balloons worked, but they weren't efficient. Five-hundred and sixteen of the balloons were launched. Only 40 of them drifted all the way across the country so they could be recovered on the other side.

Amazingly, those 40 balloons took 13,813 photos, representing about 8 percent of the land mass of the Soviet Union and mainland China. Unfortunately, the photography had been more or less random, and little usable intelligence was gathered.

The "weather" balloons were a good idea, but they just didn't pay out.

The U-2

To solve the problem, Lockheed developed a plane that could take pictures of the Soviet Union, yet fly so high that the Russian's antiaircraft guns couldn't touch it—or so it was thought. The plane made its debut in 1954.

The U-2 spy plane.

The U-2 operated at altitudes of 70,000 feet and was thought to be invulnerable to either interception by enemy fighters or destruction by enemy anti-aircraft guns and missiles. U-2s were soon overflying communist bloc countries with regularity and impunity.

The Russians, of course, were very upset at these reconnaissance missions and used every means at their disposal to shoot down the U-2s. By the spring of 1958, Russian anti-aircraft missiles had gotten dangerously close to several of the spy planes. For U-2 pilots, the job of overflying the Soviet Union was getting increasingly dangerous.

It wasn't going to be long before a new and better spy plane would be needed. In April 1958, the CIA assigned Richard M. Bissell, special assistant for planning and coordination of the U-2 spy missions, to find a replacement for the U-2. It was because of Bissell's foresight that a replacement for the spy plane was already under development by the time the U-2 became obsolete—which was rather suddenly.

> **McLean Says ...**
>
> One of the airfields for U.S spy missions was in Pakistan. One friend, attached to the American Embassy there, recalls those strange looking, long-winged planes. They were kept in a special, highly secure area. Nevertheless, they were clearly seen on takeoffs and landings. No doubt the Russians were busily taking photos of them and trying to learn whatever they could so they could eventually shoot the planes down.

Francis Gary Powers

On May 1, 1960—that is, May Day, a major Soviet holiday—a U-2 spy plane, with pilot Francis Gary Powers aboard, was shot down over the Soviet Union. There was rejoicing in Moscow and consternation in Washington.

Both the pilot and the aircraft were taken by the enemy. The U.S. at first tried to deny that it was a spy plane, saying that it was merely a plane that had wandered off course. After the Soviets found the complex photographic equipment aboard, the United States was forced to admit that Powers had been on a spy mission.

Powers was held in a Soviet prison for two years. He was released in 1962, when President Kennedy agreed to a spy swap. We got Powers back and we returned captured spy, Colonel Rudolf Abel, to the Soviets. Abel had set up a communist spy ring in New York City during the late 1950s. To those involved in the swap, the trade seemed a fair deal.

To make sure that neither side got burned during the spy swap, the exchange took place on Berlin, Germany's Glienicke Bridge, which spans the River Havel. Powers stood on the east side of the bridge and Abel stood on the west side. At a signal, both prisoners were allowed to walk across the bridge simultaneously. They passed each other at the center of the bridge silently, offering only a barely perceptible nod as they passed.

Top Secret

On May 1, 2000, U.S. Officials presented Powers' family with the Prisoner-of-War Medal, the Distinguished Flying Cross and the National Defense service medal during a 30-minute ceremony held at the Beale Air Force Base, north of Sacramento and home to the modern U.S. U-2 force. It marked the 40th anniversary of the incident.

Top Secret

Powers went into TV journalism and died in 1977 at the age of 47 when the television news helicopter he was piloting crashed in Los Angeles, California. Powers is buried in Arlington Cemetery outside Washington, D.C.

Welcome Home, Sort of

Powers was not received warmly by his CIA comrades when he arrived back at the United States. His assignment had been to make sure the plane was destroyed in case it was shot down so that the Soviets would not be able to learn anything from it. He had also been trained to take a poison pill and commit suicide if he were captured, so that he would not be able to talk.

What Next?

If the problem is the risk that your surveillance plane will be shot down and its pilot and crew captured, then there are three things you can do:

♦ You can build a plane that, somehow, is beyond the enemy's capability to shoot it down.

♦ You can put your cameras higher than a plane can go. In other words, you can attach your camera to a satellite that is orbiting the Earth.

♦ You can build your spy planes so that they run on remote control, and therefore don't need a pilot and crew.

During the latter stages of the Cold War, the U.S. intelligence services tried all three.

A New Spy Plane

The replacement for the U-2 was already on its way. The CIA's Richard Bissell had approached Lockheed and Convair aircraft companies and asked if they could make a better spy aircraft than the U-2. In the past, Lockheed had built the U-2 and Convair had built the fast, high-flying F-102 Delta Dagger.

Per the CIA's request, both companies drew up and submitted several proposals for a plane that could operate at 90,000 feet, have a top speed in excess of mach 3, or more than three times the speed of sound, and have a range of 4,000 miles.

The aircraft would stretch the design abilities of the engineers as its performance was on the edge of what was then considered aerodynamically possible. Both companies said that they would have a prototype ready only 22 months after their proposal was accepted.

> **Top Secret**
>
> Convair and Lockheed submitted their proposals for a new spy plane to the CIA under the code name Project Gusto.

And the Winner Is ...

Since the proposals were such radical departures from conventional aircraft, the CIA requested that a joint Department of Defense/U.S. Air Force board evaluate the proposals to determine cost and feasibility. The Department of Defense military experts met for several weeks, and on September 3, 1959, they recommended that the Lockheed proposal be accepted.

Code-named Project Oxcart, Lockheed went to work on the new spy plane. The head of the design team was Clarence "Kelly" Johnson, the same man who designed the U-2 and the radical P-38 Lightning. Johnson was in charge of Lockheed's *skunk works*.

Johnson assembled the best engineers, and he presented them with a daunting task. Because of the aircraft's high speed and altitude requirements, the skin of the fuselage had to withstand temperatures ranging from minus 49° Centigrade to 315° Centigrade. There was also a problem designing a fuselage that would mate harmoniously with the bigtime-thrust engines that had to be attached.

Ninety-three percent of the aircraft was covered with a skin of high-grade B-120 titanium alloy, which was expensive but could handle the extreme temperatures. The engines turned out to be specially designed Pratt and Whitney J58 turbojets with afterburners.

There was one other specification that had to be met: The new jet was to be designed so that it would leave the smallest possible signature on enemy radar screens. To accomplish this, the jet was to be shaped like a dart.

Not Your Typical Model Airplane

A full mock-up, called the A-12, was built and demonstrated for CIA officials in November of 1959. In 1960, Lockheed was told to build 12 of the jets, plus one two-seat version for training pilots. There were a few problems along the way, but the 12 prototypes were ready on April 26, 1962.

The prototypes performed without a hitch, but the engines were upgraded to make them more powerful anyway. With the new engines, the 1963 models were known as YF-12As. These new models performed well also but were eventually discontinued because they were too thirsty, and drank way too much fuel.

Fly Blackbird, Fly

The next set of changes on the jet would transform it into its final version, the SR-71A, better known as the Blackbird. The SR stands for strategic reconnaissance.

The fuselage was modified to accept several different surveillance packages: photographic, radar, electronic, or signal-intercept intelligence. In addition, the systems could be configured either as single or multiple surveillance packages. The SR-71A made its first flight on December 22, 1964. All went well.

The SR-71 Blackbird on the runway—a slender silhouette.

The new spy jet was delivered to the 4200th Strategic Reconnaissance Wing stationed at Beale Air Force Base in California.

Jet Black

The aircraft arrived wearing a special coating of black paint that had been specially developed for high-altitude flight. It was the ebony paint job that earned it its Blackbird nickname.

The SR-71A had the following specifications:

- **Wingspan:** 55 feet, 7 inches
- **Overall length:** 107 feet, 5 inches
- **Overall height:** 18 feet, 6 inches
- **Wheelbase:** 34 feet
- **Empty weight:** 60,000 pounds
- **Maximum weight:** 170,000 pounds
- **Fuel consumption:** 8,000 U.S. gallons per hour
- **Operational ceiling:** 80,000 feet

- **Maximum level speed at 30,000 feet:** 1,320 miles per hour

- **Maximum level speed at 78,740 feet:** 2,000 miles per hour

- **Typical operating radius:** 1,200 miles

- **Range without refueling:** 2,982 miles

- **Fuselage:** B-120 Series Titanium Alloy

- **Landing gear:** Retractable Tricycle type, treadless tires, Anti-skid system, braking parachute.

- **Power Plant:** Two Pratt and Whitney JT11D-20B (J58) Turbo-Ramjet engines

- **Crew:** 2 (Pilot and Recon System Officer)

- **Sensors:** photographic, infra-red, electronic

- **Armament:** None

Because there were so few of the aircraft and the maintenance and crew selection was so specialized, the Air Force consolidated all of the aircraft into one Wing. (Although the planes and missions were CIA, the Air Force's technicians and pilots were still needed to accomplish those missions.) When missions required, small one- and two-plane detachments were deployed to various bases throughout the world. Detachments operated from Midenhall, England, Seymour Johnson Air Force base in South Carolina, and Kadena Air Force Base in Okinawa, Japan.

One Smart Bird

The SR-71A Blackbird turned out to be very good at gathering intelligence, and quickly proved its value. The high speed and sophisticated intelligence gathering equipment of the aircraft allowed the military to fly routine flights over enemy nations or check out potential trouble spots very quickly. A plane could be over a target hours after that target was identified. Soon the aircraft were flying over Cuba, China, East Germany, North Korea, North Vietnam, and, of course, the Soviet Union.

> **Tradecraft**
>
> The only weapons capable of shooting down the Blackbird were anti-aircraft missiles. More than 1,000 surface-to-air missiles were fired at the SR-71A during its many missions, but none could down the aircraft.

The experience gained from these early Blackbird missions brought requests for several modifications. "B" and "C" versions were soon produced, which had improved avionics, infrared detection, and performance.

By the early 1970s there were enough Blackbirds in use to allow a reorganization of the Strategic Reconnaissance Wing. The 9th Strategic Wing took command of the SR-71s and allocated them to the 1st and 99th Strategic Reconnaissance Squadrons.

Blackbird, Bye, Bye

The Blackbirds continued flying regular missions until 1990, when they were retired from active service—retired temporarily, at least. The aircraft were expensive to operate and maintain. The CIA's experts believed that satellite reconnaissance, which we'll discuss shortly, could provide the same coverage as the SR-71 but at a lower cost.

With a touch of foresight, the Blackbirds were put in storage and carefully preserved. And it was a good thing, too, because they it wasn't long before they were called back into active duty.

Although the spy satellites in orbit around the Earth provided adequate coverage, they were not always in the proper location to photograph a chosen target. To move a satellite to a new location could take days, and that was too long given the frantic pace of world events.

In 1995, the defense department allocated $100 million to reactivate several SR-71s. They were equipped with the latest radar and high-resolution cameras. The revitalized Blackbirds began active duty again in 1996 and have been used ever since.

Aurora: Blackbird's Replacement?

Officially, there are no plans to replace the SR-71. Officially, that is. There have, however, been persistent rumors for years that Lockheed's skunk works has been developing a faster and higher-flying spy plane named Aurora. What evidence is there that Aurora really exists? Let's take a look.

In 1982 a history of Lockheed was published that stated that the company had developed a reconnaissance plane that could travel mach 6. In 1985, a line item for a program called Aurora appeared between the SR-71 and the U-2 in a Pentagon budget document. That notation was later called an "editor's error."

In 1988, the *New York Times* reported that Lockheed had a mach 6 aircraft under development. A British aircraft-recognition expert saw an unknown aircraft over the North Sea in 1989. The jet was refueling from a KC-135 tanker and was accompanied by two F-111s.

The Chinese Spy Plane Incident

One of the problems with surveillance by plane is that, if that plane is shot down, the enemy will be able to capture it and learn the methods of your intelligence gathering. This was true of the U-2, and it came up again more than 40 years later in an incident involving China.

The incident began in the skies above the Chinese island of Hainan, which is about 400 miles (640 kilometers) southwest of Hong Kong and about 200 miles (320 kilometers) east of the Vietnamese capital, Hanoi.

According to the U.S. Navy—on March 31, 2001—a U.S. EP-3E Aries surveillance plane was on a routine mission over international air space. The Chinese said that the plane was over Chinese air space.

A Chinese F-8 fighter aircraft was sent up to intercept the U.S. spy plane, but accidentally got too close and clipped the EP-3. The pilot of the jet crashed and died, while the damaged EP-3 was forced to make an emergency landing on the island of Hainan.

None of the 24-person American crew was injured. However, for the first time since Francis Gary Powers was shot down over the Soviet Union, an American spy plane had been captured. The spy plane had been based out of Kaddena Air Force Base in Okinawa, Japan.

The EP-3 was equipped with highly sensitive equipment that could monitor electronic communications and aircraft movements well into the Chinese mainland.

The incident occurred as hard-liners in both countries were urging their governments to take a tougher line toward each other. President George W. Bush had tried to redefine the relationship between China and the United States from a "strategic partner" to a "strategic competitor."

President Bush was considering whether to sell destroyers equipped with the sophisticated Aegis air defense radar system to Taiwan. At the time of the incident, a senior Chinese army officer had recently defected to the United States, and Beijing was holding a Chinese-born U.S. resident accused of spying.

The United States immediately demanded that the crew and the damaged plane be returned, but it was clear that the Chinese were not going to part with the plane until they had gleaned as much intelligence out of it as possible. The United States was disingenuous in its demands, and everyone knew it. If the roles had been reversed, the United States would be unlikely to return a Chinese spy plane.

The crew was returned to the U.S. after 11 days of interrogation. The plane eventually came back, too, although in pieces. The disassembled plane, carried inside the cargo hold of a Russian-built Antonov-124 cargo jet, was flown from China to Marietta, Georgia, in July 2001. Pentagon officials said the four-engine turboprop would be reassembled and equipped with upgraded electronics.

Remote Pilotless Vehicles

One way to reduce the risk of human casualty while spying from above is to operate a radio-controlled plane with a camera attached. Both the navigation and photography can be handled from miles away from the surveillance target without any risk to human life.

By the mid 1990s, remote pilotless vehicles (RPVs) were providing eye-in-the-sky surveillance for the CIA and other intelligence services all over the world. Pilotless planes with cameras attached were flying over parts of Northern Ireland. They were helping to counter insurgency in Israel and South Africa. The Israeli defense force maintained a 24-hour-a-day watch over South Lebanon to spot the movements of hostile armed elements trying to infiltrate the security zone adjacent to north Galilee.

War correspondent Al J. Venter reported on the eye-in-the-sky surveillance being used at that time in Zululand for the *Military Technical Journal*. He reported in 1997 that in South Africa, and specifically in Kwa-Zulu, where insurgent deaths could run into double figures over a weekend, South Africa heavily used RPVs in a series of para-military counter-insurgent programs.

Those took place in the region around the Natal capital of Pietermaritzburg and along the south coast, where gang warfare was uncontained. This was a region disputed by the pro-government African National Congress (ANC) and Chief Mongusothu Buthelezi's Inkatha movement. Some of the attacks had left 30 dead at a time. Many of the dead were innocent women and children. In those joint South African Army, Air Force and Police operations security forces had spent four to eight weeks on full-scale military operations involving helicopter-led strikes against rebel strongpoints.

Some of the gangs encountered were 2,000 strong—and almost all of them were armed. All deployments of RPVs in Southern Africa are geared so that, if necessary, there can be a quick human response. There is always the possibility for the immediate air-lifting of a reaction force to any target area where suspicious activity might have been observed by the RPV.

The Seeker

The RPV being used at that time in South Africa and in other parts of the world was called The Seeker, built by Kentron Technologies of Wilmington, Massachusetts. They each weighed 250 kilograms. If you saw one of these RPVs sitting on the ground, you might think that it's someone's toy.

The Seeker has two sets of controls, one for taking off and one for cruising. It can take off and land on any runway. Once it reaches a certain altitude, the first pilot clicks off and a second "pilot" automatically takes over.

The entire system can be operated from three mobile electronic control stations, which can be moved by truck. Because they have *infrared* capabilities, they can be used day and night.

The Seeker has what's called a thermal-imaging system, which means that it creates seeable images by judging the temperature of objects. The system can send clear pictures to the ground from as high as 18,000 feet up. The Seeker can be deployed from as far as 200 kilometers from a target and can stay aloft for more than two hours before it has to return to its home base.

> **Spookspeak**
>
> **Infrared** cameras use film sensitive to infrared light, which is made up of rays beyond those in the spectrum that are visible to the naked eye. Infrared rays are produced by heat and allow us to "see" at night. To **zero**, as a verb, means to put a target under the cross hairs of a gun, or, in this case, a camera, as in the phrase, "I'm zeroing in on it."

> **Top Secret**
>
> The Seeker's imaging system can read a license plate from 3.7 miles away.

The Seeker incorporates within its modest frame an electronic, jam-resistant microwave link with a back-up ultra-high frequency command sensor as well as an autonomous "return home" system, both ideal for wartime conditions.

The thermal-imaging system can zoom within a range of 27 degrees down to 0.8 degrees, giving it an excellent versatility when it needs to *zero* onto a specific building or a vehicle that it might be tracking.

The Seeker, of course, has its limitations. It wouldn't be effective against an enemy with a sophisticated anti-aircraft system, for example. The Seeker makes no attempt to hide itself. It can be seen from the ground, so it only works against an enemy who doesn't have the power to shoot it down.

Robot Planes Used in Afghanistan

Now, several years into the twenty-first century, the robot surveillance planes have advanced. They are now no longer just curious. They are curious and dangerous at the same time.

These new robot planes don't just locate a target and take pictures of it. If necessary, they will locate a target, take pictures of it, and then blast the target to smithereens.

McLean Says ...

Black shoes are bad news. Cops wear black shoes. At least bartenders, waiters, lots of average citizens, and probably most foreign spies, think so.

One time I had been to a formal event and then changed from suit to casual clothes, but neglected to change shoes. I stopped at a pub on the way home, and I observed that a bartender kept looking at my shoes. Finally, I asked the bartender what the problem was. He shrugged and just said, "Nothing, you cops got a right to drink beer."

While praising the work of the CIA one day recently during an appearance on CNN, Senator Bob Graham (D), the chairman of the intelligence committee, said, "I think the CIA has done a wonderful job and I think there are several things that have been done that will end up being harbingers of things that will be done in the future. For one thing, the use of the Predator ..."

The CIA-owned Predator drone is a robotic plane that is equipped for surveillance and attack. It can locate a target and it can take it out—all without the risk of U.S. casualties.

Here are some facts about the Predator:

◆ **Length:** 27 feet

◆ **Weight:** 2,250 pounds

◆ **Speed:** 84–140 miles per hour

◆ **Range:** Can operate 454 miles from its controller.

◆ **Ceiling:** 25,000 feet.

◆ **Armament:** Two 100-pound hellfire laser-guided tankbusting missiles.

◆ **Personnel:** While no humans fly inside the Predator, a crew of 55 is needed to operate one.

The drone planes can patrol over a country such as Afghanistan for up to 24 hours without a rest and can fire sophisticated guidance missiles. It is given credit for locating and knocking out a Taliban convoy.

Drones Are Shrinking

The Predators, with their 49-foot wingspans, were formerly used with great effectiveness to support U.S. military forces in Kosovo, Iraq, and Afghanistan. Future robot flying surveillance—MAVs, Micro Air Vehicles—will be much smaller. The smaller size will make them increasingly difficult to detect from the ground. After all, you get better pictures of the enemy when he doesn't know he is being photographed. The Rand Corporation, MIT Lincoln Laboratory, and the Defense Advanced Research Projects Agency have studied ways to shrink cameras, chemical sensors, communications gear, and weapons for mini-drones.

> **Top Secret**
>
> On February 4, 2002, President Bush sent Congress a $2.13 trillion budget, which included a $48 billion hike in military and paramilitary spending. Among the things that Bush called for in his budget was $1.1 billion more for remote-controlled aircraft, 22 new Predators, and three new Global hawk surveillance drones, which work much like the Predator but at a much higher altitude.

They would be able to do things that the Predator can't because of their size. For example, the new mini-bots would be able to fly *into* buildings like small packs of hummingbirds. And the aerial robots could track radioactive, chemical, or germ-filled clouds, for example, all the time.

Gnats and P-3s

The war on terrorism in the Philippines has made maximum use of aerial surveillance as well. During the spring of 2002, as 160 U.S. special op troops aided 5,000 Philippine troops in their fight on the island of Basilan against the Al Qaeda-linked Abu Sayyaf Muslim bandit guerillas, the land war was being aided from above not only through satellite surveillance, a subject we will deal with in depth later in this chapter, but also through drone planes and Navy reconnaissance aircraft.

The spy plane being used is the P-3 Orion, which was originally designed for long-range anti-submarine warfare. The drone is called the GNAT unmanned aerial vehicle, which is smaller than the Predators used in Afghanistan, but not as small as some of the mini-drones under development.

The GNAT unmanned aerial vehicle, such as those used in the Philippines, has been equipped with a fine-resolution, real-time radar developed by Sandia National Laboratories.

(Photo by Randy Montoya/ courtesy Sandia National Laboratories)

Turbojets the Size of Shirt Buttons

The agency is spending $35 million over 4 years to come up with cheap 6-inch vehicles that can fly for 2 hours at 90 m.p.h. and relay images from a distance of 6 miles. These mini planes could be launched by hand, via catapult, or even launched with a weapon.

Some designs call for spy planes that weigh as little as 11 ounces. IGR, Inc., a firm in Ohio, is working on a mini-fuel cell to power them. Meanwhile, the brains at the Massachusetts Institute of Technology are working on a turbojet that is the size of a shirt button!

Organic Drones

Another $6 million has been allocated in the CIA budget for the development of mini-spy drones called OAVs, or Organic Air Vehicles. These would not need to be radio controlled from a "pilot" on the ground.

Rather, they would be pre-programmed via a computer to react to a countless number of situations. Then they could be sent out on their own, where they would no longer need instructions. The OAVs will be designed to take off vertically, so they could land on a window sill, look inside, and then take off again.

The Marines and the Navy have similar drones under development. The Marines' is called Dragon Eyes and the Navy has plans for a "Robofly." The Navy's flying spy is the smallest of all and has been called a "micromechanical flying insect."

Future Predators

But not all of the research and development had to do with mini robots. Drone spy planes the size of the Predator have a future as well. The Predator, which is built by General Atomics Aeronautical Systems of San Diego, California, is currently undergoing an upgrade.

Expect future Predators to be "cloaked" so that they are more difficult to pick up on radar. They will also be equipped with superior weapons.

The system of getting the photos back to earth is constantly improving as well. A new chip is being prepared by the Sarnoff Corporation of West Windsor, New Jersey. Working with Windows software, the chip overlays target images onto maps for precise targeting. The chip replaces a cumbersome system in which images had to be stitched together.

Top Secret
There was a time when some believed that the follow-up to the U-2 would be a robot plane, and so Northop Grumman designed the pilotless Global Hawk, which once flew from the United States to Australia on its own. The Global Hawk, can cruise at 65,000 feet, and has three sensors so that it can see through any weather.

Modern Satellite Surveillance

In August 1960, thousands of feet over the Pacific Ocean, a U.S. Air Force C-119 closed in on a parachute falling from the sky. Using a trailing nylon cable, the aircraft tried to snag the parachute to reel it in, but missed.

The pilot turned around and tried a second time, but missed again. The parachute was at 8,500 feet altitude when the pilot tried for a third time and this time was successful.

The retrieved parachute held a roll of 70mm film that had been taken by a satellite called Corona over the then Soviet Union. These were the first reconnaissance photos ever taken from a satellite.

Giving Instant Film Processing a Twist

Corona was the result of a series of Air Force studies conducted from 1946 to 1956, when the Air Force formally began the satellite reconnaissance program called

Weapons System 117L. It was originally intended to photograph a target, develop the film on board, scan the images electronically, and then broadcast them down to Earth.

But after the launch of the Soviet Union's Sputnik, the first artificial satellite to orbit the Earth, in 1957, the U.S. decided that it couldn't wait for the 117L to be developed and instead switched to an interim plan. This satellite would use a Thor rocket and return its unprocessed film to Earth.

In early 1958 President Dwight D. Eisenhower ordered that the satellite be developed jointly by the CIA and the Air Force. (The CIA and the Air Force has previously teamed to build and operate the U-2 spy plane.)

The project was named Corona, after the brand of the typewriter upon which the proposal was written. This was the classified name. The public knew only of a satellite called Discoverer.

Tradecraft

Corona's camera had a 24-inch focal length and was designed by the Itek Corporation. As the satellite orbited, the camera would sweep a narrow slit over a long strip of film. The film would advance, and the camera would sweep over the next piece of film. When the individual strips of film were placed next to one another, they formed a picture of a vast area. The resulting photos had a resolution of 25 feet (an object had to be 25 feet or larger—a house, maybe—to be seen). The film from this camera was wound on a film cassette inside a re-entry capsule. The capsule re-entered the atmosphere, where its ablative—that is, meant to melt away—coating shielded it from the heat of atmospheric friction. At 60,000 feet, the re-entry shield was jettisoned and a spherical "bucket" was yanked clear with a small parachute called a drogue. A larger chute quickly opened and a radio beacon was activated. The beacon allowed a nearby aircraft to fly by and snag the film as it descended. The film was flown to Pearl Harbor in Hawaii, and from there was transported to Eastman Kodak in Rochester, N.Y., where it was developed.

The Itek Corporation designed Corona's cameras and Fairchild built them. Lockheed was responsible for overall satellite integration. There were 11 failures before the system worked in 1960, and during this time the urgency to get the system up increased when Gary Powers was shot down over the Soviet Union in his U-2 spy plane.

Soviet Bomber Base Photographed

That first successful secret spy mission, known to the public as Discoverer 14, photographed the Soviet bomber base at Mys Schmidta as well as other areas. Both the camera designers and the photo-interpreters were somewhat disappointed with the quality of the initial photos.

The designers upgraded the camera twice before finally achieving their goal of creating a camera that took photos with a resolution of 25 feet.

The satellite reconnaissance system received another major upgrade in 1962. This involved the addition of a second camera, which rotated in the opposite direction of the first. Now two images of the same location could be taken from slightly different angles. When viewed through a stereoscopic microscope, the resulting images revealed a third dimension and could determine the height of objects.

Several upgrades were to come as photos became sharper and sharper. The final Corona mission flew in 1972, at which time it was replaced by a new satellite reconnaissance program.

There were 145 Corona missions in all. Those missions photographed strategic targets within the Soviet Union such as missile complexes, bomber bases, shipyards, and plutonium production facilities.

The Soviet Spy Satellite: Zenit

Although we didn't know it at the time, the Soviet Union was working on space surveillance as well. The first Soviet reconnaissance satellite was adapted from the Vostik manned spacecraft that took the first man to orbit the earth, Yuri Gagarin, into space. The reconnaissance satellite was called Zenit (or, in English, Zenith).

The satellite weighed five and a half tons, as opposed to Corona, which weighed just under one ton. The Zenit satellite contained four cameras, two high-resolution and two low-resolution. Like Corona, Zenit parachuted its exposed film back to Earth.

The Soviets first attempted to put the Zenit satellite into orbit on December 11, 1961, but the mission failed because of a malfunction in the third stage of the booster rocket. The second attempt, which lasted from March 16 until March 19, 1962, went better, but still no cigar.

> **Top Secret**
>
> Later Soviet reconnaissance satellites were called Resurs-F and Kometa.

On the second mission everything worked except the orientation of the satellite, so, although the satellite returned beautiful photographs to Earth, none of those images were of the intended targets. The third try, which blasted off on July 28, 1962, was a winner, and the first useful photographs were returned.

Latest Satellites

Today's surveillance satellites transmit their images directly to receivers on Earth, and they do it in real time. The current U.S. satellites are called KH-11s and KH-12s. Using film that picks up the electromagnetic spectrum, these satellites can be set so that they could read a license plate from space.

Of course, using satellites isn't the most efficient way to read a license plate, and for purposes of intelligence, photos of larger areas are usually required, so a lower resolution and larger scope is usually used.

The KH-11s and KH-12s orbit hundreds of miles above the Earth, in synch with the Earth's revolution so that they remain parked over a single spot on the planet. They were moved to a spot over Iraq during the Gulf War.

During the Gulf War, CIA spy satellites provided the first-ever real-time images of enemy movements taken from space. These images gave the U.S. a tremendous advantage, and saved hundreds of American lives on the ground.

The United States got off to an early lead against the Soviets in surveillance from space, even if the Soviets were, for a time, winning the space race. When it comes to spies in the sky, it was a technological advantage that the United States never gave up. Right up until the fall of the Soviet Union, the United States had superior reconnaissance satellites in space.

Tradecraft

KH-12 spy satellites cost more than $1 billion apiece.

The Least You Need to Know

◆ The U-2 was the first U.S. spy jet. It photographed the Soviet Union and Cuba during the Cold War.

◆ The U-2 was replaced in the U.S. arsenal by the Blackbird.

◆ Ever since the early days of space travel, satellites have been used for reconnaissance.

◆ The war in Afghanistan was aided by drone planes that photograph the enemy without a risk to friendly life.

Part 4

Watergate and Other Black Eyes

The CIA got knocked around in the 1970s, and by the time the decade was over, it had been severely bruised by a series of congressional investigations into its Cold War activities.

Making matters worse, the agency found itself embroiled in the Watergate scandal. To this day, it hasn't been able to shake off the unfounded allegations that it was somehow involved in the break-in at the Democratic National Headquarters.

Things didn't get much better for the company in later decades, as it discovered traitors in its midst and lost its prime directive with the end of the Cold War.

Chapter 16

Black Eyes for the CIA

In This Chapter

- ◆ Domestic activities
- ◆ Government investigations
- ◆ Leaky plumbers
- ◆ Call from the White House

By the 1970s, the secretive nature of the CIA had caught up with it, and the agency was battered with accusations that it had been in violation of its charter, which led to several government investigations.

To make matters worse, there was a scandal involving the White House, which involved characters familiar to CIA payrolls, and which eventually brought down a president.

Rocky's Punch

On December 22, 1974, *The New York Times* published a front-page article that charged that the CIA had been engaging in domestic spying, which it was forbidden by law to do. The author or the article, Seymour Hersh, alleged that the CIA had been spying upon and maintaining files on U.S. citizens in the United States, all because they were active protesters against the unpopular war in Vietnam. Hersh's article was called, "Huge CIA Operation Reported in U.S. Against Anti-War Forces, Other Dissidents in Nixon Years."

Spookspeak

The **Rockefeller Commission** was formed on January 5, 1975. Future president Ronald Reagan served on the Commission.

A commission was formed in reaction to the article. Called the *Rockefeller Commissions* (actually, the Commission on CIA Activities Within the United States, chaired by Vice President Nelson Rockefeller), it determined that the CIA had, indeed, illegally opened the mail of U.S. citizens and installed illegal surveillance systems to spy on Americans.

There had been a huge domestic operation—it was called Operation Chaos—to keep tabs on anti-war demonstrators in the United States. The CIA's defense was that, yes, they had undertaken missions that were in defiance of the rules in their charter, but they had done it in order to address what they called "serious national security questions."

It turned out, for example, that President Lyndon B. Johnson had put pressure on the agency to create files on dissident students. Okay, should have been an FBI job. But the Rocky Commission was just the first punch.

The CIA Goes to Church

The findings of the Rockefeller Commission caused such a stir that it was quickly followed up by a second, more thorough, investigation into the CIA, this one by the U.S. Senate and chaired by Senator Frank Church, a Democrat from Idaho. Now that the cat was out of the bag regarding the CIA and its refusal to color inside the lines when it came to its own bylaws, politicians saw the CIA as an easy target. Now, in addition to the stories of the CIA's domestic spying, there were rumors that the CIA had also conspired to assassinate foreign leaders.

The official name of the committee was the Senate Select Committee to Study Governmental Operations with Respect to Intelligence Activities, but it was dubbed the Church Committee. The committee's hearings started in 1975 and stretched on until the next year, despite the fact that some of the revelations coming out in the public hearings were compromising operations and the fact that President Gerald Ford had personally called Church, asking that the hearings be halted.

Top Secret

Senator Frank Church served in Army Intelligence along the Burma Road during World War II.

Details of the hearings were printed in the press, and it was during this time that many Americans learned that the CIA was more than an intelligence-gathering organization, but also was expert at small yet critical covert actions, as well (see Chapter 11 for more on covert actions).

Using Journalists

Also exposed during the hearings was the CIA's fondness for using journalists as agents working overseas. For years newspaper reporters and electronic media journalists had been used as assets. Now, as a result of these hearings, the CIA was forbidden by law to put U.S. journalists working abroad on their payroll. When George Bush became DCI, the rules against using reporters for clandestine purposes were further tightened.

Professor Spies

The Church Committee also uncovered a thorough infiltration by the CIA of the U.S. academic community. The report stated:

> The Central Intelligence Agency has long-developed clandestine relationships with the American academic community, which range from academics making introductions for intelligence purposes to intelligence collection while abroad, to academic research and writing where CIA sponsorship is hidden. The Central Intelligence Agency is now using several hundred American academics ('academics' includes administrators, faculty members and graduate students engaged in teaching), who in addition to providing leads and, on occasion, making introductions for intelligence purposes, occasionally write books and other material to be used for propaganda purposes abroad.

> Beyond these, an additional few score are used in an unwitting manner for minor activities. These academics are located in over 100 American colleges, universities, and related institutes. At the majority of institutions, no one other than the individual concerned is aware of the CIA link. At the others, at least one university official is aware of the operational use made of academics on his campus. In addition, there are several American academics abroad who serve operational purposes, primarily the collection of intelligence. Although the numbers are not as great today as in 1966, there are no prohibitions to prevent an increase in the operational use of academics. The size of these operations is determined by the CIA.

With the exception of those teachers, scholars and students who receive scholarships or grants from the Board of Foreign Scholarships, the CIA is not prohibited from the operational use of all other categories of grantee support under the Fulbright-Hays Act (artists, athletes, leaders, specialists, etc.). Nor is there any prohibition on the operational use of individuals participating in any other exchange program funded by the United States Government.

The Committee is disturbed both by the present practices of operationally using American academics and by the awareness that the restraints on expanding this practice are primarily those of sensitivity to the risks of disclosure and not an appreciation of dangers to the integrity of individuals and institutions.

Other of the CIA's alleged sins made public by the Church Committee were:

◆ Projects designed to control the human mind.

◆ Drugging unsuspecting human guinea pigs (see Chapter 14).

◆ Conspiracy to assassinate foreign leaders.

There were two other investigatory bodies functioning at about the same time as the Rockefeller Commission and the Church Committee. These were House of Representative bodies called the Pike Committee and the Nedzi Committee, both of which covered much of the same ground as their larger predecessors, and both of which further sullied the CIA's reputation.

An Undeserved Black Eye

The CIA perhaps has received no bigger—and undeserved—black eye than it did after Watergate, the scandal that brought down President Nixon.

Break-In at the Watergate

The Watergate scandal began on June 17, 1972, when five burglars broke into Democratic National Committee headquarters at the Watergate Hotel in Washington, D.C. They were captured and arrested.

The five arrested men, who eventually became known as the "White House Plumbers" (because they "plugged leaks") were Eugenio Martinez, Virgilio Gonzalez, Frank Sturgis, Bernard Barker, and James McCord. Several had worked for the CIA—which obviously caused a great deal of suspicion that the CIA was involved. Sturgis, McCord, and Martinez all were or had been on the CIA payroll. A media frenzy ensued, and it was alleged that since so many of the Watergate plumbers had at one time been associated with the CIA, the CIA had to be a sponsor of the crime.

Tradecraft

Here's an example of what not to do: The Watergate burglars had placed tape over a door lock in the building's parking garage—so the door would not lock behind them—and the burglary was discovered in progress by a guard after he noticed the tape.

In terms of the growing scandal, McCord's name was the most significant, as he worked for the Committee to Re-Elect the President (CRP for short, although it was later dubbed by the media as CREEP). Two others with agency backgrounds—E. Howard Hunt and G. Gordon Liddy—also were later arrested as part of the plot. They worked for CRP and had supervised the burglary.

Spookspeak

A **front** is an organization that serves to provide a legend or disguised identification for a CIA operation or project.

A Political Dirty Trick?

The investigation into the burglary, the purpose of which has never been definitely nailed down, looked right away like dirty politics. An investigation into the burglary and the crime's subsequent cover-up led all the way to the Oval Office and eventually resulted in the resignation from office of President Richard Nixon on August 9, 1974.

When the investigations were finally over, it was determined that the CIA had nothing to do with the Watergate break-in or its subsequent cover up. Even the mass media have admitted that the first charges of CIA involvement were unfounded. In the climate of distrust among the American people during the 1970s stemming from the Vietnam War, the assassination of President Kennedy, and by the Watergate scandal itself, people were quick to assume the worst about the CIA.

Stoic Agency

Following the Watergate burglary, Nixon's aides called a meeting with DCI Richard Helms. They asked that he call the FBI Director, L. Patrick Gray, and ask that the FBI investigation be restricted, since a full investigation might reveal CIA secrets. Helms knew this was not true and refused to make the call. Not long thereafter Helms was fired by Richard Nixon and was reassigned as U.S. ambassador to Iran. So, given an opportunity to obscure the facts regarding Watergate, the CIA's director said no, and took his punishment for not playing ball.

McLean Says ...

We were living in a small New Jersey town so we could raise our children in the country while I worked in New York and flew elsewhere periodically. The town needed some volunteers for the Republican Party, and that seemed like a pleasant sidelight in the community. I thought a bit of political work might be insightful. Besides, at that time my wife had no clue about the quiet intel work I did. For all public knowledge, I was a syndicated columnist and radio broadcaster.

One day the phone rang. The caller identified himself as calling from The White House. He asked whether I could come to Washington to be interviewed for a speech writers job at the White House. I agreed.

There I finally received some answers. I wouldn't really be a speech writer. Actually the job would entail working on special projects for CREEP—the Committee to Re-Elect the President!

"What duties?" I asked.

"That will be determined as needs arise," I was told.

After more polite chatter, I asked to think it over, shook hands and cabbed back to the airport.

My wife didn't favor living or working in D.C. I liked my present work and family roots in the Garden State. So, I called and politely declined the offer for a GS-16, which was a political appointment with no Civil Service protection. Nice pay, but no way!

Looking back, that job could have led me into that wonderful Watergate mess. Considering who ran the Committee to Re-Elect, I probably was being recruited as another Dirty Tricks guy. Intel was one thing. Political Nixon games were another.

The Least You Need to Know

◆ The Rockefeller Commission investigated domestic CIA activities that were in violation of the agency's charter.

◆ The Church Committee investigated CIA covert actions overseas.

◆ Watergate started when five Republican burglars were caught inside Democratic national headquarters.

◆ The CIA received an undeserved black eye over the Watergate scandal.

Chapter 17

Traitors

In This Chapter

- ◆ The Cambridge Spy Ring
- ◆ This Ames untrue
- ◆ Turncoat teacher
- ◆ Selling codes

Traitors come in two categories: those who betray your side to help the other guys, and those who betray the other guys to help you. This chapter concerns the former group, those in the U.S. intelligence community who betrayed their country—usually for profit.

Probably the most famous traitors in the modern history of intelligence were the four members of the Cambridge Spy Ring. They were respected British Spies, one of them knighted, who sold secrets to the Russians. The four were Guy Burgess, Donald Maclean, Harold "Kim" Philby (the son of an explorer and adventurer, sometimes referred to as the "Third Man"), and Anthony Frederick Blunt (a.k.a. the "Fourth Man").

Guy Burgess brought suspicion upon himself, and his fellow traitor Kim Philby, in 1950 when he insulted the wife of the CIA's William King Harvey in the presence of CIA anti-mole expert James Angleton. This scrutiny eventually led to the exposure of Burgess and Maclean as spies in 1951. The pair fled to the Soviet Union.

In 1962, Kim Philby confessed in exchange for immunity from prosecution. He moved to the Soviet Union and remained there for the rest of his life. Two years later, Blunt also confessed in exchange for immunity from prosecution. His knighthood was taken away from him and, although he remained in England, he lived until 1983 in virtual isolation.

Unfortunately, however, we have had our share here in the United States, too.

Top Secret
In 1990, the Soviet Union issued a Kim Philby postage stamp to honor his work for the KGB.

The Aldrich H. Ames Case

The most damaging mole in CIA history was Aldrich H. Ames. A CIA employee for 31 years, working predominantly out of the Directorate of Operations, Ames agreed to sell classified information to the KGB in 1985.

His treasonous activities were not discovered until nine years later, by which time he had compromised more than 100 CIA operations targeting the Soviet Union. Ten CIA agents inside the Soviet government were captured and executed because of Ames' traitorous deeds. Sadly, it was all for money: Ames began to betray his country because of financial pressures caused by a divorce and remarriage.

A Common Scofflaw

Ames never did like rules. In a CIA psychological profile of the turncoat, it says: "In his routine behavior as an Agency employee, Ames seemed predisposed to accidentally violate or deliberately ignore many rules and regulations. This was not done for personal profit, however. So far as is known, there was no petty theft or fraud typical of a predisposition toward antisocial or criminal behavior. It appears to be more a case of grandiosity, of feeling that he was above the rules, that security and other mundane procedures followed by others did not merit his attention."

Profit Not Only Motive

The report went on to say that financial gain was not Ames' only motive for betrayal:

> There were a number of other facilitating factors. Given the nature of his position, Ames could have no doubt that he would be welcomed and handsomely rewarded by the KGB. The opportunity to meet with Soviet officials and enter the Soviet Embassy with CIA approval made the initial contact invitingly simple; it eliminated a significant element of risk in initiating and maintaining the

contact. Ames understood and knew how to avoid the routine counterintelligence measures intended to catch Soviet spies.

As other factors that facilitated his decision, Ames cited his lack of concern that he would soon be subject to a reinvestigation polygraph and his fading respect for the value of his Agency work as a result of lengthy discussions with Soviet officials.

Ames was first investigated in 1989 when information was received through an agency employee that Ames was living beyond his means. (He bought a Jaguar and a half-million dollar home.) Unfortunately, the inquiry stalled and was tabled for more than a year, exposing difficulties in the CIA's counterintelligence department.

Top Secret
Because of the Ames case, the CIA revamped its polygraph policies and stiffened its concentration on computer security.

Tradecraft

Scientists have discovered a new way to remotely eavesdrop on computer data. Flickering light from a common screen reflected off a wall can reveal whatever appears on the screen of a computer monitor. And computer users who rely on external modems with blinking lights to connect to the Internet are also vulnerable. It is said that images of this blinking and reflecting can be captured with a telescope or long-distance lens and processed to reveal all the data passing through the device.

One intelligence expert said, "Data communication equipment, and even data encryption devices, sometimes emit modulated optical signals that carry enough information for an eavesdropper to reproduce the entire data stream. It requires little apparatus, can be done at a considerable distance, and is completely undetectable."

Ames was convicted of treason and sentenced to life in prison without a chance for parole.

Harold J. Nicholson

Harold J. Nicholson was a CIA teacher who appeared to be having an extremely successful CIA career until it was discovered that he had been selling the names of his students to the Russians.

Nicholson was arrested in 1996 and charged with espionage. He was 46 years old at the time and had been a CIA employee for 16 years. He had served in Manila, Bangkok, Tokyo, Bucharest, and Kuala Lumpur and as an instructor of CIA Trainees.

Nicholson made a meteoric rise in the agency, advancing from trainee to station chief in less than 10 years. He was the only CIA station chief ever to be charged with spying against the United States.

The most troubling part of the Nicholson case is that he carried out his betrayal after the Ames's case was discovered—in effect, when CIA counterintelligence was on the alert. However, Nicholson was captured, in part, because of new polygraph rules put in place after the Ames's case was discovered.

Because of Nicholson's activities, there are many U.S. intelligence officers whose entire careers will be impeded because of the suspicion that their names might be known in Moscow.

At his trial, Nicholson said that he had handed over names to make money for his kids. Because he had cooperated fully with the investigation into the damage he had caused, he was spared the death penalty. In 1997, Nicholson was sentenced to 23 years in prison.

Joseph G. Helmich

The CIA doesn't have a monopoly on U.S. traitors. Former U.S. Army Warrant Officer Joseph G. Helmich was arrested in 1981 and charged with selling U.S. codes to the Soviet Union between 1963 and 1966.

Helmich had been working with codes both at Fort Bragg, North Carolina, and in France, and it is said that he initiated contact with officials at the Soviet Embassy in Paris. Helmich gave up the "KL-7" code system in exchange for $131,000.

He was investigated in 1964 because—he was living beyond his means, but he was cleared at the time. Seventeen years later his treasonous activities were finally stopped. Helmich was sentenced to life in prison.

Robert Hanssen

Robert Hanssen was a 27-year FBI veteran. He spent more than half of that 27 years as a counterintelligence agent, selling secrets to the Soviet Union. On July 6, 2001, he pleaded guilty on to 13 separate acts of espionage against the United States.

He was a devout Catholic, a member of the conservative Opus Dei organization. He was arrested by FBI agents on February 18, 2001, as he tried to leave a package of classified documents at a drop location in a park near his Vienna home.

Experts say that Hanssen sold out his country for more than just the money. He did it for thrills as well.

> **Top Secret**
>
> Hanssen almost got away with his double life. He was only months away from retirement when he was arrested.

Assessing the Damage

Just how much damage did Hanssen do? Experts are still trying to figure that out. A damage assessment team is still trying to establish comprehensive details of Hanssen's access to classified information.

In order to do this, the traitor's full range of official and unofficial activities must be studied, along with his computer skills and his relationships with others. It may be a long time before we know exactly how much damage one man did.

Karl F. Koecher: Czech Mole in the CIA

Karl F. Koecher got a job as a translator with the CIA in 1973. What the CIA did not know when they hired him was that Karl, along with his gorgeous wife Hana, were already working for the Czech Intelligence Service.

The 1970s were swinging times and there were many wild parties, in which Americans with various levels of knowledge blabbed what they knew. What wasn't said in front of Karl was said in front of Hana.

Koecher's activities went unabated until the early 1980s when another Czech, who was working for the FBI, figured out what Koecher was up to and turned him in. The CIA didn't have enough evidence to confront him, however, so they followed him, instead. They followed him for years but could come up with no additional evidence that he was a double agent.

So they tried to get him to confess. FBI officers told Koecher—insincerely, apparently—that he would not be prosecuted if he gave full details

> **Top Secret**
>
> Through his job as a translator, Koecher learned that a Soviet diplomat in the United States was working as a CIA agent. When Koecher ratted on the man to the KGB, the agent committed suicide—taking a poison pill from the inside of a CIA pen—rather than face capture.

of his activities. He could become a triple agent, he was told, actually working for the CIA while pretending to work for Czech Intelligence.

The Czech never did talk, but the false promise of immunity was enough to prevent prosecution, and the United States ended up trading Koecher for a U.S. agent held behind the Iron Curtain.

The real question was: How did an agent for Czech intelligence get hired by the CIA in the first place? An investigation revealed that the polygraph examination that Koecher had taken before he was hired was improperly administered.

The Barnett Case

In 1976, a retired CIA operations officer named David H. Barnett supplemented his income by selling the Soviets information regarding the CIA's operation in Indonesia. He had quit the CIA to start his own business, but business was not good.

Having already committed treason, Barnett applied to re-join the CIA. If he had received the same background check as other prospective employees, and a second polygraph test, he probably would not have been hired.

Evidence that he had been less than discreet with the information that he already knew probably would have surfaced. But, because he was a former employee, no new background check and no new polygraph examination were administered.

During his second career with the CIA, he became a teacher, training prospective CIA operations officers before they were shipped overseas. In that capacity he knew the identity of many future operations officers and, as might be expected, he offered those names for sale to the Soviets. He was spotted in Vienna during a meeting with the KGB to sell them the names.

He was arrested in 1980. Barnett has the distinction of being the only CIA operations officer to ever be prosecuted. He pleaded guilty to treason in 1981 and was sentenced to 18 years in prison.

And you better believe that it is now standard policy to do a new background check and administer a new polygraph examination for all former CIA employees who are seeking to be re-hired.

Boyce and Lee: a.k.a. Falcon and Snowman

In order to protect itself from espionage, the agency not only has to be extremely careful about the honesty of its own employees, but it has to be careful about the honesty of all employees who work for CIA contractors as well.

CIA contractor employees were responsible for the breach of security that was later made into the Hollywood movie, *The Falcon and the Snowman*.

Christopher J. Boyce was employed by TRW, Inc., in a low-level position. TRW did contract work for the CIA. Despite the fact that Boyce did not work for the CIA and did not have a high-level position at TRW, he still had access to the classified code material used to transmit photos from one of the CIA's surveillance satellites.

Boyce gave the info to his friend, Andrew Daulton Lee, a drug addict, who sold the info to KGB agents in Mexico City—then split the proceeds with Boyce. Later, testifying before Congress, Boyce said that security was lax at TRW, where boozey parties were held in the same rooms with top-secret information.

Spilling the Beans in Bed

In 1983, Sharan M. Scranage, a 30-year-old CIA operations support assistant assigned to Ghana, began to date the first cousin of Ghana's prime minister, who was also an agent for Ghana intelligence.

> **McLean Says ...**
>
> Churches are seldom used as drop off points or meeting places, though perhaps they should be utilized more. Row Four about three feet in on the left pew was one of my favorite spots to tape a message. Simply kneel, bow, reach under the pew seat in front of you and press the pre-taped message into position. Within an hour or so, as pre-arranged, your devout contact simply comes to pray, picks up the message and goes on his way. Frankly, some dedicated spooks don't like using churches in the "business."

Before she was done blabbing as she bobbed in bed, she had compromised eight CIA agents in Ghana, who were imprisoned. She and her boyfriend were eventually caught and arrested by the CIA's Office of Security.

She was sentenced in 1985 to five years in prison, a sentence that was later lowered to two. Her boyfriend was released in exchange for the eight arrested CIA agents in Ghana.

> **Tradecraft**
>
> Regarding the war on terrorism, the State Department's head of counterterrorism, Frank Taylor, said in 2002, "We will close the seams in which these groups operate—and by that I don't just mean the physical places, but the cracks where intelligence isn't shared and countries don't cooperate."

Ana Belen Montes

The most recent traitor to be exposed from within the U.S. intelligence community is one Ana Belen Montes, a 45-year-old DIA analyst. In 2001, it was discovered that she had been working for Cuba for 16 years.

According to the Association of Former Intelligence Officers newsletter, Montes "received information from Cuba by listening to high-frequency encrypted transmissions on short-wave radio. She sent her purloined information out by using pay phones in Northwest Washington and Bethesda (Maryland), transmitting encoded messages to an electronic page number."

Montes was caught because of an undisclosed tip. Why did she do it? Of Puerto Rican descent, Montes said that she was morally outraged by U.S. policy toward Cuba.

> **McLean Says ...**
>
> Some beggars make great spies. Think about it. They are on the street, wandering here and there and just about everywhere. Local authorities don't think too much about them and let them beg.
>
> Beggars with brains can report the departures of trains and planes. They can look at a photo, stick it in their pocket, and then report when that person enters or leaves certain buildings where they hang out begging.
>
> One beggar I worked with sat every day on a cushion on a flat fire hydrant connection that jutted out from a building. For a $10 fee, he watched for certain people we knew commuted by subway, came out that exit, and picked up coffee at the Dunkin' Donuts next to where the beggar sat. He was valuable eyes and ears for us over the years.

Again, according to the Association newsletter: "Montes was believed to have been recruited by Cuban intelligence when she worked in the Freedom of Information office at the Justice department between 1979 and 1985, and was asked by the Cubans to work at an agency that would provide more useful information to Cuba. Thus she was a Cuban spy when she entered DIA, a deep cover mole, who never, in any public utterance, offered any opinion on U.S. policy towards Cuba. She just transmitted U.S. classified information to Cuban intelligence."

Montes had not yet been sentenced as we hit the presses, but, to avoid the death penalty, she has agreed to cooperate with her case's damage-control investigation. That process is currently ongoing.

The Least You Need to Know

◆ The most famous traitors in the modern history of intelligence were the four members of the Cambridge Spy Ring, who betrayed Great Britain in favor of the Soviet Union.

◆ The most damaging mole in CIA history was Aldrich H. Ames.

◆ Harold J. Nicholson was a CIA teacher who appeared to be having an extremely successful CIA career until it was discovered that he had been selling the names of his students to the Russians.

◆ In 1976, a retired CIA operations officer named David H. Barnett supplemented his income by selling the Soviets information regarding the CIA's operation in Indonesia.

◆ CIA contractor employees were responsible for the breach of security that was later made into the Hollywood movie, *The Falcon and the Snowman*.

◆ The most recent traitor to be exposed from within the U.S. intelligence community is one Ana Belen Montes, a 45-year-old DIA analyst who spied for Cuba.

Part 5

Keeping the Terror at Bay

The CIA was slow to let go of the Cold War mentality that had been so deeply ingrained in its fabric.

What the company needed was a kick in the pants, which, figuratively, of course, was provided on September 11, 2001, when terrorists attacked the World Trade Center in New York and the Pentagon in Washington, killing thousands of innocent people.

If ever there was a clear indication that the Cold War was over and the world now faced a new and deadly enemy, this was it. To its credit, despite the shock felt by the rest of the world, the CIA's reaction to the crisis was immediate and appropriate.

18

Terrorism: The New Enemy

In This Chapter

- ◆ Briefing the president
- ◆ Outline for a war
- ◆ CIA on the ground
- ◆ A Russian surprise

On September 13, 2001, two days after the September 11 attacks in New York and Washington, President Bush received a briefing from his chief of staff. The CIA had just sent over a warning from a foreign intelligence service that Pakistani jihadists (Muslim extremists) were planning an attack on the White House. The director of the Secret Service advised President Bush to evacuate the White House, but he refused to leave. The nonessential employees at the White House were allowed to go home, but government activity continued. It was agreed that Vice President Cheney should not be in the White House, so he was moved to his now-famous "undisclosed location."

DCI George Tenet had also given the president a briefing that morning in the White House situation room, one floor below the chief of staff's office in the southwest corner of the west wing. At that meeting, Tenet mapped out what was to become the United States' war on terrorism.

Using the Northern Alliance

On the morning of September 13, 2001, Tenet told the president that the war must include a combined usage of the CIA's paramilitary operations, covert action, and technology. The United States also had to maximize its use of forces from Afghanistan who were battling the Taliban already. These forces were known as the Northern Alliance.

The problem was that unifying the Northern Alliance was a bit like getting dry sand to stick together. The Northern Alliance consisted of about 20,000 soldiers divided among about 25 factions, out of which 5 were powerful enough to have a say in things. To make matters worse, the Northern Alliance's most charismatic leader, Ahmed Shah Massoud, was assassinated two days before the September 11 attacks by two suicide bombers who had been posing as journalists.

The United States, as it turned out, was already giving some aid to the Northern Alliance in their ongoing fight against the Taliban for control of Afghanistan. For four years, CIA paramilitary teams had been meeting in secret with the leaders of the Northern Alliance. But that aid was going to have to be greatly increased now that the United States was eager to have the Taliban vanquished, along with the terrorist Al Qaeda organization and especially its leader, Osama bin Laden.

> **Top Secret**
>
> George Tenet has been DCI under two presidents. He submitted his reports to President Clinton in writing, and the two men rarely spoke. In contrast, he meets in person with President Bush every morning, and the two have become close allies in the war on terrorism.

A CIA team would accompany each warlord of each faction of the Northern Alliance, Tenet told the president. These teams would be the United States' "eyes on the ground" and help coordinate attacks. With CIA money and training, it was hoped that the Northern Alliance troops could be turned into a strong enough army that most of the ground fighting could be done without U.S. personnel. (This strategy was not entirely successful, because the Northern Alliance remained a hesitant lot.)

The Cofer Counterterrorism Briefing

When Tenet's briefing of the president was over, Cofer Black, head of the CIA's counterterrorism center, briefed President Bush. Black described the benefits of covert action to the president. According to Black, the more U.S. personnel stationed on the ground in Afghanistan, the better.

"You give us the mission," Black said to the president, "and we can get 'em! We'll rout 'em out." The president gave Black the nod, and the war began.

> **McLean Says ...**
>
> The hulking Cofer Black is a hero among CIA employees because he captured one of the world's most deadly terrorists, Carlos the Jackal. Carlos is now serving a life sentence in France.

The Camp David Briefing

On September 15, 2001, Tenet again met with Bush, this time at Camp David. The briefing concerned Osama bin Laden. Bush wanted to know all there was to know about the world's most dangerous terrorist, and Tenet had four years' worth of intelligence to report. The briefing lasted for 30 minutes during which Tenet outlined a plan for a global war on terrorism focusing initially on Al Qaeda, Osama bin Laden, and the Taliban government in Afghanistan. He also brought with him to Camp David a draft of the presidential intelligence finding that Bush would have to sign to give Tenet formal permission to carry out the CIA's plan.

> **McLean Says ...**
>
> The famed CIA operative Duane Clarridge, in his 1997 book *A Spy For All Seasons*, wrote that the CIA "will be reinvented or restored to competency only after some appalling catastrophe befalls us." The September 11 attacks were that catastrophe.

Tenet's global "attack matrix" involved combating terrorism through covert action in 80 different countries. These actions sometimes would involve no more than dissemination of propaganda, but in other countries, plans called for preliminary CIA strikes in preparation for larger military actions. The ground war in Afghanistan, it was agreed, would begin with six or so CIA paramilitary teams.

A full-scale attack on the finances of organized terrorism was also outlined in Tenet's plan. He suggested clandestine computer surveillance and electronic eavesdropping to locate the assets of Al Qaeda and other terrorist groups. His plan also included clamping down on the assets of charitable groups that had been supporting Al Qaeda.

The plan also proposed that the CIA maximize its use of cooperative foreign intelligence services. Again, as had been true in the past, this plan would put the CIA in a working relationship with people of questionable character, including past human rights violators.

> **McLean Says ...**
>
> During the past too many years, the CIA has been hamstrung by presidential orders and congressional leaders' wishes not to deal with human rights violators. But the fact is that the people who have access to the information that the CIA needs are not saints—they are thieves and worse. Insisting that only "good guys" should be helping U.S. intelligence efforts is one of the dumbest restrictions ever placed on the CIA.

Tenet told the president that the CIA had somewhat of a head start in Afghanistan because it had already been doing a great deal of work in the area and already had officers in place. Tenet said that the Predator robot surveillance plane (see Chapter 15), which was equipped with Hellfire missiles, could be used not only to find Osama bin Laden, but to kill him as well.

Tenet also told the president that cooperation from Pakistan as well as the former Soviet states of Tajikistan and Turkmenistan would be necessary to restrict the travel of fleeing terrorists. Tenet then described in detail how much money, weapons, and advisors would be needed to coagulate the noncohesive Northern Alliance into a successful fighting army.

> **Tradecraft**
>
> If you want to know how some people in the Arab world see U.S. foreign policy, check out the website of Al-Jazeera, the popular Qatari satellite TV station, although be aware that the website is peppered with photos of slain Afghan and Palestinian children.

On September 14, 2001, only three days after the September 11 attacks, President Bush signed the directive that gave the CIA units orders to "use all necessary means to destroy Osama bin Laden and Al Qaeda." This directive gave the CIA an unprecedented amount of power, including permission to use deadly force. In this way, CIA officers became full-fledged soldiers in the war on terrorism.

The Sad Story of Abdul Haq

During the early days of United States involvement in Afghanistan, the CIA got off to a rocky start. According to the press, Abdul Haq, a 1980s mujahedin leader who had recently returned to the region, asked the CIA for weapons and air support. He said he had a plan to slip back into Afghanistan and organize anti-Taliban resistance among the Pashtuns in the southern part of the country. The CIA, still on unfamiliar footing, turned him down.

Rejection by the CIA did not discourage Haq, who decided to proceed with his plan anyway. He snuck behind enemy lines in Afghanistan with only 19 men and a handful of guns. It was not long before he was surrounded by Taliban troops.

New York Post columnist Peter Beinart describes what happened next: "Haq called his nephew, who called an American friend, who called [former] National Security Adviser Robert McFarlane, who called the CIA operations center, which dispatched an unmanned aircraft. Too late. Haq was captured and executed." Haq died on October 26, 2001.

McFarlane later criticized the CIA over the affair, stating that it was unprepared for the crisis in Afghanistan despite a healthy budget provided by Congress. He said, "They spend $30 billion and don't have anybody out there who can speak Dari or who understands who these players are."

The Battle Plan in Afghanistan

After President Bush signed off on Tenet's plans for fighting terrorists in Afghanistan, the CIA went to work putting the plans into action. The CIA had many important roles to perform in this war, which differed in many ways from previous conflicts.

Deploying Special Activities Division Teams

The CIA paramilitary units, all of which—both in Afghanistan and elsewhere—were covert until after the September 11 attacks, consisted of teams of about a half dozen men each who didn't wear military uniforms. The teams came from the Special Activities Division (please don't call them SAD), which was made up of about 150 fighters, pilots, and specialists. They came with state-of-the-art helicopters and their own personal surveillance satellites. Most of the people involved were retired military men—retired, as they say, but active.

Although details are sketchy, it is known that on at least two occasions the Special Activities teams fought side by side with their Northern

> **Top Secret**
>
> Full retirement is possible for those who served in military services for 20 years. People who enlist at 18 years old are only 38 when they retire from the service; these people are still at physical peak for special duties. ROTC college or West Point graduates who become officers at 21 years old are only 41 or 42 after completing their 20 years of service.

Alliance allies in some of the fiercest firefights of the Afghan-istan war. The Pentagon was highly appreciative of the CIA units, who did the dirty work most often reserved for the U.S. military. A Pentagon spokes-man said, "The CIA men on the ground have denied Taliban food and ammunition. Without the SAD the Northern Alliance would have taken many more weeks to reach Kabul and other important cities."

Choosing the Sites to Strike

Although the great bulk of news coverage regarding the war against terrorism featured the aerial attack of selected sites in Afghanistan, the greatest achievement of the war was the precise selection of those sites. Determining targets for the hundreds of sorties flown in Afghanistan was the job of the CIA—along with some members of the U.S. Army and the Navy Special Forces—working behind the scenes and in the shadows, with the effort being run from CIA headquarters in Virginia.

Almost a month passed after the September 11 attacks before the air war against the Taliban and Al Qaeda began. The Taliban were given that long to cough up Osama bin Laden. Had they turned the terrorist over, the U.S. offered, no air war would be necessary. The time was also useful for the United States and its allies to get their military forces in place.

The air war did not start until October 7, 2001. By mid-November, more than 10,000 bombs or missiles had been dropped or fired into Afghanistan. Sorties had been flown by fighter jets such as the F-14 and F-18, many based upon the aircraft carrier USS *Enterprise*. Also eight B-1 and B-2 bombers and ten B-52s were in action. Only a total of 600 or so sorties had been flown, so targets were very select. To illustrate this point, remember that, during the Gulf War, the Air Force was flying 3,000 sorties a day.

> ### Top Secret
>
> Former CIA official Frank Anderson said, "The war in Afghanistan is almost certainly the most intelligence-intensive war that we've ever fought."

Given the circumstances, finding adequate targets was a lot like finding a needle in a haystack. Afghanistan is a large country and is very easy to hide in. In order to wage an effective air campaign, U.S. pilots had to know where to drop the bombs, and U.S. sailors had to know where to point the missiles.

Maintaining Secrecy

Secrecy has been essential to the CIA's operations in Afghanistan. Obviously, it's easier to figure out what the enemy is going to do when they don't know they are being watched. We certainly won't know details of any CIA units' location or activities until long after the war in Afghanistan is over. We may never find out, not if the CIA used any methods that they would like to use again someday.

According to CNN, the CIA's presence in Afghanistan has been close to 100 percent clandestine. Despite the fact that hundreds of CIA agents are stationed on the ground in Afghanistan, CIA operatives have overtly appeared only once in all of the news coverage of the war. That moment came after the capture of the American Taliban John Walker Lindh when two CIA agents were shown interrogating the new prisoner. (Coincidentally and tragically, one of those agents was Mike Spann, the CIA man who, moments after the videotape was made, became the first U.S. fatality in Afghanistan when he was murdered during a prisoner uprising. Chapter 19 describes this event.)

Forging Relationships

Obviously, the CIA alone on the ground in Afghanistan was not going to gather the kind of intelligence to bring about the downfall of the Taliban in that government. In order to accomplish this task, CIA operatives in Afghanistan forged relationships with anti-Taliban leaders, as well as with Pakistani, Russian, and other intelligence operatives.

These relationships between the CIA men and others in the region were not only important because of the extremely high quality of the intelligence that was being gathered as a result of them, but also because they created the sort of war in which it has been possible to keep U.S. combat fatalities, as of early 2002, to a minimum.

Tradecraft

According to former CIA official Frank Anderson, "One of the tactical differences in the war on terrorism is that we have to be more security conscious when it comes to prisoners." The United States learned in the Pacific during World War II that taking prisoners when fighting a suicidal enemy can be extremely risky.

A Surprise from the Russians

The city of Kabul, a Taliban stronghold, was among the very first sites chosen for air strikes by U.S. fighters and bombers. The bombings began during the first week of October, 2001. By the following month, the enemy was fleeing from the city and opposition forces—made up almost exclusively of non-American soldiers—were able to march into the city. After the Taliban and Al Qaeda retreated from Kabul, Afghanistan, the first Americans to enter the city were from the CIA's Special Activities teams. They went directly to the building that had formerly been used by Al Qaeda's commanders and were surprised to discover that a sizable Russian intelligence unit had already set up camp in Kabul. The unit included 80 military intelligence officers and 20 other military personnel.

The Russian intelligence team had flown into an Afghanistan airport north of the city. The team had moved into place inside the city even before all of the Taliban left, posing successfully as construction workers who were there to repair damage done to the Russian embassy.

The Russians were not there just to keep abreast of the United States' actions in Afghanistan. They were there to protect their own interests by looking for evidence of Al Qaeda involvement with the rebels who were fighting in Chechnya.

> **Tradecraft**
>
> A good intelligence analyst learns to read between the lines. The fact that the Russians came to Kabul on their own without an invitation was their way of telling the United States and the United Nations that the Russians were going to play a role in this war whether they were invited or not.

Although surprised to find the Russians in Kabul, the United States quickly offered cooperation with their effort, and the two countries shared information gathered in Afghanistan about Al Qaeda. The Russians also supported the U.S. effort by supplying tanks and ammunition to the country's Northern Alliance to help that assemblage of factions combat the Taliban government and the Al Qaeda terrorists they were protecting.

The Least You Need to Know

♦ Within days of the September 11 attacks, DCI Tenet had outlined for President Bush his plans to defeat Osama bin Laden and Al Qaeda.

♦ The CIA contribution would involve both gathering of intelligence and the use of paramilitary units on the ground known as Special Activities Divisions.

♦ The Special Activities Divisions used satellites, drone planes, and helicopters and fought side by side with their Northern Alliance allies in Afghanistan.

♦ When the CIA entered Kabul following the Taliban's withdrawal, it was surprised to find an old enemy already there, agents from now-friendly Russian intelligence.

CIA on the Front Lines

In This Chapter

- ◆ Remembering a CIA hero
- ◆ Understanding the enemy
- ◆ Searching for Osama
- ◆ Interrogating prisoners

Ever since its inception, the CIA has put its people in harm's way. And as we learned during our tour of the CIA in Chapter 3, many agency people have lost their lives in the line of duty. But it wasn't until the war on terrorism that the death of a CIA officer made front page news as the first American fatality in Afghanistan.

The Company Loses a Man

The officer was 32-year-old Mike Spann, who was married with three young children. Spann grew up in the small Alabama town of Winfield, which is about 75 miles northwest of Birmingham. He played football at Winfield City High School, graduating in 1987. At Auburn University, he earned a degree in criminal justice and law enforcement in 1992. Immediately after college he entered the Marine Corps, and he joined the CIA in June 1999.

"We Are Here To Kill You"

Spann was killed on November 25, 2001 in Mazer-i Sharif when he and a fellow officer were interviewing prisoners captured during the war. The CIA officer working with Spann that day will be remembered only as "Dave." One Northern Alliance soldier, who witnessed Spann's murder, described it this way: "The fighting started when the Taliban were being questioned by two men from the CIA. The agent asked where they had come from, and whether or not they may be Al Qaeda."

The witness claimed that Spann asked one of the prisoners why he was in the country. "We are here to kill you," was the chilling reply. The man then jumped at Spann, who pulled a gun and shot the man dead with a single shot. But this action was a cue for the other prisoners to jump in.

More than a dozen prisoners charged at the two CIA officers. The Americans managed to shoot four of them. "Dave" got away but Mike was soon overpowered. The Northern Alliance witness continued, "The Taliban wrestled him [Spann] to the ground and then beat, kicked, and bit him to death." According to CIA reports, Spann was also shot.

All of the prisoners began attacking in a full-fledged revolt during which many Northern Alliance guards were killed. Before the prisoners could get out of the compound however, Air Force fighters attacked them. Three days passed before the prisoner revolt was completely vanquished, and that was not accomplished until almost all of the Taliban prisoners had been killed. One of the few survivors was the American turncoat John Walker Lindh who, because he could speak English with an American accent, may have had an easier time surrendering than the others.

> **Tradecraft**
>
> The prison revolt was costly for everyone. A U.S. missile missed its intended target (the prisoners) and ended up killing eight Northern Alliance guards and two American G.I.s.

An American Hero

CIA Director George J. Tenet wasted no time calling Spann an American hero:

> Mike Spann, who worked in the Directorate of Operations, was where he wanted to be: on the front lines, serving his country. Given the nature of the CIA's mission, I can publicly discuss his activities and the circumstances surrounding his death only in broad terms.

> Mike was in the fortress of Mazer-i Sharif, where Taliban prisoners were being held and questioned. Although these captives had given themselves up, their

pledge of surrender—like so many other pledges from this vicious group they represent—proved worthless.

Their prison uprising—which had murder as its goal—claimed many lives, among them that of a very brave American ...

Another Officer Wounded

On January 4, 2002, another CIA officer, one who remained unidentified, was seriously wounded in Afghanistan. The injury came in the same action that killed an Army Special Forces soldier: a brief midafternoon firefight in the eastern portion of the country.

The Al Qaeda ambush in which the officer was injured came a short time after a small group of Americans and Afghan allies met with Afghan leaders near Khost in an attempt to learn the location of Al Qaeda leaders thought to be in the area.

This was a busy section of the country. Only a few miles away from the firefight, American jets were bombing an Al Qaeda training camp near Khost.

The Hunt for Osama

After scattering from previous U.S. attacks, Al Qaeda forces started regrouping in a compound of buildings, caves, and bunkers only three miles from the Pakistani border in the Tora Bora region of eastern Afghanistan. In late December 2001, CIA officers reported that their sources were telling them that Osama bin Laden was hiding out in the Tora Bora region as well.

The United States military undertook a major assault on the region, but it never found the Al Qaeda leader. It's possible that Osama was never in the Tora Bora region, and the information was deliberately given to CIA operatives to lead them in the wrong direction. Nonetheless, the U.S. military did succeed in taking out a number of Al Qaeda people and destroying a lot of their weapons.

> **Spookspeak**
>
> A **legend** is the artificial background created for CIA officers as cover. Intelligence officers under commercial cover of U.S. companies learn the lingo of their trade and bone up on the business with help from the cooperating cover firm officials who are privy to the program.

Is That Him?

On January 3, 2002, a CIA unmanned Predator spy plane photographed an Al Qaeda military convoy that aroused the interest of those who were monitoring the images.

The convoy appeared to be made up of high-level Al Qaeda leaders including one "significant figure" who appeared to be completely shielded by stringent security. Was the "significant figure" Osama?

Although there was no solid evidence that the figure was Osama, the United States didn't ask for identification. Instead, it bombed the convoy. If the person was bin Laden, he was blown to smithereens. We'll never know for sure.

Panic in Kabul

As the ground war in Afghanistan progressed efficiently, the CIA's Special Activities Division on the ground began to pick up Taliban and Al Qaeda messages that were most encouraging. There was panic in the ranks for Al Qaeda as Northern Alliance soldiers began to close in on key cities occupied by the terrorists. Among the messages picked up were plans for Al Qaeda members to retreat out of Afghanistan and to regroup in northern countries to start up their activities once again.

> **Top Secret**
>
> According to German intelligence, approximately 70,000 people have graduated from the Al Qaeda terror camps in Afghanistan. And for every member of Al Qaeda there are 10 wannabes willing to carry out smaller terrorist missions to prove themselves to Al Qaeda or, in their own minds, to Allah.

When those terrorists left their positions in Kabul and tried to flee to other countries, the Special Activities Division members called in their locations, and they were sitting ducks for strikes from the air. Despite this effort, U.S. intelligence chiefs reported that "hundreds" of bin Laden's top men successfully escaped from Afghanistan by using unchecked corridors in Pakistan and Tajikistan.

Tradecraft

Never underestimate the importance of psychological warfare. Given the opportunity, the CIA never fails to exploit a crack in the psyche of the enemy. The war in Afghanistan was only days old when a Predator drone plane took a photo of Taliban leader Muhammed Omar getting into his SUV. The CIA put a close-up of Omar's face and a close-up of his license plate, so close that the number could be read, on a leaflet that was printed by the thousands and dropped over Afghanistan. The message on the leaflet was simple, saying: "We are watching." This idea, proud to say, originated with a few retired officers. In the meantime, the shrinks at Langley, when planning new psychological warfare campaigns, took special note of the fact that Omar, though he ordered his troops in Kandahar to fight to the death, withdrew before his defenses were overrun.

Among the Pashtun ... Or in Pakistan ... Or ...

On January 15, 2002, an intelligence source leaked to the press that new sources on the ground were saying that bin Laden was hiding among Pashtun tribes, who live in the Northwest Frontier province of Pakistan where there are only tribal laws. CIA analysts, on the other hand, were telling ABC News that bin Laden might have left the area entirely and was in neither Afghanistan or Pakistan. Of course, bin Laden might have already been dead by this time, buried by U.S. bombing beneath a mountain somewhere in Afghanistan.

POWS: A Great Source of Intelligence

Some of the best intelligence regarding Al Qaeda activities is expected to come from prisoners of war taken during the war in Afghanistan. The prisoners are being housed in *Guantánamo Bay*, Cuba. The site was chosen so that intelligence officers stationed stateside could interview the prisoners, who are considered to be extremely dangerous, without having to travel all the way to Pakistan.

By January 2002, the United States was holding approximately 300 prisoners in temporary facilities on the naval base until a permanent maximum-security prison could be built. As the prison was being built, President Bush asked the Pentagon, the Justice Department, and his National Security Office to write guidelines for how to sort out the detainees and determine which ones might be eligible for military tribunals and which ones might be tried in federal court.

The Geneva Convention states that all detainees shall be treated humanely until their status is determined by a screening tribunal of three commissioned officers. It also requires that a written record be made of the proceedings and that the prisoner be advised of his rights, be allowed to attend the tribunal, have access to an interpreter, be able to call witnesses, and that his status shall be determined by a majority vote based on a preponderance of evidence. It makes no reference as to whether a detainee can have a lawyer.

> **Spookspeak**
>
> **Guantánamo Bay,** where the U.S. Navy has a base, is the only portion of Cuba that is not controlled by Fidel Castro.

> **Tradecraft**
>
> The Vienna Convention on Consular Access, which the United States has signed, requires the United States to notify consular officials when their nationals are detained by any law enforcement agency or other branch of the federal government. On January 12, 2002, the United States notified Great Britain that one of the detainees in Guantánamo Bay was a British citizen.

U.N. Group Files Scary Report

On January 22, 2002, even as it appeared that U.S. military action in Afghanistan was winding down, intelligence gathered by the United Nations' monitoring group in Afghanistan seemed almost designed to sustain the edge of terror that had set the teeth of Americans with the attacks of September 11. The U.N. group reported that Osama bin Laden's terror network may have nerve gas and short-range missiles capable of carrying warheads. The weapons, plus popular support among some of the people, would give Al Qaeda, it was suggested, a means to an uprising, despite being decimated by U.S. air and ground attacks.

In its report the group said, "Due to the strength of this support, the Taliban and Al Qaeda are likely to remain a threat for some time to come. These missiles may be fitted with conventional, chemical, or nuclear warheads." The missiles had a range of 45 to 200 miles. The report said that the group had not learned whether the missiles were operational or where they were located. The report also claimed that the Taliban had Sarin and VX nerve gas projectiles that could be fired with artillery.

The Least You Need to Know

- The first American to be killed in Afghanistan during the war on terrorism was a CIA officer named Mike Spann.

- Al Qaeda detainees are an important source of information on the terrorist organization and its future plans.

- Despite being defeated in Afghanistan, the Al Qaeda terror network remains capable of major terrorist acts.

Chapter 20

The Ongoing War

In This Chapter

- ◆ NYC office destroyed
- ◆ Germ warfare precautions
- ◆ Suspects rounded up
- ◆ Taking Osama's temperature

The attacks of September 11 had provided the CIA with the "kick in the pants" it needed to get out of its long-time Cold War mind set and refocus its efforts on the war against terrorism. The impact of the attacks was profound for all CIA personnel around the globe, but it was particularly powerful for several CIA employees based in New York City.

The most immediate effect that the September 11 attacks had on the CIA domestically was the complete destruction of the CIA's secret New York station, which had been located in the 47-story building at 7 World Trade Center, adjacent to the twin towers. The offices had been listed as being rented by another federal organization. Luckily, all of the CIA employees who worked there (who had watched in horror from their office windows as the twin towers burned) were safely evacuated before their own building collapsed.

A Secret CIA Site

The New York station, which was the largest in the United States outside the Washington area, had been used to recruit agents from among the diplomats working at the United Nations. It also debriefed willing American businesspeople who were returning from trips overseas. During the Cold War, the office had been involved in espionage operations against Russian intelligence officers, who were also found frequently in the vicinity of the United Nations.

The New York station also had been involved in counterterrorism efforts in conjunction with the FBI and other agencies, including investigations of the August 1998 bombings of two U.S. embassies in East Africa, as well as the bombing of the USS *Cole* in Yemen. It is ironic indeed that this site was destroyed by the Al Qaeda attacks of September 11. However, there is no evidence that the terrorists knew that the office was there or that it had anything to do with their choice of the World Trade Center as their target.

Following the collapse of the building, the CIA sent a special team into the rubble in search of secret documents and intelligence reports that had been stored in the CIA offices. Although morale was pretty low among the New York CIA employees in the days following the attack, the crisis gave them a new and intensified sense of mission.

> **Top Secret**
>
> The procedures used in recovering secret documents from the World Trade Center wreckage were put in place following the security disaster in 1979 when the U.S. embassy in Tehran was taken over by Iranian troops before CIA officers could destroy all of the classified material.

The CIA employees of lower Manhattan (led by the first female station chief in the agency's history, by the way) now had a problem they shared with many of their neighbors in the World Trade Center area: They needed to find new office space. As an interim move, some moved into the United States Mission at the United Nations and into spare space at other federal agency sites. A new location for the office was not immediately chosen, and when it is, the new address naturally will not be publicized.

Soon, however, the CIA had more important issues to contend with.

CIA Anthrax Reaction

On October 26, 2001, with anthrax-laced letters showing up in the offices of powerful people in the government and media, CIA spokesman Bill Harlow reported that the CIA, too, had identified anthrax in its mail. Fortunately, it was only a trace amount (not enough to cause the deadly inhalation anthrax). On top of finding a new location for its NYC office and battling terrorism abroad, the CIA had to focus its attention on the domestic anthrax nightmare.

When criminal profilers pretty much agreed that the anthrax threat was a domestic one, a lot of the weight was taken off the CIA's shoulders. Anthrax became an FBI problem. The CIA didn't mind; after all, it already had its hands full with battling terrorism around the world.

Al Qaeda Suspects Rounded Up

Amidst all the other events in the fall of 2001, the CIA was busy making up a master list of people suspected of being Al Qaeda operatives or terrorists working for other organizations whose whereabouts were known. The names on that list were then sent to foreign intelligence services and police agencies around the world.

The result was the rounding up and detention of 360 suspects. That number accounted for only those arrested from the CIA list and not those who might have been arrested by foreign intelligence services on their own.

The process of getting all suspects off the streets was similar to the program carried out simultaneously by the FBI that led to 1,100 people being detained within the United States. (The FBI's number is larger because the bureau was responsible for picking up all Middle Eastern nationals who were in violation of the immigration laws, regardless of that person's possible connection to terrorism.)

Top Secret
The 360 detainees from the CIA's counterterrorism list were arrested on nearly every continent. The numbers broke down this way: ◆ Europe: More than 100 ◆ Near East: More than 100 ◆ Latin America: 30 ◆ Africa: 20

Top Secret
President Bush and CIA were pleased with the ease with which the worldwide roundup was accomplished. It had been unclear how much international cooperation there would be with the U.S. roundup, but cooperation, it turned out, was almost without exception. The Jordanian General Intelligence Department (GID), for example, was involved in more than a dozen arrests. The hard line that President Bush had drawn—you are either with us or against us—encouraged cooperation in some countries that otherwise might not have been so helpful. Some countries that had previously denied they had an Al Qaeda presence in their country realized after September 11 that, in fact, they did, and arrests were made there.

An interesting sidelight to these arrests is that even though some foreign governments didn't want to admit they had terrorists living in their country, CIA reports made it crystal clear that they did. According to some reports, officials who had "looked the other way" now realized that they may have a problem in their countries. For example, Al Qaeda members have long been active against Egypt, the Phillipines, and several other countries. With the vivid TV scenes of September 11, many foreign officials seem to have realized that the same thing could happen in their own countries, which prompted better cooperation than might have been accomplished without the dramatic assault on the twin towers.

Making Do Without Assistance

One country refused to give the location of a terrorist who was suspected of having foreknowledge of the September 11 attacks. The CIA didn't let that hold it back, however. It sent a team into the country and reportedly stole the information it needed.

The information was given to a cooperative intelligence agency in the area, which made the arrest. The country that refused to cooperate—a smart guess would be a country whose name is four letters long and ends in *q*—made it clear which side of President Bush's fence it was on, a piece of intelligence in itself, but the agency got its man anyway.

The war against terrorism was working. At least four planned terrorist attacks had to be aborted because of interference from the civilized world between September 11 and the end of the year. The most publicized of these was a planned attack on the U.S. embassy in Paris.

Keeping Nukes Out of the Wrong Hands

Even before the September 11 attacks, the CIA was concerned about the possibility a terrorist group might obtain a nuclear weapon. Since the attacks, the CIA has focused its work in this area on Osama bin Laden and Al Qaeda. The CIA has not been alone in its pursuit of information regarding Osama bin Laden and his nuclear capabilities. Both Mossad (Israeli intelligence) and British intelligence (MI5) have also been deeply involved.

The Search for Suitcase Nukes

Nothing sets a CIA officer's teeth on edge like the thought of small nuclear weapons in the hands of terrorists. (I say small, but remember, a "small" atom bomb, if exploded in the center of a city, would kill 100,000 or more people. Such a device, experts say, would destroy everything within a half mile of ground zero.)

The subject has received top priority at the CIA since at least 1997, when a former Russian national security adviser, Aleksandr Lebed, told CBS news show *60 Minutes* that the former Soviet Union had built a series of small nuclear devices. The devices, which measured 24 inches by 16 inches by 8 inches, were small enough to be stored inside suitcases. They were intended to be carried by Soviet military intelligence units and had been designed so that they could be detonated by one person. The detonation process, it was said, took about a half hour.

> **Tradecraft**
>
> As far as we know, the smallest nuclear device ever developed by the United States was the Special Atomic Demolition Munition. It weighed between 80 and 100 pounds and was said to fit inside a duffle bag. With about the same strength as the Russian suitcase nuke, the U.S. duffle bag bomb had the explosive charge of approximately 1,000 tons (1 kiloton) of TNT.

The Russians had built 250 or so of the suitcase nukes. That was frightening enough, but the truly scary part was that 100 of the devices were missing. Lebed told *60 Minutes*, "I'm saying that more than 100 out of a supposed number of 250 are not under the control of the armed forced of Russia. I don't know their location. I don't know whether they have been destroyed or whether they are stored or whether they've been sold or stolen; I don't know."

Dirty Rumors of Dirty Bombs

The story of the 100 missing suitcase nukes, when combined with persistent reports that Osama bin Laden had been seeking a nuclear capability, was terrifying. Then there was the story published in the Arabic language newspaper *Al-Watan al-Arabi* in July 2000, which said that Osama bin Laden, using money he had acquired from the selling of opium, had purchased 20 nuclear warheads from renegades within Russia.

The article said that the weapons had been transported by land through Russia and Uzbekistan to get to Afghanistan. In addition, the story reported that bin Laden had an international team of nuclear scientists hard at work to develop portable nuclear weapons. The device bin Laden was rumored to be attempting to build is called a *dirty bomb*.

> **Spookspeak**
>
> A **dirty bomb** is a nuclear device that doesn't kill the majority of its victims with its explosion. Instead the intense cloud of radiation it leaves around the site of its detonation delivers a lethal level of radiation to every living thing in the area.

After September 11, it was obvious that Osama bin Laden did not necessarily need a nuclear bomb in order to use radiation as a weapon of mass destruction. Just as he had used our own commercial airliners as weapons against us, he could use that same method to crash a plane into a nuclear power plant here in the United States. Thus, he could use our own radiation to kill us. Indeed, plans for just such an attack were found in Afghanistan.

Probe in Pakistan

In December 2001 the Associated Press reported that the CIA had intelligence that said there were nuclear scientists in Pakistan capable of creating weapons of mass destruction who had links to Osama bin Laden. DCI George Tenet delivered the tip in person to Pakistan. As a result, Pakistan started an all-out search for those scientists. Two scientists, both of whom had been former members of Pakistan's Atomic Energy Commission, were taken into custody. Two other scientists were questioned but not detained.

On January 29, 2002, Pakistan announced that it had decided not to press criminal charges against the two scientists. The scientists, it was determined, broke a secrecy oath when they made journeys into Taliban-controlled sections of Afghanistan, but no evidence could be found that implicated that the scientists had released information that was necessary to build weapons of mass destruction.

Another not-so-small factor in the "release" of the scientists was Pakistani national security: It was determined that a trial might expose Pakistani nuclear secrets. "We were forced to ignore their action in the best interest of the nation," was the comment of one senior Pakistani official. Yet the scientists were not free to go anywhere they pleased. The pair remained under the close watch of the Pakistani government, living in a safe house for their own protection.

> **McLean Says …**
>
> Is there life after the CIA? You bet! Take David Cohen, for example. The recently retired Cohen was the former Deputy Director for Operations, with 35 years in the agency. In 2002, Cohen was appointed to the new post of Deputy Commissioner for Intelligence in the New York Police Department. He will investigate terrorism, international crime, drug trafficking, and money laundering.

Tradecraft

When Osama bin Laden and his Al Qaeda terror group have been disposed of forever, don't be surprised if the United States' next target is Imad Mugniyah, who is Lebanese and a leader in the Hezbollah guerrilla group as well as the Islamic Jihad. Mugniyah's anti-American violence includes bombings of the American embassy and Marine barracks in Beirut in 1983, torture and murder of the CIA station chief in Beirut in 1984, a possible role in the bombing of Khobar Towers in Saudi Arabia in 1996, and the hijacking in 1985 of a TWA flight in which an American was killed and 39 Americans were held hostage.

Operation Curdled Milk

One of the more interesting things that Al Qaeda left behind when it evacuated Kabul was a desktop computer containing four years' worth of text and video files. The computer's hard drive held many correspondences with militant Muslims around the world. Al Qaeda, despite its medieval dogma, imitated big corporations in its lingo, calling Al Qaeda "the company" and its leadership "the general management."

Users of the computer included two top lieutenants of Mr. bin Laden: Dr. Zawahri and Mohammed Atef. Zawahri is a former Cairo surgeon who merged his own Egyptian terror outfit with Al Qaeda in 1998 and is widely regarded as bin Laden's chief strategist. Atef, killed in a November bombing raid near Kabul, headed Al Qaeda's military wing. U.S. officials believe he masterminded the lethal 1998 bombings of U.S. embassies in Kenya and Tanzania.

The hard drive did not contain any details of the plotting of the September 11 attacks, but it did contain plans to execute a biological and chemical warfare program called *Zabadi*, which means "curdled milk."

Excuse Me, Mr. bin Laden, Could You Pee in This Cup?

It is standard tradecraft to learn as much about your enemy's leaders as you can, including the details of their health. If a foreign leader is sick and cannot run the country, it's essential to find out who is calling the shots and how that new personality entering the mix affects the situation. For this reason countries are often less than forthcoming when it comes to their leaders' health. It's considered a weakness, a loosening of national security, to let it be known that your leader is in poor health.

Taking that into consideration, you can imagine how the faces in Langley lit up when the first reports came in that Osama bin Laden had a severe kidney problem. The reports, relayed through Pakistani intelligence, said that on September 10, 2001, the day before the attacks in New York and Washington, bin Laden underwent secret treatment for kidney disease in a military hospital in Rawalpini, Pakistan. At least some of the information came from a nurse in the hospital's urology department.

Top Secret
According to information acquired by British Intelligence (MI6), bin Laden purchased a dialysis machine for the treatment of kidney disease in early 2001.

This information put together with the fact that recent videos showed him walking with a cane, the reports of a dialysis machine, and bin Laden's gaunt appearance during one of his later videos led the CIA to suspect that bin Laden was in failing health. That is, if he wasn't already as flat as a pancake under some mountain.

Tenet's Warning

On February 6, 2002, DCI George Tenet spoke before the Senate Select Committee on Intelligence for the first time since September 11 and warned America that Al Qaeda was not finished, despite the appearance of a military victory in Afghanistan. The terrorist organization was still capable of reorganizing and plotting another deadly attack on the United States. Tenet also reported that almost 1,000 Al Qaeda operatives had been arrested or detained in 60 different countries since the September 11 attacks, although many of the organization's leaders remained at large.

Tradecraft

As all veteran Spooks know and appreciate, appearances can be deceiving. Media reports picked up by eager reporters may be rushed into print to make headlines for the day without being thoroughly checked. However, some media reports, especially those of astute investigative reporters with good sources may be as factual as solid CIA information. That's one reason the CIA has people who regularly read all major U.S. media as well as key foreign media. Nobody wants to overlook important facts picked up by talented reporters with reliable secret sources.

Tenet said that there was a chance that future terrorist attacks could take place in the United States, but the targets, he said, could also be Americans abroad. "Operations against U.S. targets could be launched by Al Qaeda cells already in place in major cities in Europe and the Middle East," Tenet said. "Al Qaeda can also exploit its presence or connections to other groups in such countries as Somalia, Yemen, Indonesia, and the Philippines."

In Afghanistan, Tenet said, the United States had recovered documents that showed that Osama bin Laden was pursuing a sophisticated biological and chemical weapons research program. He was uncertain whether Mr. bin Laden was still alive, but the CIA believed that Mullah Muhammad Omar, a Taliban leader, was still alive. (A major portion of Tenet's testimony before the Senate Select Committee on Intelligence is included as Appendix C.)

> **Top Secret**
>
> "We welcome the committee's review of our record on terrorism," Tenet told the Senate Select Committee on Intelligence on February 6, 2002. "It is a record of discipline, strategy, focus, and action. We are proud of that record."

Bringing Hellfire to Al Qaeda

On February 4, 2002, a CIA Predator drone (for details on this intelligence tool that has turned into a powerful weapon see Chapter 15) used its TV camera to send pictures back to a CIA outpost. The pictures were of a stretch of land 11,000 feet into the mountains and near the Zawar Kili Al Qaeda camp, which had been recently evacuated.

Below the robot plane, an Al Qaeda convoy had halted, and many of the men had gotten out of their vehicles. There was a group of seven men in one cluster. Among them was a very tall man dressed in white, and he appeared to be the center of attention.

Naturally, this man caused a great deal of fuss at the CIA because Osama bin Laden is 6 feet and 5 inches tall and generally towers over the men around him. Also, bin Laden is known to dress in white and is usually the center of attention no matter where he is.

As noted in Chapter 15, the Predator surveillance plane does more than spy. It also attacks when it is equipped with AGM-114 Hellfire missiles. The Hellfire can be equipped with three types of warheads: single explosive, double explosive (for new armored vehicles with reactive armor), and a "delayed-blast fragmentation" warhead. The Predator's CIA controllers didn't have to look for long at the monitor with the pictures of the group of Al Qaeda leaders, including the tall one dressed in white, before they made a decision: They shot a Hellfire missile at the cluster of men.

> **Top Secret**
>
> The Predator drones were specially equipped with the Hellfire missiles for the war in Afghanistan. The missiles were mounted underneath the drone plane's wings. The Hellfire missiles weighed 100 pounds apiece and were laser-guided.

Parts Are Parts

The missile struck a direct hit and blew the seven men to smithereens. Was the tall guy Osama bin Laden? The answer to that question was going to be difficult to determine. Not only had the Hellfire missile transformed big evidence into many, many pieces of small evidence, but the region where the convoy had stopped was very difficult to get to. The terrain was mountainous, and attempts to get there were further hampered by bad weather.

On the ground, there were complaints—propaganda, as it turned out—that the men hit by the Hellfire missile were not Al Qaeda big shots, but rather innocent peasants. This report set off a string of criticisms of the CIA.

When the approximately 50 troops from the U.S. Army's 101st Airborne Division arrived on the scene, they found that the site had already been visited—although they couldn't be sure if the visitors were humans or animals. The body parts they found there were described as small pieces of bone and human flesh. There could be no way to tell right away if one of the men killed was bin Laden. But the pieces of flesh were picked up and sent back to Langley, where their DNA would be compared against DNA samples of members of bin Laden's family.

> **Top Secret**
>
> The Hellfire is known as a tank-buster missile, but it could also be used effectively against a target as large as an enemy ship.

The troops did find that the dead men weren't innocent peasants. At the site, troops found English-language documents including credit card applications and airline schedules that indicated that the men killed by the Hellfire missile were up to no good.

The Taliban Change Turbans

By mid-February 2002, word out of Afghanistan was that the Taliban were regrouping. According to Afghanistan's foreign minister, the Taliban's leaders had formed two new political organizations in Pakistan.

Gathering intelligence in a foreign land can be complicated in unexpected ways. There are occasions when you have to deal with communities of people whose beliefs are not only very different from yours, but drastically different from those of the people in the next town. The CIA could take nothing for granted when dealing with a tribe known as the Pashtuns during the war on terrorism in Afghanistan.

McLean Says ...

In order to fight organized crime—and that is what terrorism is—various law enforcement agencies must cooperate with one another. In 2002, Interpol (an international police force with headquarters in England and France, dedicated to creating a safer world) provided the world's police agencies with lists of terrorist financiers. These lists are the first follow-up on the December 2001 initiative between Interpol and the U.S. Department of Treasury to strengthen the international efforts to crack down on terrorism financing.

It is difficult for some Americans to understand that, in other parts of the world, there are people who do not identify with any nation—people who do not even recognize the borders between countries. The Pashtuns, a large tribe that lives in both Afghanistan and Pakistan, has never acknowledged the 900-mile border between the two countries. They do not acknowledge a nationality, and they certainly are not members of any particular political party or military force. The Pashtuns were thought to be pro-Taliban when the war in Afghanistan started, but they proved to be adept at leaning toward the side that's winning.

After the Taliban's collapse, most of that movement's members switched sides, and laid low in Afghanistan's cities. Senior Taliban commanders, fearing they would be arrested by Americans, made a run for it. Abdul Sahadi, the former Taliban Defense Minister who is now in Pakistan, revealed how their getaway had been arranged:

> We shaved off our beards, changed our turbans from Taliban white to Kandahari green, got in cars, and drove across the border. We're not broken; we're whole. Now we are just waiting. We are regrouping. We still have arms and many supporters inside [Afghanistan], and when the time is right, we will be back.

The Least You Need to Know

♦ The CIA's New York office was flattened on September 11, but a plan was immediately put in place to make sure national security was uncompromised.

♦ There is much concern regarding missing Russian nuclear devices and reports that Al Qaeda have been seeking to purchase or build nuclear weapons.

♦ Intelligence regarding bin Laden's failing health has been considered particularly significant.

♦ DCI Tenet says future Al Qaeda attacks could take place in the United States or against U.S. targets abroad.

Global Flashpoints in the War on Terror

In This Chapter

- ◆ Suspect in Indonesia
- ◆ Osama, phone home
- ◆ Return to Iraq?
- ◆ Chechnya camps

In their valiant attempt to put a spy shield around the United States, the CIA's war against terrorism quickly expanded to global proportions. As Joe Louis once said of a lesser opponent whose attempts at flight were impeded by the four corners of the boxing ring: "He can run, but he can't hide." The same is true for terrorists, confined as they are to the four corners of the Earth.

Traveling Tenet

George Tenet has personally met with world leaders regarding the war on terrorism. On February 16, 2002, DCI Tenet met with Egyptian President Hosni Mubarak and then traveled to Yemen to meet with President Ali Abdullah Saleh.

Yemen, which has recently been trying to distance itself from its image as a haven for Islamic militants, has been among the possible targets for Al Qaeda terrorist activity. A manhunt for Al Qaeda members in Yemen started in December 2001.

By March, although the military operation in Afghanistan had a "clean-up" feel, there were signs that Al Qaeda was regrouping. By mid-March 2002, CIA surveillance of financial and Internet activity indicated that Al Qaeda might still have been attempting to finance further terrorist attacks.

On March 17, former CIA counterterrorist chief Vincent Cannistraro told the Associated Press: "There's lots of signs Al Qaeda is reconstituting itself. Internet traffic has picked up enormously. Money is moving around. There is some evidence that leadership is active." Al Qaeda still had enough money to be dangerous, working with what remained of Osama bin Laden's fortune, donations from Islamic groups, and profits from commodity trading, mostly in gold and honey.

The Far Eastern Front

As the war on terrorism moved into Asia, so did the CIA—not that it wasn't already there, but now it acted with urgency. With the dual objective of fighting terrorism and maintaining regional stability, U.S. political and military leaders had talks with Malaysia, Singapore, and Indonesia. U.S. troops also accompanied Philippine soldiers in pursuit of local rebels. Congress passed a bill that established a counterterrorism training program for officers in Southeast Asian armies, and the CIA began to arm and train counterterrorist teams and intelligence services in Southeast Asia nations.

Terrorist Suspect Picked Up in Indonesia

One of the men CIA surveillance kept an eye on following the September 11 attacks was Muhammad Saad Iqbal Madni. The CIA had information from Indonesian officials and foreign diplomats that Iqbal, a stocky 24-year-old man with a beard, was an agent of Al Qaeda who had worked with "shoe bomber" Richard C. Reid, the Briton charged with trying to detonate explosives in his shoes on an American Airlines flight from Paris to Miami on December 22, 2001.

In mid-November 2001, Iqbal—who carried both an Egyptian and a Pakistani passport—traveled from Pakistan to Jakarta, Indonesia. His stated reason was to give an inheritance to his father's ex-wife. That transaction was taken care of quickly, but he remained in Indonesia, moving into a clean but run-down boarding house. He spent his time visiting a nearby mosque and watching television at a friend's house.

He handed out business cards that identified him as a radio personality at an Islamic radio station.

Iqbal also visited Solo, a city in central Java, Indonesia's main island, saying he was going to see his stepmother. The city is regarded by Western and Asian intelligence officials as a base for Jemaah Islamiah, a militant Muslim group with bases in Indonesia, Singapore, and Malaysia that is alleged to be affiliated with Al Qaeda. The group is accused of plotting to blow up Western embassies and U.S. naval vessels in Singapore and of aiding two of the September 11 hijackers during a trip they made to Malaysia in 2000.

Top Secret

In February 2002, a joint congressional inquiry "to ascertain why the intelligence community did not learn of the September 11 attacks in advance" was announced. According to the announcement, this inquiry would investigate the intelligence community's response to terrorist threats dating back to 1985, and hearings would be public when possible. The White House pledged full cooperation and stated that the inquiry's scope and direction would have no constraints.

Following the shoe bomber's arrest, the CIA urged Indonesia to apprehend Iqbal. Egypt asked Indonesia to extradite Iqbal, saying that he was a suspected terrorist in activities unrelated to those of the shoe bomber. Indonesian intelligence apprehended Iqbal in early 2002, and he was flown to Egypt aboard an American jet. The official story was that he was being deported because of visa problems.

Iqbal remains in custody in Egypt. He is one of dozens of suspected terrorists who have been taken off the streets through the combined effort of the CIA and foreign intelligence services with which it is friendly.

Flights over the Philippines

In mid-February 2002, the U.S. began intelligence-gathering flights over the southern Philippines as part of the war on terrorism in that country. The surveillance flights complemented the more than 500 U.S. soldiers on the ground, a number projected to peak at 660 troops in coming months.

The flights are being made by Navy and Air Force aircraft based in Okinawa and elsewhere in Asia. The United States is hoping to track down the Abu Sayyaf group, which has been linked to Osama bin Laden and Al Qaeda and had taken several hostages, including two American missionaries.

In June, 2002 Phillipine forces attempted a rescue. One of the American missionaries died in the attack on the miliant group Abu Sayyaf near a fishing village on the island of Mindanao, about 50 miles south of Manila. The second missionary was shot in the leg but was rescued. According to Phillippine military forces, four guerrillas were killed out of an estimated 30 to 50 in the group. News reports claim that there may be as many as 1,200 U. S. forces in the Phillippines on counterterrorism training missions.

Phone Records Are Key

Between 1996 and 1998, Osama bin Laden and a handful of top lieutenants, including Egyptian sidekicks Ayman al-Zawahiri and the late Muhammad Atef, stayed in touch with the outside world from their hideouts in Afghanistan using a Compact-M portable satellite telephone. Their billing records were obtained by U.S. investigators probing the 1998 U.S. Embassy bombings in Africa, and a country-by-country analysis of the bills provided U.S. authorities with the key to important Al Qaeda cells around the world.

" " McLean Says ...

A friend had a price put on his head in 1998 by Osama bin Laden while he was in Afghanistan working on a business project. A radio program had announced that he and another American business associate were wanted. The price on their heads was five million Afghanis, which was a lot of money to Afghans, but not much in terms of U.S. dollars.

A business meeting had been scheduled for the next day on the project they had been negotiating with Taliban officials. In fact, they were in the country at the invitation of the Taliban to help them with the country's communications system. Instead of going to the afternoon meeting they decided to go in the other direction from Kabul, out of the country as fast as possible.

They knew airports would be watched. So would major roads. The best bet seemed to do what Al Queda would not expect. They drove to Jalalabad, the center of Osama bin Laden's organization. Once there they decided to stay at a medium-size hotel that supposedly was run by bin Laden. They checked in, had a good night's sleep, dressed in their next change of Afghani clothes that had been made by an Afghan tailor, and headed down the valley.

By the time they were missed at the meeting, they were well beyond most who would have heard that radio broadcast announcing they were wanted men. By the next day they had traveled up and over the Khyber Pass, slipped through checkpoints in the Pakistan border, and caught a flight out of that country. Lesson learned: Sometimes the lion's den is the safest place to hide, especially when everyone is searching all the most likely escape routes.

The most calls, 238 out of 1,100, were to hard-wired and mobile phones in England. The recipient of most of those calls, bin Laden associate Khalid al-Fawwaz, has been in British custody for years awaiting extradition to the United States, where he is wanted for conspiracy to murder U.S. citizens through acts of terrorism.

The second largest group of outgoing calls (221) was to numbers in Yemen. Some calls went to a Yemeni phone number that investigators now believe was used as a switchboard by conspirators involved in the three deadliest Al Qaeda attacks since 1998:

- The embassy bombings in Africa
- The bombing of the USS *Cole*
- The September 11 attacks in New York and Washington D.C.

The switchboard number was reportedly registered to Ahmad Mohammad Ali al-Hada, the patriarch of a Yemeni terrorist clan. Intelligence sources say al-Hada fought as an Islamic guerrilla against Soviet occupation forces in Afghanistan where, in 1999, he sat next to bin Laden at a banquet.

One of al-Hada's sons-in-law, Khalid Almidhar, was a member of the team that crashed an American Airlines plane into the Pentagon on September 11. Another son-in-law is among 13 men named by the Justice Department in February 2002 as members of a terror team feared to be plotting an imminent attack against American targets.

Other countries called on bin Laden's phone included Azerbaijan, Pakistan, Saudi Arabia, Sudan, and Egypt. Interestingly, nearly 10 percent of the outgoing calls went to numbers in Iran. A Bush administration official said that U.S. intelligence has believed for years that hard-line anti-American factions inside Iran helped the bin Laden organization operate an "underground railroad" to smuggle terrorists to Al Qaeda training camps in Afghanistan. Iran has claimed to have cracked down on Taliban and Al Qaeda forces attempting to flee Afghanistan, but the United States remains skeptical.

> **Top Secret**
>
> The CIA and FBI have begun jointly developing a new super-computer system designed to improve their ability to both cull and share information.

Osama Search in Kashmir

The CIA learned in January 2002 from India intelligence that Osama bin Laden reportedly had fled Afghanistan and had gone to the strife-torn Indian state of

Kashmir, where he was being protected by the extremist Islamic group called Harkat ul-Mujahedeen.

In response to the report, President Bush—through his agent, U.S. Secretary of State Colin Powell—and British Prime Minister Tony Blair decided to send U.S. and British commandos to Kashmir to hunt for bin Laden. The story first became public in the British newspaper, *The Daily Telegraph*, possibly alerting bin Laden and his followers of the plans and giving them time to find another hideout. After all, bin Laden and his followers are not stupid people, and they do have access to the world's media.

Meanwhile, in Iraq

At the beginning of March 2002, it was announced to the press that the CIA had begun covert operations designed to topple Saddam Hussein in Iraq. President Bush gave the project the green light in February.

The action, which was still in its formative stages at the time of the announcement, would arm and finance groups inside Iraq that were hostile to Saddam Hussein's regime. The plan could take as long as four or five years.

Bush administration officials also said that the CIA covert action did not, in any way, mean that Bush had ruled out an invasion of Iraq and the toppling of Saddam Hussein the old-fashioned way: with brute force.

> ### Top Secret
>
> "We know terrorists can and will hit us overseas where we are sometimes overextended and security is less than is needed," one senior operative noted on condition of anonymity. "When we get hit with another Big Bang of whatever kind in our own country, no doubt we'll finally wake up. If we are lucky, Bush and his team are awake already and quietly working investing in homeland security at a faster pace. We may not see or hear about budget diversions, but let's hope we are getting things and people in place."

Georgia on My Mind

According to the Association of Former Intelligence Officers newsletter, another flash point in the global war on terrorism could be the Pankisi Gorge, a lawless area in the former Soviet Republic of Georgia that abuts the state of Chechnya. The newsletter reported, "[In March 2002], the U.S. chargé d'affaires in Georgia, Philip Remler, told a local newspaper that dozens of Arab terrorists 'connected with bin Laden' are holed up in the gorge."

According to Russian security officials, there are between 600 and 1,500 hard-core foreign fighters in Chechnya, who are funded and armed by Al Qaeda and other groups through the same shadowy channels that prepared the September 11 attacks on the United States. Before Russian forces invaded and occupied Chechnya in 1999, there were 15 terror-training camps in Chechnya all using the same instructors and textbooks that U.S. forces have found in Al Qaeda camps in Afghanistan.

Tradecraft

The 2002 annual report from the National Intelligence Council (NIC), which is required by Congress, gave mixed reviews when it came to the Russians' ability to keep their nuclear materials secure. The report indicated that the Russians were performing adequately in protecting their nuclear weapons from an outside threat, but their security measures "are not designed to counter the preeminent threat faced today—an insider who attempts unauthorized actions."

"We are talking about an international network that shares the same sources of funding, political support, weapons, training, and ideology, operating in Chechnya, Afghanistan, and many other places," says Sergei Ignatchenko, spokesman of Russia's FSB security service, the domestic successor of the Soviet KGB that oversees Moscow's counterinsurgency operation in Chechnya. "These are not nationalists or independence-seekers. They are disciplined international terrorists, united by a single aim: to seize power and bring in a new world order based on sharia [Islamic] law."

Gauging the Nuke Threat

Robert Walpole, the National Intelligence Officer for Strategic and Nuclear Programs, told a Congressional panel that "the missile threat will continue to grow" and that the chance that a missile with a nuclear, chemical, or biological warhead will be used against U.S. forces or interests was "greater than during most of the Cold War." Walpole's public remarks were based on a still-classified CIA report to Congress that covered the threat during the next 15 years.

The report identified Iran and North Korea as "probably" being capable of having a missile that could reach the United States by the year 2015 and Iraq as "unlikely but possibly" capable. North Korea was farthest along technologically, the report said, and might be ready to test the Taepo Dong-2, a missile capable of delivering a nuclear payload to the United States. The country is believed to possess one and perhaps two nuclear weapons and has undertaken chemical and biological weapons programs. The report said that Iran was at least five years away from testing a missile capable of reaching the United States.

Safety First and Always

Which brings us back to our original point. The CIA has a hugely important role when it comes to the safety of the United States, and that role has never been more important than it is today.

Unfortunately, in the days since September 11, far too much time has been wasted searching for a scapegoat. Who was responsible? Well, it was the terrorists, of course. Everyone else should stop pointing fingers and concentrate on maximizing American security.

As we go to press, we learn that one Jose Padilla, a 31-year-old Muslim also known as Abdullah al Muhajir, had been plotting to steal and explode a radioactive "dirty bomb" in Washington, D.C. Padilla will never have that opportunity, however, as he was arrested and remains in jail. Remember, the catastrophes that never happen are the U.S. Intelligence Community's greatest reward.

The Least You Need to Know

- Dozens of suspected terrorists have been taken off the streets through the combined effort of the CIA and CIA-friendly foreign intelligence services.

- Between 600 and 1,500 hard-core foreign fighters in Chechnya are funded and armed by Al Qaeda and other groups.

- According to estimates, the chance that a missile with a nuclear, chemical, or biological warhead will be used against U.S. forces or interests is greater than during most of the Cold War.

CIA Abbreviations and Acronyms (and What They Mean)

A-2   Air Force Intelligence

AEC   Atomic Energy Commission

AFSA   Armed Forces Security Agency

AFTAC   Air Force Technical Applications Center

AIA   Air Intelligence Agency

ASA   Army Security Agency

ASSA   Armed Services Security Agency

BI   Background Investigation

CARG   Covert Action Review Group

CEA   Council of Economic Advisers (to the President)

CEP   Circular error probability (when judging probable accuracy of a warhead strike)

CIA   Central Intelligence Agency, often called internally, "The Company"

CIC   The U.S. Army's Counterintelligence Corps

CIO   Central Imagery Office, now under the NIMA

CS   Clandestine Services

COCOM   Coordinating Committee on Multilateral Export Controls

COMINT   Communications Intelligence

Commo   CIA communications apparatus

COMSEC   Communications Security

COS   Chief of Station, CIA

DA   Directorate of Administration

D-Branch   Counterespionage Branch of MI5, Great Britain, U.K.

DCI   Director of Central Intelligence

DCID   Director of Central Intelligence Directive

DDA   Deputy Director of Administration

DDI   Deputy Director of Intelligence

DDO   Deputy Director for Operations

DDPO   Defense Dissemination Program Office, now under the NIMA

DDS&T   Deputy Director for Science and Technology

DI   Directorate of Intelligence

DIA   Defense Intelligence Agency

DIS   Defense Investigative Service

DMA   Defense Mapping Agency, now under the NIMA

DS&T   Directorate of Science and Technology

DST   French Counterespionage Service, similar to MI5 of the United Kingdom

ELINT   Electronic Intelligence

EPQ   Embarrassing Personal Question

ERIR   Economic Research Intelligence Report

FBI   Federal Bureau of Investigation, also called "The Bureau"

FBIS   Foreign Broadcast Information Service

FCC   Federal Communications Commission

FSO   Foreign Service Officer

G-2   Army Intelligence

GAO   General Accounting Office

GPS   Global Positioning System

GPU   See OGPU, Forerunner of KGB

GRU   Soviet Military Intelligence

HUMINT   Human Intelligence

IAM   Intelligence Analytical Memorandum

IC   Intelligence Community

ICBM   Intercontinental ballistic missile

INR   Bureau of Intelligence and Research (the State Department intelligence agency)

INSCOM   Army's Intelligence and Security Command

JCS   Joint Chiefs of Staff

JJ   James Jesus Angleton, the legendary CIA searcher for "moles" and penetration of the CIA by foreign intelligence operatives

KGB   Komitet Gosunderstvennoy Bezopasnosti, the Committee of State Security of USSR (Russia)

LASP   Low Altitude Surveillance Platform

LDC   Less developed country

MCIA   Marine Corps Intelligence Activity

MI5   British Security service, formerly Section 5 of Military Intelligence, which gave the service the name still used today

MI6   British Secret Intelligence Service, formerly Section 6 of Military Intelligence, which today is a civilian organization with functions similar to the CIA

MBO   Management by objective

NAIC National Air Intelligence Center

NFAC National Foreign Assessment Center

NFIB National Foreign Intelligence Board

NFIP National Foreign Intelligence Program

NHB New CIA headquarters office building, compared to the OHB, the old or original CIA headquarters building

NIAM National Intelligence Analytical Memorandum

NIC National Intelligence Council

NID *National Intelligence Daily*

NIE National Intelligence Estimate

NIMA National Imagery and Mapping Agency

NKVD Another forerunner name of KGB of USSR

NPIC National Photographic Interpretation Center

NRO National Reconnaissance Office

NRP National Reconnaissance Program

NSA National Security Agency, primarily a global Hi-Tech Intel Listening organization, based at Fort Meade, Maryland

NSC National Security Council

NSCID National Security Council Intelligence Directive

OCI Office of Current Intelligence

OGPU Another forerunner of the KGB of USSR

OGSR Office of Geographic and Societal Research

OHB Old CIA headquarters building

OIS Office of Intelligence Support (Department of the Treasury)

ONI Office of Naval Intelligence

ONNI Office of National Narcotics Intelligence

ONS Office of National Security (Department of the Treasury)

OPC Office of Policy Coordination

ORR   Office of Research and Reports

OSI   Office of Scientific Intelligence

OSR   Office of Strategic Research

OSS   Office of Strategic Services, the World War II forerunner of the CIA

OTR   Office of Training

PDB   *President's Daily Brief*

PIC   Photographic Interpretation Center, now known as the NPIC

PFIAB   President's Foreign Intelligence Advisory Board

PLO   Palestine Liberation Organization

RADINT   Radar Intelligence

RPV   Remote pilotless vehicles, used for spying from the air

SALT   Strategic Arms Limitation Treaty

SDECE   French secret Intelligence Service, similar to British MI6

SIGINT   Signals Intelligence

SNIE   Special National Intelligence Estimate

TDY   Temporary duty assignment

TELINT   Telemetry Intelligence, gathered by the National Security Agency

Related Intelligence Organizations

There are a couple of fine organizations dedicated to providing services for intelligence officers and former intelligence officers. They are the Association of Former Intelligence Officers and the National Military Intelligence Association.

The Association of Former Intelligence Officers

The Association of Former Intelligence Officers (AFIO) is a nonprofit, nonpolitical educational association with some 3,000 members throughout the United States. AFIO was founded in Virginia in 1975 and is recognized as a tax exempt educational organization by the IRS. AFIO's educational mission is to foster public understanding of the role and importance of U.S. Intelligence for National security and world stability. The focus is two-fold, on intelligence activities abroad and on security at home.

Intelligence and Security

Education on the role of U.S. intelligence abroad is accomplished in historic, contemporary, and future contexts. This includes U.S. policy and decision-making, support for Presidential and National Security Directives and Congressional laws, organization for the collection, analysis, and dissemination of intelligence, and study of critical issues.

In addition, AFIO focuses on understanding the critical need for effective counterintelligence and security against foreign, political, technological, or economic espionage, as well as lawfully authorized clandestine actions and covert, terrorist, or criminal operations threatening U.S. security, the national infrastructure, or corporate and individual safety.

Since foreign intelligence, counterintelligence, and covert activities are necessarily conducted in secrecy in an ever-present silent war, education on the vital need for effective institutions conducting U.S. intelligence and counterintelligence operations is an ongoing, challenging, necessary, and important mission.

Men and Women of Distinction

AFIO is an association of people with active intellectual lives, many of whom have participated, or are still actively participating in events of historic significance. Many have played roles of leadership and served their country with high distinction.

They are men and women dedicated to worthy principles and objectives. AFIO members include primarily individuals from U.S. Government Departments, but also State and local government, corporate or private professionals, and supporters.

Volunteers of America

Aside from a small professional staff and central office, the AFIO organization and its chapters throughout the country are run by volunteers who donate their time and talents to the cause of furthering AFIO's objectives with the fellowship of professional colleagues and supporters.

The Honorary Board of Direction is a Who's Who of notable Americans. The Co-Chairmen are The Honorable George H. W. Bush and The Honorable Gerald R. Ford. Other members include Mr. John Barron, The Hon. Shirley Temple Black, The Hon. Frank C. Carlucci, Dr. Ruth M. Davis, Amb. Richard Helms, Adm. Bobby R. Inman, USN (Ret), Professor Ernest May, Mr. John Anson Smith, The Hon. William H. Webster, and The Hon. R. Woolsey.

Purpose: Fostering Understanding

AFIO members subscribe to the values of patriotism, excellence, integrity, dedication, and loyalty represented by the active intelligence establishment of the United States engaged in the execution of national policies and the advancement and defense of the vital interests and security of the country, its citizens, and its allies.

AFIO's principal objective is to foster understanding by intellectual, political, and business community leaders and the general public of the continuing need for a strong and responsible national intelligence/counterintelligence establishment to deal with a variety of short and long-term threats and issues in the current world environment and the new Information Age.

Within this context AFIO stresses education on the need for effective long-term intelligence strategies and capabilities to support national decisionmakers and to guard against surprise.

Ongoing Intelligence Programs

AFIO seeks to implement its objectives by conducting a variety of programs. These are designed to contribute balance and expert insight into the public and media discourses on intelligence-related issues, support educational courses, seminars, symposia and research on intelligence and counterintelligence topics, and promote public understanding of intelligence and counterintelligence roles, needs, and functions. In addition, the programs encourage the exchange of information among intelligence professionals and promote the study of the history and current role of U.S. intelligence.

In support of the objectives and programs, AFIO issues periodic informative publications. There is a Weekly Intelligence Notes with email commentaries on intelligence issues that keeps members posted on news they seldom see in local media.

For members, AFIO conducts a National Convention, symposia, seminars, and workshops. There also are mini symposia with luncheon speakers in the Washington, D.C., area, plus AFIO Chapter meetings and conferences throughout the United States. To further extend the information efforts, key members also participate in TV, radio, and printed news media discussions.

Academic Support

Academic support and outreach programs also are conducted through the Institute for Intelligence Education, the Harold P. Ransburg Memorial Education Agenda, AFIO videos, audio tapes, and printed material for high school and college use.

To encourage study of intelligence, AFIO has set up tuition scholarships, meritorious educational awards for students and instructors, and developed an overview course on intelligence & counterintelligence.

Two Categories of Membership

There are two categories of membership: Members and Associate Members. Both Members and Associate Members may be officers or directors of the Association. Members are former U.S. intelligence, counterintelligence, and related (for example security personnel of any rank or level may become Members). Associate members are U.S. citizens in private, civil, academic, or corporate pursuits. Americans currently in government employment at any level or military service may become Associate Members.

Membership information is available at the website, www.afio.com, where you'll also find useful links to other intelligence agencies and organizations.

Chapters Are Semi-Autonomous

AFIO chapters are semi-autonomous extensions of AFIO, consisting of AFIO members who have banded together to form a chapter chartered by AFIO National to conduct activities as authorized by, and in consonance with, AFIO bylaws, principles, and educational objectives. These chapters are located throughout the United States. Chapters are both collegial and promote the AFIO mission. Chapters generally conduct two kinds of activity. Chapters conduct informative educational programs of meetings and newsletters for their members.

Peace Through Vigilance: The NMIA

The National Military Intelligence Association is an organization designed to lend support to intelligence professionals in the military services and intelligence agencies, office of the United States government, Congress, industry, and academia.

The organization provides those professionals with a forum to share and exchange ideas for their individual professional enhancement and the good of the entire Intelligence Community. Their theme is basic: "Peace Through Vigilance!"

For several decades NMIA has been the sole professional association of all the U.S. armed services. This is appropriate because the intelligence function is a basic element of all military operations: on land, at sea, in the air, and even in space.

Goals

NMIA's goals are to serve as a means to exchange ideas between members, to provide a public outlet for information about the profession, and to support the intelligence effort of the United States through the enhancement of the members' professional role and stature.

In its first 25 years, NMIA has made many contributions to the United States intelligence field. For the next decade, the organization is ready for new initiatives to improve service to all who serve or have served the defense intelligence and national security community, and to the public in their understanding of the role and importance of intelligence to the nation.

How to Join

Full membership in the National Military Intelligence Association is available to military and civil service personnel, as well as to reserve, national guard, retired and former service personnel, and to U.S. civilians in the industrial sector supporting the U.S. Intelligence system.

U.S. citizens who have an interest in historical, literary, technical, or academic aspects of intelligence and who support the purposes and principles of the Association may also be eligible for membership. Associate membership may be available to personnel of allied nations. Subscriptions are available to libraries as well.

An application form to join the NMIA is posted on the NMIA website at www.nmia.org.

Tenet's Testimony Before Congress

Testimony of George J. Tenet, Director of Central Intelligence, to the Senate Select Intelligence Committee, February 6, 2002.

MR. TENET: Mr. Chairman, I appear before you this year under circumstances that are extraordinary and historic for reasons I need not recount. Never before has the subject of this annual threat briefing had more immediate resonance. Never before have the dangers been more clear or more present.

September 11 brought together and brought home literally several vital threats to the United States and its interests that we have long been aware of. It is the convergence of these threats that I want to emphasize with you today: The connection between terrorists and other enemies of this country, the weapons of mass destruction they seek to use against us, and the social, economic and political tensions across the world that they exploit in mobilizing their followers.

September 11 demonstrated the dangers that arise when these threats converge and remind us that we overlook, at our own peril, the impact of crises in remote parts of the world. This convergence of threats has created a world I will present to you today, a world in which dangers exist not only in those places we have most often focused our attention, but also in other areas that demand it; in places like Somalia, where the absence of a national government has created an environment in which groups sympathetic to Al Qaeda have offered terrorists an operational base and potential safe haven; in places like Indonesia, where political instability, separatist and ethnic tensions and protracted violence are hampering economic recovery and fueling Islamic extremism; in places like Colombia, where leftist insurgents who make much of their money from drug trafficking are escalating their assault on the government, further undermining economic prospects and fueling a cycle of violence; and finally, Mr. Chairman, in places like Connecticut, with the death of a 94-year-old woman in her own home of anthrax poisoning, can arouse our worst fears about what our enemies might try to do to us.

These threats demand our utmost response. The United States has clearly demonstrated since September 11 that it is up to the challenge. But make no mistake: Despite the battles we have won in Afghanistan, we remain a nation at war. Last year I told you that Osama bin Laden and the Al Qaeda network were the most immediate and serious threat this country faced. This remains true, despite the progress we have made in Afghanistan and in disrupting the network elsewhere.

We assess that Al Qaeda and other terrorist groups will continue to plan to attack this country and its interests abroad. Their modus operandi is to continue to have multiple attack plans in the works simultaneously and to have Al Qaeda cells in place to conduct them.

We know that the terrorists have considered attacks in the U.S. against high-profile government or private facilities, famous landmarks and U.S. infrastructure nodes such as airports, bridges, harbors and dams. High-profile events such as the Olympics or last week's Super Bowl also fit the terrorists' interests in striking another blow within the United States that would command worldwide media attention.

Al Qaeda also has plans to strike against U.S. and allied interests in Europe, the Middle East, Africa and Southeast Asia. American diplomatic and military installations are at high risk, especially in East Africa, Israel, Saudi Arabia and Turkey. Operations against U.S. targets could be launched by Al Qaeda cells already in place in major cities in Europe and the Middle East. Al Qaeda can also exploit its presence or connections to other groups in such countries as Somalia, Yemen, Indonesia, and the Philippines.

Although the September 11 attacks suggest that Al Qaeda and other terrorists will continue to use conventional weapons, one of our highest concerns is their stated readiness to attempt unconventional attacks against us. As early as 1998, bin Laden publicly declared that acquiring unconventional weapons was a religious duty. Terrorist groups worldwide have ready access to information on chemical, biological and even nuclear weapons via the Internet, and we know that Al Qaeda was working to acquire some of the most dangerous chemical agents and toxins.

Documents recovered from Al Qaeda facilities in Afghanistan show that bin Laden was pursuing a sophisticated biological weapons research program. We also believe that bin Laden was seeking to acquire or develop a nuclear device. Al Qaeda may be pursuing a radioactive dispersal device, what some call a dirty bomb.

Alternatively, Al Qaeda or other terrorist groups might also try to launch conventional attacks against the chemical or nuclear industrial infrastructure of the United States to cause widespread toxic or radiological damage.

We are also alert to the possibility of cyber warfare attack by terrorists. September 11 demonstrated our dependence on critical infrastructure systems that rely on electronic and computer networks. Attacks of this nature will become an increasingly viable option for the terrorists as they and other foreign adversaries become more familiar with these targets and the technologies required to attack them.

The terrorist threat goes well beyond Al Qaeda. The situation in the Middle East continues to fuel terrorism and anti-U.S. sentiment worldwide. Groups like the Palestinian Islamic Jihad and Hamas have escalated their violence against Israel, and the intifada has rejuvenated once-dormant groups like the Popular Front for the Liberation of Palestine. If these groups feel that U.S. actions are threatening their existence, they may begin targeting Americans directly, as Hezbollah's terrorist wing already does.

We're also watching states like Iran and Iraq that continue to support terrorist groups. Iran continues to provide support, including arms transfers, to the Palestinian rejection groups and Hezbollah. Tehran also has failed to move decisively against Al Qaeda members who have relocated to Iran from Afghanistan. Iraq has a long history of supporting terrorists, including giving sanctuary to Abu Nidal.

The war on terrorism, Mr. Chairman, has dealt severe blows to Al Qaeda and its leadership. The group has been denied its safe haven and strategic command center in Afghanistan. Drawing on both our own assets and increased cooperation from allies around the world, we are uncovering terrorist plans and breaking up their cells. These efforts have yielded the arrest of nearly 1,000 Al Qaeda operatives in over 60 countries and have disrupted terrorist operations and potential terrorist attacks.

Mr. Chairman, bin Laden did not believe that we would invade his sanctuary. He saw the United States as soft, impatient, unprepared, and fearful of a long bloody war of attrition. He did not count on the fact that we had lined up allies that could help us overcome barriers of terrain and culture. He did not know about the collection and operational initiatives that will allow us to strike with great accuracy at the heart of the Taliban and Al Qaeda. He underestimated our capabilities, our readiness and our resolve.

That said, I must repeat that Al Qaeda has not yet been destroyed. It and other like-minded groups remain willing and able to strike at us. Al Qaeda's leaders, still at large, are working to reconstitute the organization and resume its terrorist operations. We must eradicate these organizations by denying them their sources of financing, eliminating their ability to hijack charitable organizations for their terrorist purposes. We must be prepared for a long war and we must not falter.

Mr. Chairman, we must also look beyond the immediate danger of terrorist attacks to the conditions that allow terrorism to take root around the world. These conditions are no less threatening to U.S. national security than terrorism itself. The problems that terrorists exploit—poverty, alienation, and ethnic tensions—will grow more acute over the next decade. This will especially be the case in those parts of the world that have served as the most fertile recruiting grounds for Islamic extremist groups.

We have already seen in Afghanistan and elsewhere that domestic unrest and conflict in weak states is one of the factors that creates an environment conducive to terrorism. More importantly, demographic trends tell us that the world's poorest and most politically unstable regions, which include parts of the Middle East and sub-Saharan Africa, will have the largest youth populations in the world over the next two decades and beyond. Most of these countries will lack the economic institutions or the resources to effectively integrate these youth into their societies.

All of these challenges come together in parts of the Muslim world, and let me give you just one example. One of the places where they converge that has the greatest long-term impact on any society is its educational system. Primary and secondary education in parts of the Muslim world is often dominated by an interpretation of Islam that teaches intolerance and hatred. The graduates of these schools, madrases, provide the foot soldiers for many of the Islamic militant groups that operate throughout the Muslim world.

Let me underscore what the president has affirmed. Islam itself is neither an enemy nor a threat to the United States. But the increasing anger toward the West and toward governments friendly to us among Islamic extremists and their sympathizers clearly is a threat to us. We have seen and continue to see these dynamics play out across the Muslim world. Our campaign in Afghanistan has made great progress, but the road ahead is fraught with challenges. The Afghan people, with international assistance, are working to overcome a traditionally weak central government, a devastated infrastructure, a grave humanitarian crisis, and ethnic divisions that deepened over the last 20 years of conflict. The next few months will be an especially fragile period.

Let me turn to Pakistan, Mr. Chairman. September 11 and the response to it were the most profound external events for Pakistan since the Soviet invasion of Afghanistan in 1979 and the U.S. response to that. The Musharraf government's alignment with the United States and its abandonment of nearly a decade of support for the Taliban represent a fundamental political shift with inherent political risks because of the militant Islamic and anti-American sentiments that exist within Pakistan.

President Musharraf's intention to establish a moderate, tolerant Islamic state, as outlined in his January 12 speech, is being welcomed by most Pakistanis, but we still have to confront major vested interests. The speech is energizing debate across the Muslim world about which vision of Islam is the right one for the future of the Islamic community. Musharraf established a clear and forceful distinction between a narrow, intolerant, conflict-ridden vision of the past and an inclusive, tolerant, and peace-oriented vision of the future. The speech also addressed the jihad issue by citing the distinction the prophet Mohammad made between the smaller jihad involving violence and the greater jihad that focuses on eliminating poverty and helping the needy.

Although September 11 highlighted the challenges that India and Pakistan and their relations posed for U.S. policy, the attack on the Indian parliament on December 13 was even more destabilizing, resulting as it did in new calls for military action against Pakistan and subsequent mobilization on both sides. The chance of war bet-ween these two nuclear armed states is higher than at any point since 1971. If India were to conduct large-scale offensive operations into Pakistani Kashmir, Pakistan might retaliate with strikes of its own, in the belief that its nuclear deterrent would limit the scope of an Indian nuclear counter-attack. Both India and Pakistan are publicly downplaying the risks of nuclear conflict in the current crisis. We are deeply concerned, however, that a conventional war, once begun, could escalate into a nuc-lear confrontation, and here is a place where diplomacy and American engagement has made an enormous difference.

Let me turn to Iraq. Saddam has responded to our progress in Afghanistan with a political and diplomatic charm offensive to make it appear that Baghdad is becoming more flexible on U.N. sanctions and inspection issues. Last month, he sent Deputy Prime Minister Tariq Aziz to Moscow and Beijing to profess Iraq's new openness to meet its U.N. obligations and to seek their support. Baghdad's international isolation is also decreasing as support for the sanctions regime erodes among other states in the region. Saddam has carefully cultivated neighboring states, drawing them into economically dependent relationships in the hopes of further undermining their support for sanctions. The profits he gains from these relationships provide him with the means to reward key supporters, and more importantly to fund his pursuit of weapons of mass destruction. His calculus is never about bettering or helping the Iraqi people.

Let me be clear. Saddam remains a threat. He is determined to thwart U.N. sanctions, press ahead with weapons of mass destruction, and resurrect the military force he had before the Gulf War. Today he maintains his vice grip on the levers of power through a pervasive intelligence and security apparatus, and even his reduced military force, which is less than half of its pre-war size, remains capable of defeating more poorly armed internal opposition and threatening Iraq's neighbors.

As I said earlier, we continue to watch Iraq's involvement in terrorist activities. Baghdad has a long history of supporting terrorism, altering its targets to reflect changing priorities and goals. It has also had contacts with Al Qaeda. Their ties may be limited by diverging ideologies, but the two sides mutual antipathy towards the United States and the Saudi royal family suggest that tactical cooperation between them is possible, even though Saddam is well aware that such activity would carry serious consequences.

In Iran, we are concerned that the reform movement may be losing its momentum. For almost five years, President Khatami and his reformist supporters have been stymied by Supreme Leader Khatami and the hard-liners. The hard-liners have systematically used the unelected institutions they control—the security forces, the judiciary, and the guardians council—to block reforms that challenge their entrenched interests. They have closed newspapers, forced members of Khatami's cabinet from office, and arrested those who have dared to speak out against their tactics.

Discontent with the current domestic situation is widespread, and cuts across the social spectrum. Complaints focus on the lack of pluralism and government accountability, social restrictions and poor economic performance. Frustrations are growing as the populace sees elected institutions such as the—(inaudible)—and the presidency, unable to break the hard-liners' hold on power.

The hard-line regime appears secure for now because security forces have easily contained dissenters and arrested potential opposition leaders. No one has emerged to rally reformers into a forceful movement for change, and the Iranian public appears to prefer gradual reform to another revolution, but the equilibrium is fragile and could be upset by a miscalculation by either the reformers or the hard-line clerics.

For all of this, reform is not dead. We must remember that the people of Iran have demonstrated in four national elections since 1997 that they want change, and have grown disillusioned with the promises of the revolution. Social, intellectual, and political developments are proceeding. Civil institutions are growing, and new newspapers open as others are closed.

The initial signs of Teheran's cooperation in common cause with us in Afghanistan are being eclipsed by Iranian efforts to undermine U.S. influence there. While Iran's officials express a shared interest in a stable government in Afghanistan, its security forces appear bent on countering American presence. This seeming contradiction in behavior reflects a deep-seeded suspicion among Teheran's clerics that the United States is committed to encircling and overthrowing them, a fear that could quickly erupt in attacks against our interests.

We have seen little sign of a reduction in Iran's support for terrorism in the past year. Its participation in the attempt to transfer arms to the Palestinian Authority via the Karine A probably was intended to escalate the violence of the intifada and strengthen the position of Palestinian elements that prefer armed conflict with Israel.

The current conflict between Israel and Palestinians has been raging for almost a year and a half, and it continues to deteriorate. The violence has hardened the public's positions on both sides and increased the long-standing animosity between Israeli Prime Minister Sharon and Palestinian leader Arafat. Although many Israelis and Palestinians say they believe that ultimately the conflict can only be resolved through negotiations, the absence of any meaningful security cooperation between Israel and the Palestinian Authority, and the escalating and uncontrolled activities of the Palestinian Islamic Jihad and Hamas, make progress extremely difficult.

We're concerned that this environment creates opportunities for any number of players, most notably Iran, to take steps that will result in further escalation of violence by radical Palestinian groups. At the same time, the continued violence threatens to weaken the political center in the Arab world and increases the challenge for our Arab allies to balance their support for us against the demands of their public.

Mr. Chairman, let me now turn to the subject of proliferation. I would like to start by drawing your attention to several disturbing trends. Weapons of mass destruction programs are becoming more advanced and effective as they mature, and as countries of concern become more aggressive in pursuing them. This is exacerbated by the diffusion of technology over time, which enables proliferators to draw on the experience of others, and develop more advanced weapons more quickly than they could otherwise. Proliferators are also becoming more self-sufficient, and they are taking advantage of the dual-use nature of weapons of mass destruction and missile related technologies to establish advanced production capabilities and to conduct WMD and missile related research under the guise of legitimate commercial or scientific activity.

With regard to chemical and biological weapons, the threat continues to grow for a variety of reasons and to present us with monitoring challenges. On the nuclear side, we are concerned about the possibility of significant nuclear technology transfers going undetected. This reinforces our need for closely examining emerging nuclear programs for sudden leaps in capability.

On the missile side, the proliferation of ICBM and cruise missile design and technology has raised the threat to the United States from weapons of mass destruction delivery systems to a critical threshold. As outlined in our recent national intelligence estimate on the subject, most intelligence community agencies project that by 2015 the U.S. will most likely face ICBM threats from North Korea and Iran, and possibly Iraq. This is in addition to the long-standing missile forces of Russia and China. Short- and medium-range ballistic missiles pose a significant threat right now.

Mr. Chairman, Russian entities continue to provide other countries with technology and expertise applicable to CW, BW, nuclear and ballistic missile and cruise missile projects. Russia appears to be the first choice of proliferant states seeking the most advanced technology and training. These sales are a major source of funds for Russian commercial and defense industries and military research and development. Russia continues to supply significant assistance on nearly all aspects of Tehran's nuclear program. It is also providing Iran with assistance on long-range ballistic missile. Chinese firms remain key suppliers of missile-related technologies to Pakistan, Iran and several other countries. This, in spite of Beijing's November 2000 missile pledge not to assist in any way countries seeking to develop nuclear-capable ballistic missiles. Most of China's efforts involve solid propellant ballistic missile, developments for countries that are largely dependent on Chinese expertise and materials. But it has also sold cruise missiles to countries of concern, such as Iran.

North Korea continues to export complete ballistic missiles and production capabilities, along with related raw materials, components and expertise. Profits from these sales help Pyongyang to support its missile and probably other WMD development programs, and in turn generate new products to offer its customers, primarily Egypt, Libya, Syria and Iran.

North Korea continues to comply with the terms of the agreed framework that are directly related to the freeze on its reactor program. But Pyongyang has warned that it is prepared to walk away from the agreement, if it concluded that the United States was not living up to its end of the deal.

Iraq continues to build and expand an infrastructure capable of producing weapons of mass destruction. Baghdad is expanding its civilian chemical industries in ways that could be diverted quickly into CW production. We believe Baghdad continues to pursue ballistic missile capabilities that exceed the restrictions imposed by UN resolutions. With substantial foreign assistance, it could flight test a longer-range ballistic missile within the next five years.

We believe that Saddam never abandoned his nuclear weapons program. Iraq maintains a significant number of nuclear scientists, program documentation, and probably some dual-use manufacturing infrastructure that could support a reinvigorated nuclear weapons program. Baghdad's access to foreign expertise could support a rejuvenated program. But our major near-term concern is the possibility that Saddam might gain access to fissile material.

Iran remains a serious concern because of its across-the-board pursuit of weapons of mass destruction and missile capabilities. Tehran may be able to indigenously produce enough fissile material for a nuclear weapon by later this decade.

Mr. Chairman, both India and Pakistan are working on the doctrine and tactics for more advanced nuclear weapons, producing fissile material and increasing their stockpiles. We have continuing concerns that both sides may not be done with nuclear testing. Nor can we rule out the possibility that either country could deploy their most advanced nuclear weapons without additional testing.

Mr. Chairman, I want to talk about Russia, China and North Korea, and then we will go to question. And I appreciate the patience, but I think it's important.

Mr. Chairman, with regard to Russia, the most striking development, aside from the issues I have just raised, regarding Russia over the past year has been Moscow's greater engagement with the United States. Even before September 11, President Putin had moved to engage the United States as part of a broader effort to integrate Russia more fully into the West, modernize its economy, and regain international status and influence. This strategic shift away from a zero-sum view of relations is consistent with Putin's stated desire to address many socioeconomic problems that could cloud Russia's future.

During his second year in office, he moved strongly to advance his policy agenda. He pushed the Duma to pass key economic legislation on budget reform, legitimizing urban property sales, flattening and simplifying tax rates, and reducing red tape for small businesses. His support for his economic team and its fiscal rigor positioned Russia to pay back wages and pensions to state workers, and amassed a Soviet high—a post-Soviet high of almost $39 billion in reserves. He has pursued military reform. And all of this is promising, Mr. Chairman. He is trying to build a strong presidency that can ensure these reforms are implemented across Russia, while managing a fragmented bureaucracy beset by internal networks that serve private interests.

In his quest to build a strong state, however, we have to be mindful of the fact that he is trying to establish parameters within which political forces must operate. This managed democracy is illustrated by his continuing moves against independent national television companies. On the economic front, Putin will have to take on bank reform, overhaul Russia's entrenched monopolies and judicial reform to move the country closer to a Western-style market economy, and attract much-needed foreign investment.

Putin has made no headway in Chechnya. Despite his hint in September of a possible dialogue with Chechen moderates, the fighting has intensified in recent months, and thousands of Chechen guerrillas and their fellow Arab mujaheddin fighters remain. Moscow seems unwilling to consider the compromises necessary to reach a settlement, while divisions among the Chechens make it hard to find a representative interlocutor. The war meanwhile threatens to spill over into neighboring Georgia.

After September 11, Putin emphatically chose to join us in the fight against terrorism. The Kremlin blames Islamic radicalism for the conflict in Chechnya, and believes it is to be a serious threat to Russia. Moscow sees the U.S.-led counterterrorism effort, particularly the demise of the Taliban regime, as an important gain in countering radical Islamic threat to Russia and Central Asia.

So far Putin's outreach to the United States has incurred little political damage, largely because of his strong domestic standing. At the same time, Mr. Chairman, Moscow retains fundamental differences with us, and suspicion about U.S. motive persists among Russian conservatives, especially within the U.S. military and the security services. Putin has called the intended U.S. withdrawal from the ABM Treaty a mistake, but has downplayed its impact on Russia. At the same time, Russia is likely to pursue a variety of countermeasures and new weapons system to defeat a U.S.-deployed missile defense.

With regard to China, Mr. Chairman, I told you last year that China's drive to become a great power was coming more sharply into focus. The challenge, I said, was that Beijing saw the United States as the primary obstacle to its realization of that goal. This was in spite of the fact that the Chinese leaders at the same time judged that they needed to maintain good ties with us. A lot has happened in U.S.-China relations over the past year, from the tenseness of the EP3 episode in April, to the positive image of President Bush and Jiang Zemin standing together in Shanghai last fall, highlighting our shared fight against terrorism.

September 11 changed the context of China's approach to us, but it did not change the fundamentals. China is developing an increasingly competitive economy, and building a modern military force with the ultimate objective of asserting itself as a great power in East Asia. And although Beijing joined the coalition against terrorism, it remains skeptical of U.S. intentions in Central and South Asia. It fears that we are gaining regional influence at China's expense, and views our encouragement of a Japanese role—a Japanese military role in counterterrorism—as a support for Japanese rearmament, something that the Chinese firmly oppose.

On the leadership side, Beijing is likely to be preoccupied this year with succession jockeying, as top leaders decide who will get what positions, and who will retire at the Party Congress, and in the changeover in government positions that will follow next spring. This preoccupation is likely to translate into a cautious and defensive approach on most policy issues. It probably also translates into a persistent nationalist foreign policy, as each of the contenders in the succession context will be obliged to avoid any hint of being soft on the United States.

Taiwan also remains the focus of China's military modernization programs. Over the past year, Beijing's military training exercises have taken on an increasingly real-world focus, emphasizing rigorous practice and operational capabilities, and improving the military's actual ability to use force. This is aimed not only at Taiwan, but at increasing the risk to the United States itself in any future Taiwan contingency. China also continues to upgrade and expand the conventional short-range ballistic missile force it has arrayed against Taiwan.

Finally, Mr. Chairman, let me say that with regard to North Korea, the suspension last year of engagement between Pyongyang, Seoul, and Washington reinforced the concerns I cited last year about Kim Jong Il's intentions towards us and our allies in Northeast Asia. His reluctance to pursue a constructive dialogue with the South, or to undertake meaningful reforms suggests that he remains focused on maintaining internal control at the expense of addressing the fundamental economic failures that keep the North Koreans mired in poverty, and pose a long-term threat to the country's stability.

North Korea's large standing army continues to be a primary claimant on scarce resources, and we see no evidence that Pyongyang has abandoned its goal of eventual reunification of the peninsula under the North's control.

Mr. Chairman, I skipped some things, and I'll end there, because I think we want to move to questions as soon as you can. I wonder, Mr. Chairman, if I can just respond for a minute to both of your opening statements on the whole terrorism issue and how we proceed ahead, because I think it's important. And you get to speak to the American people—so do I—and I think it's important that they hear us on this question.

We welcome the committee's review of our record on terrorism. It's important we have a record. It is a record of discipline, strategy, focus and action. We are proud of that record. We have been at war with Al Qaeda for over five years. Our collective successes inside Afghanistan bear a reflection of the importance we attach to the problem, and a reflection of a demonstrated commitment to expanding our human assets, technical operations, fused intelligence, and seamless cooperation with the military. These are things we have been working on very hard over the last five years.

During the millennium threat, we told the president of the United States that there would be between 5 and 15 attacks against American interests both here and overseas. None of these attacks occurred—primarily because of the result of heroic effort on the part of the FBI and the CIA inside the United States and overseas to ensure that those attacks were not successful.

A year later the *Cole* was bombed. We lost a battle there. Part of the problem that we need to address as you look at this is not only to assess what we can do unilaterally, or in conjunction with our military and law enforcement colleagues, but the countries out there who have often deflected us, or have not recognized there was a terrorism problem, who didn't help us solve problems that we could not solve simply on our own. In the last spring and summer we saw—in the spring and summer of 2001— again we saw spectacular threat reporting about massive casualties against the United States. These threat reportings had very little texture with regard to what was occurring inside the United States. We again launched a massive disruption effort. We know that we stopped three or four American facilities from being bombed overseas. We know we saved many American lives. We never had the texture that said the date, time and place of the event inside the United States would result in September 11. It was not the result of the failure of attention and discipline and focus and consistent effort, and the American people need to understand that.

What Tom Ridge is doing today in protecting the homeland, in thinking about our Border Patrol policies, our visa policies, the relationship between all our organizations—airport security—all of these things must be in place—intelligence will never give you 100 percent predictive capability on terrorist events. This committee has worked diligently over the last five years, and the American people need to understand that with the resources and authorities and priorities the men and women of the FBI and the CIA performed heroically. Whatever shortcomings we may have, we owe it to the country to look at ourselves honestly and programmatically. But when people use the word "failure"—"failure" means no focus, no attention, no discipline—and those were not present in what either we or the FBI did here and around the world. And we will continue to work at it. But when the information or the secret isn't available, you need to make sure your backside is protected. You need to make sure there is a security regime in place that gives you the prospect of succeeding—and that's what we all need to work on together.

The decision of the president to go inside the sanctuary and take the war to the Taliban and Al Qaeda may be the most significant thing that happened, because all of this preparation has resulted in destroying that sanctuary, even as we chase everybody around the world. We have disrupted numerous terrorist acts since September 11, and we will continue to do so with the FBI. And we welcome the committee's review. It is important for the American people. But how we paint it is equally important, because they need to know that there are competent men and women who risk their lives and undertake heroic risks to protect them. Thank you, Mr. Chairman. Thank you, Mr. Vice Chairman.

CIA Medals and What They Signify

Distinguished Career Intelligence Medal   For service reflecting a pattern of increasing levels of responsibility or increasingly strategic impact and with distinctly exceptional achievements.

Distinguished Intelligence Cross   For a voluntary act or acts of extraordinary heroism involving the acceptance of existing dangers with conspicuous fortitude and exemplary courage.

Distinguished Intelligence Medal   For performance of outstanding services for achievement of a distinctly exceptional nature in a duty or responsibility.

Intelligence Star   For a voluntary act or acts of courage performed under hazardous conditions or for outstanding achievements or services tendered with distinction under conditions of grave risk.

Intelligence Medal of Merit   For the performance of especially meritorious service or for an act of achievement conspicuously above normal duties.

Career Intelligence Medal   For a cumulative record of service which reflects exceptional achievement.

Intelligence Commendation Medal   For the performance of especially commendable service or for an act of achievement significantly above normal duties which results in an important contribution to the Mission of the agency.

Exceptional Service Medallion   For injury or death resulting from service in an area of hazard.

Gold Retirement Medallion   For a career of 35 years or more with the agency.

Silver Retirement Medallion   For a career of 25 years or more with the agency.

Bronze Retirement Medallion   For a career of more than 15 years but less than 25 years with the agency.

Foreign Terrorist Organizations

The following list was released by the Office of the Coordinator for Counterterrorism, U.S. Department of State, October 8, 1997. You may have seen some of these groups mentioned in the news. For reference, this is a basic list. Greater details can be found on the Loyola University website and the Counterintelligence website (listed at the end of this appendix).

- **Abu Nidal Organization (ANO)**   Militant Palestinian group that split from the PLO in 1974. It has carried out terrorist acts in 20 countries—including the United States, United Kingdom, and Israel—claiming 900 lives.

- **Abu Sayyaf Group (ASG)**   Islamic group fighting for an Islamic state on the island of Mindanao in the Philippines.

- **Armed Islamic Group (GIA)**   Islamic extremist group fighting to replace the current regime in Algeria with an Islamic state.

- **Aum Shinrikyo (Aum)**   Japanese religious sect. Carried out Sarin gas attacks in the city of Matsumoto, Japan in 1994.

- **Euzkadi Ta Askatasuna (ETA)**   Basque group fighting Spain for an independent Basque state.

◆ **Democratic Front for the Liberation of Palestine-Hawatmeh Faction (DFLP)** Marxist-Leninist group supporting the birth of a Palestinian state through revolt of the masses.

◆ **HAMAS (Islamic Resistance Movement)** Outgrowth of the Muslim Brotherhood. Believes in establishing a Palestinian state through violent means. Known for its suicide bombers.

◆ **Harakat ul-Ansar (HUA)** Islamic group based in Pakistan and operating in Kashmir against Indian troops.

◆ **Hizballah (Party of God)** Group of Lebanaese Shi'ite Muslims fighting Israel since the 1982 Lebanon War.

◆ **Gama'a al-Islamiyya (Islamic Group, IG)** Militant Islamic group seeking Islamic rule in Egypt by force. The leader of this group was arrested for the 1993 World Trade Center bombing.

◆ **Japanese Red Army (JRA)** International terrorist group dedicated to the overthrow of the Japanese government and world revolution. The leader lives in Lebanon and supports militant Islamic causes.

◆ **al-Jihad** Militant Islamic group operating in Egypt against the Egyptian government, as well as Christian, Israeli, and Western targets on Egyptian soil.

◆ **Kach** Radical Israeli group seeking the overthrow of the Israeli government and restoration of the biblical state of Israel.

◆ **Kahane Chai** Offshoot of Kach (see previous entry).

◆ **Khmer Rouge** Radical Cambodian political group. Their attempt to purify the "Khmer race" resulted in millions dead.

◆ **Kurdistan Workers' Party (PKK)** Communist group of Turkish Kurds seeking an independent Kurd state in southeastern Turkey.

◆ **Liberation Tigers of Tamil Eelam (LTTE)** Revolutionaries in Sri Lanka.

◆ **Manuel Rodriguez Patriotic Front Dissidents (FPMR/D)** Armed wing of the Chilean Communist Party; it has attacked U.S. businesses in Chile, mostly fast food restaurants.

◆ **Mujahedin-e Khalq Organization (MEK, MKO)** Radical Iranian revolutionaries based in Iraq.

◆ **National Liberation Army (ELN)** Marxist guerrilla group operating out of Colombia. They kidnap foreign businessmen for ransom.

- **Palestine Islamic Jihad—Shaqaqi Faction (PIJ)**   Militant Palestinians originally based in the Gaza Strip, now operating throughout the Middle East.

- **Palestine Liberation Front—Abu Abbas Faction (PLF)**   Conducts attacks against Israel. Attacked cruise ship *Achille Lauro* in 1985, murdering U.S. citizen Leon Klinghoffer.

- **Popular Front for the Liberation of Palestine (PFLP)**   Group based in Syria, Lebanon, and Israel. They attack Israeli and moderate Arab targets.

- **Popular Front for the Liberation of Palestine-General Command (PFLP-GC)**   Based in Syria and active since 1968. Believes in the violent destruction of Israel.

- **Revolutionary Armed Forces of Colombia (FARC)**   Military wing of the Colombian Communist Party, which has, since 1964, committed terrorist acts against Colombian targets.

- **Revolutionary Organization 17 November (17 November)**   Based in Greece and named after the 1973 student uprising in Athens, this group supports radical causes in Greece through assassinations and bombings.

- **Revolutionary People's Liberation Party/Front (DHKP/C)**   Offshoot of the Turkish People's Liberation Party/Front. This radical anti-U.S. group attacks Turkish military targets (as well as U.S. targets during the Gulf War).

- **Revolutionary People's Struggle (ELA)**   Greek leftist group. Bombs the Greek government and economic targets.

- **Shining Path (Sendero Luminoso, SL)**   Maoist group in Peru. Conducts bombings and assassinations. Has claimed 30,000 lives in Peru.

- **Tupac Amaru Revolutionary Movement (MRTA)**   Radical Peruvian group seeking to rid Peru of imperialism through kidnapping, assassinations and commando-style military operations.

To learn more about Terrorism and Counterterrorism check into the Loyola University website at www.loyola.edu/dept/politics/intel.html#govt. It is one of the most comprehensive sources and archives available. The following list provides just a few samples of the intelligence information that you can research on the site, and additional reports are added regularly:

- Combating Terrorism: Threat and Risk Assessments Can Help Prioritize and Target Program Investments (GAO Report, April 1998).

- Combating Terrorism: Need for Comprehensive Threat and Risk Assessments of Chemical and Biological Attacks (GAO/NSIAD-99-163).

- Foreign Terrorist Organizations, 1999, via U.S. Department of State.

- Heritage Foundation Library on Intelligence/Counter-Terrorism.

- National Commission on Terrorism Report, 2000 (pdf, 3.2 mb).

- Patterns of Global Terrorism, 1996, 1997, 1998, 1999, 2000, via State Department.

- Public Health Emergency Preparedness and Response Site (Centers for Disease Control).

- Terrorism and Intelligence Operations, before Joint Economic Committee, May 20, 1998.

- Toward a National Strategy for Combating Terrorism, Advisory Panel to Assess Domestic Response Capabilities for Terrorism Involving Weapons of Mass Destruction Second Annual Report to Congress, Dec. 2000.

Intelligence Agencies Around the Globe

The following tables organize intelligence agencies around the world according to the kind of intelligence they focus on. Although the list isn't comprehensive, it is intended to give readers a sense of the number and kinds of agencies various countries have. Some agencies appear in more than one table because they are responsible for more than one kind of intelligence.

Offensive Domestic Counterintelligence Operations

Acronym	Name	Country
AVH	Allavedelmi Hatosag	Hungary
CSIS	Canadian Security Intelligence Service	Canada
DS	Durzhavna Sigurnost	Bulgaria
DGSE	Direction Generale de Securite Exterieure	France
FBI	Federal Bureau of Investigation	U.S.
FSZA	Federal Directorate of Intelligence Services	Czech.
MSS	Ministry of State Security	China
PSIA	Public Security Investigation Agency	China

continues

Offensive Domestic Counterintelligence Operations   (continued)

Acronym	Name	Country
SHIN BETH	Sherut Bitachon Klali	Israel
SB	Sluzba Bezpiecezenstwa	Poland
SISDE	Servizio Informazioni Generali e Sicurezza	Italy
SISMI	Servizio perle Informazioni e la Sicurezza Militaire	Italy
Special Branch	Scotland Yard	U.K.
SS	Security Service	U.K.

Offensive Counterintelligence Foreign-Operations Agencies

Acronym	Name	Country
AVH	Allavedelmi Hatosag	Hungary
CSIS	Canadian Security Intelligence Service	Canada
CIA	Central Intelligence Agency	U.S.
DGSE	Direction Generale de la Securite Exterieure	France
HSR	Hlavni Sprava Rozvedky	Czech.
ILD	International Liaison Department	China
NCNA	New China News Agency	China
PSIA	Public Service Investigation Agency	Japan
SHIN BETH	Sherut Bitachon Klali	Israel
SB	Sluzba Bezpiecezenstwa	Poland
SISDE	Servizio Informazioni Generali e Sicurezza	Italy
Special Branch	Scotland Yard	U.K.
SIS	Secret Intelligence Service	U.K.

Principle Human Foreign Intelligence Collection (HUMINT)

Acronym	Name	Country
AVH	Allavedelmi Hatosag	Hungary
BND	Bundesnacrichtendienst	West Germany
CIA	Central Intelligence Agency	U.S.

Acronym	Name	Country
DIA	Defense Intelligence Agency	U.S.
CSIS	Canadian Security Service	Canada
DGSE	Direction Generale de la Securite Exterieure	France
ILD	International Liaison Department	China
Mossad	Mossad Letafkidim Meouychadim	Israel
Naicho	Cabinet Research Office	Japan
SIS	Secret Intelligence Service	U.K.
SISDE	Servizio Informazioni Generali e Sicurezza	Italy
SISMI	Servizio perle Informazioni e la Sicurezza Militaire	Italy

Non-SIGINT Analysis Organizations

Acronym	Name	Country
AMAN	Agaf Modiin	Israel
CIA	Central Intelligence Agency	U.S.
DIA	Defense Intelligence Agency	U.S.
DGSE	Direction Generale de la Securite Exterieure	France
FIB	Foreign Intelligence Bureau	Canada
HSR	Hlavni Sprava Rozvedky	Czech.
Mossad	Mossad Letafkidim Meouychadim	Israel
Naicho	Cabinet Research Office	Japan
RI	Research Institutes	China
SIS	Secret Intelligence Service	U.K.
SISDE	Servizio Informazioni Generali e Sicurezza	Italy
SISMI	Servizio perle Informazioni e la Sicurezza Militaire	Italy

SIGINT Collection Organizations

Acronym	Name	Country
AMAN	Agaf Modiin	Israel
Chobetsu	Ground Self-Defense Forces Division	Israel

continues

SIGINT Collection Organizations (continued)

Acronym	Name	Country
CSE	Communications Security Establishment	Canada
DGSE	Direction Generale de la Securite Exterieure	France
GCHO	General Communications Headquarters	U.K.
GCR	Groupement de Communications	France
HSR	Hlavni Sprava Rozvedky	Czech.
NSA	National Security Agency	U.S.
SIOS	Secondo Reparto	Italy
SISMI	Servizio perle Informazioni e la Sicurezza Militaire	Italy
TD	Technical Department	China

Imaging and Imaging Analysis Organizations

Acronym	Name	Country
AMAN	Agaf Modiin	Israel
CIA	Central Intelligence Agency	U.S.
DMA	Defense Mapping Agency	U.S.
ID	Intelligence Division	Japan
JARIC	Joint Air Reconnaissance Intelligence Centre	U.K.
MID	Military Intelligence Department	China
Nibetsu	Ground Self-Defense Forces	Japan
NRO	National Reconnaissance Organization	U.S.

Covert Action Agencies

Acronym	Name	Country
CIA	Central Intelligence Agency	U.S.
CSIS	Canadian Security Intelligence Service	Canada
DGSE	Direction General de la Securite Exterieure	France
HSR	Hlavni Sprava Rozvedky	Czech.
ILD	International Liaison Department	China

Acronym	Name	Country
Mossad	Mossad Letafkidim Meouychadim	Israel
SIS	Secret Intelligence Service	U.K.
SISDE	Servizio Informazioni Generali e Sicurezza	Italy
SISMI	Servizio perle Informazioni e la Sicurezza Militaire	Italy
UFWD	United Front Work Department	China

Military Intelligence Collection Organizations

Acronym	Name	Country
AMAN	Agaf Modiin	Israel
DIA	Defense Intelligence Agency	U.S.
Nibetsu	Ground Self-Defense Forces	Japan
RUMNO	Intelligence Division	Bulgaria
VKF/II	General Staff Directorate II	Hungary
WSW	Woiska Sluzby Wewnetraznei	Poland
Z-II	ZARZAD-II	Poland
ZSGS	Zpravodajska Sprava Generalniko Stabu	Czech.

Security Screening Organizations

Acronym	Name	Country
CSIS	Canadian Security Intelligence Service	Canada
FBI	Federal Bureau of Investigation	U.S.
DGSE	Direction Generale de la Securite Exterieure	France
SISDE	Servizio Informazioni Generali e Sicurezza	Italy
SS	Security Service	U.K.

Counterterrorism Organizations

Acronym	Name	Country
DELTA	Special Forces Detachment	U.S.
CT	Counterterrorism	U.S.
Mossad	Mossad Letafkidim Meouychadim	Israel
SAS	Special Air Service	U.K.
SISDE	Servizio Informazioni Generale e Sicurezza	Italy
SISMI	Servizio perle Informazioni e la Sicurezza Militaire	Italy

Appendix G

Spookspeak: A Glossary

abwehr   German Intelligence Service.

agent   A person recruited by CIA Officers to provide information and intelligence needed by the United States and, if necessary, to betray their own countries. An agent may also be known as an asset.

analysis   Determining the significance of collected information. Putting information together with other known facts to gauge its intelligence value. To make conclusions based on collected information.

asset   See Agent.

backstopping   Taking steps and arranging information to back up false information given out about a person. This can include placing records and documents at colleges, businesses, public offices and elsewhere so that anyone checking will find the "facts" that they had been given.

bigot list   A term used by some to identify a select group of key people who have access to intelligence reports from or about a particularly sensitive operation or project.

blot out   A rather old term that describes using radio to "blot out" or otherwise interfere with recordings of conversations which makes understanding the recording difficult without use of special electronic equipment.

blowback   Bad publicity. Also known as flap.

bug   Small electronic listening or recording device. Such a device may be placed in an area where valuable information may be recorded and used to obtain information from conversations at meetings, individual phone calls, or other situations. A bug is usually considered an electronic device. Many types have been invented and perfected by the technical experts at the CIA. The FBI also has experts in bugging for investigations of crimes.

Camp Perry   The legendary training base outside Williamsburg, Virginia, where career CIA officer trainees are given courses in many aspects of Intelligence work. These include detecting explosives, surveillance and countersurveillance, and training in a wide variety of conventional and sometimes unconventional weapons. Officer trainees also are taught how to conduct counterterrorism, paramilitary operations, recruit and run agents, and otherwise gain basic training for their CIA careers. Also used for refresher course training. Often called "the Farm," a nickname for this facility.

case officer   A member of an intelligence organization who is responsible for recruiting and handling agents or assets. Sometimes also called an Operations Officer.

Center for the Study of Intelligence   Division of the CIA that maintains the agency's historical materials and promotes the study of intelligence as a legitimate and serious discipline.

CIA   The Central Intelligence Agency was created in 1947 with the signing of the National Security Act by President Harry Truman. The National Security Act charged the Director of Central Intelligence, the DCI, with coordinating the nation's intelligence activities and correlating, evaluating, and disseminating intelligence that affects national security. The CIA is an independent agency responsible to the President through the DCI and accountable to the American people through the intelligence oversight committees of the U.S. Congress

clandestine   Secret, secretly.

clandestine operations   Operations carried out in secret, or without general public knowledge. Sometimes referred to as undercover or covert operations.

classification   A division of sensitive intelligence, military, or policy information that usually includes three levels: Confidential, Secret, and Top Secret.

classified documents   Documents, maps, and information that has been classified by a government primarily for its importance to that government. This is the type of secret information that often has value to U.S. leaders and is the target of CIA activities in many parts of the world, especially in foreign countries viewed as adversaries or potential threats to America.

collect   Acquire information.

commercial cover   A protective device whereby a person is given a job and title with a business or other organization and uses that position to hide his or her real work as an intelligence operative. In such cases the person does not have the benefit of Diplomatic immunity.

The Company   Nickname for the CIA.

confidential   The lowest security classification, defined as information the unauthorized disclosure of which reasonably could be expected to cause damage to the national security.

consumer   Client who obtains information from the intelligence-gathering service. Basically this is the person or organization that receives intelligence and uses it.

contract employee   Most members of the CIA are full-time staff employees, but some specialists from the military or with expertise in needed certain fields may be hired under contract. Often military officers are assigned to the CIA for specific projects and tours of duty.

counterintelligence   Activities undertaken by an agency or organization to thwart or foil efforts by hostile intelligence services or individuals to penetrate a country's or organization's intelligence service, files, and operations. This includes the penetration of a foreign service with a "mole" or agent who reports to U.S. Intelligence, CIA, or other, on the work of or activities of the hostile government service.

cover   A protective guise or façade given or assumed by an individual or activity to conceal the true nature of the person or organization. For example, an intelligence operative may have credentials and identification as a teacher, student, worker for another government agency, a business, or other activity than his/her true intelligence work.

covert action   A clandestine activity designed to influence events in foreign countries without the U.S. or CIA or other Intelligence agency role being known. Such actions can range from placement of propaganda in media to attempts to overthrow a government that is deemed unfriendly to this country.

cowboy   An unflattering term that denotes an intelligence person who defies rules, regulations, and convention and conducts himself in an unprofessional, flamboyant way. Otherwise called a "loose cannon".

cryptonyms   Code names. Sometimes called "crypts" for short.

current intelligence   Looks at day-to-day events.

dead drop   Basically, a place where a Case Officer and Agent agree to leave or deposit messages, film, or other material that is to be picked up by the other. It may include directives, payments, and necessary communications. The objective is to leave and retrieve information somewhere that is accessible and without having to meet in person with the risk of being observed.

debriefing   The word used to cover questioning of people with possible worthwhile intelligence information that can range from asking questions of business people who have traveled to foreign countries to interrogating defectors or captured spies.

debug   A term that describes the finding and eliminating of secret recording devices.

defector   A person who has repudiated his own country and citizenship and provides information of intelligence value to another country. There may be defectors who leave their country to be given new names, identification, and even a job in the country whose intelligence service has recruited them to become agents and, therefore, traitors to their homeland.

Defense Intelligence Agency   The coordinating agency in the Defense Department that reports to the Secretary of Defense with intelligence collected from all military services, but also is subject to coordinating authority of the DCI.

Deputy Director for Intelligence   The head of the CIA's analytic directorate, which evaluates and summarizes raw intelligence reports.

Deputy Director of Central Intelligence   Person who assists the Director in his duties as head of the CIA and the Intelligence Community and exercises the powers of the Director when the Director's position is vacant or in the Director's absence or disability.

Deputy Director of Operations   The head of the CIA's clandestine branch, known as the Directorate of Operations. This person manages the CIA stations abroad and also covert operations and assists in other sensitive intelligence collecting abroad.

diplomatic immunity   Immunity from criminal prosecution on foreign soil granted to diplomats and key employees of government agencies.

direction finder   Device that locates the source of electronic emissions using triangulation.

Directorate of Intelligence   The analytical branch of the CIA, responsible for the production and dissemination of all-source intelligence analysis on key foreign issues.

Directorate of Operations   Branch of the CIA that is responsible for the clandestine collection of foreign intelligence.

Directorate of Science and Technology   Branch of the CIA that creates and applies innovative technology in support of the intelligence collection mission.

Director of Central Intelligence   The top person who oversees and coordinates all U.S. intelligence agencies, heads the Central Intelligence Agency, and is usually considered the President's chief intelligence advisor.

disinformation   False information purposefully disseminated to mislead.

dissem   A document that may be disseminated to consumers.

dissemination   Distribution of intelligence to consumers via oral, written, or electronic methods.

dumping   A term used to describe sending information or messages in short electronic bursts.

espionage   Most commonly, clandestine intelligence collection. Also can be taken to mean destructive activities against an organization or country. Some forms of espionage are used by commercial companies against their competition, especially in foreign business situations.

estimate   An intelligence product that analyzes and assesses future potential developments and courses of action for review by an intelligence consumer.

Estimative Intelligence   Looks at what might be or what might happen.

evaluation   The determination of probable validity and utility of intelligence information, which is subjective and some believe is merely a "best bet" or guesstimate.

Executive Director of the Central Intelligence Agency   The EXDIR manages the CIA on a day-to-day basis.

finding   A written determination by the President of the United States that is required before covert action may be undertaken. This is usually a brief written directive in which the President states that he "finds" a certain "covert action" is important for national security.

flap   Bad publicity. Also known as blowback.

foreign intelligence   Intelligence concerning or involving areas and activities outside the United States.

front   An organization that serves to provide a legend or disguised identification for a CIA operation or project.

Human Source Intelligence   Also called HUMINT, this is intelligence collected by means of agents or informers. There has been an ongoing debate about the loss of HUMINT because of a focus on using satellite and high tech intelligence and not investing in the use of human sources on the ground.

imagery   Representations of objects produced on film, optical displays, radar or other electronic means for viewing, interpretation, and analysis.

information   Unevaluated raw data which has not been subjected to analysis and evaluation of sources and content.

intelligence   The finished product of collection, evaluation, and analysis of information that is useable by the recipient. See difference between intelligence and information, above.

Intelligence Community   IC, generally used as a term referring to all the U.S. intelligence agencies and employees, of which the Director of Central Intelligence is the senior member.

Intelligence Finding   Order by the President of the United States to the CIA to perform a covert action.

Langley   Location of CIA headquarters in Virginia (suburban Washington, D.C.).

laundering   A process of hiding sources, transmittal, and persons involved in financial matters and transfers of money for intelligence, and today more commonly for criminal purposes, primarily associated with terrorist activity and narcotics trafficking.

legend   A cover story made up to provide provable background about an intelligence officer, which can include college attended, home town, family connections, all of which may be fabricated and memorized to become a different person, i.e. "a legend in one's own time," so to speak.

light disguise   A simple disguise of wigs and glasses, change of clothing, superficial cover, and appearance changes.

light legend   Another basic phrase that refers to a superficial cover story of identify and background.

magnum   CIA spy satellite that can eavesdrop on sound signals from earth.

marginalia   Method by which one studies the history of a document, by examining the notes, initials etc. that have been jotted in the margins.

mole   A person inside a government agency, usually an intelligence agency, who is obtaining information about that organization's secrets and activities.

molehunting   See Counterintelligence.

Mossad   The Israeli Intelligence agency.

National Foreign Intelligence Board (**NFIB**)   Made up of the heads of all U.S. Intelligence agencies. In effect, this acts as a "Board of Directors" for U.S. Intelligence and is chaired by the DCI. Members include representatives from CIA, NSA, DIA, NRO and the intelligence services of the Navy, Army, Air Force, Marines, FBI and Departments of State, Energy and Treasury.

National Imagery and Mapping Agency (**NIMA**)   Provides maps of the world from satellite collection, both government and commercial sources.

National Intelligence Daily (**NID**)   A top-secret summary of the main intelligence items from the previous days, with a very limited distribution.

National Intelligence Estimate (**NIE**)   A formal written forecast of future potential events in countries or of various intelligence, military, or economical problems. It presents the best collective judgement of all the U.S. intelligence agencies.

National Reconnaissance Office (**NRO**)   A lower-profile agency responsible for satellite and aerial overhead intelligence gathering. It reports to the Secretary of Defense with coordination by the DCI.

National Security Council (**NSC**)   Includes the President and his senior foreign policy makers, with the DCI and Chairman of the Joint Chiefs of Staff as advisors.

noforn   Document that is not to be seen by foreign eyes.

nonofficial cover   Intelligence officers who pose as entrepreneurs or employees of private companies to hide their real activities. Also called Commercial cover, this is riskier than when using a cover of another U.S. government agency, because it provides no diplomatic immunity.

officer   A member of an intelligence organization who is responsible for recruiting and handling agents or assets. Sometimes also called an operations officer.

open sources   Refers to news, books, public information of all kinds that is available to intelligence officers as well as the public.

operations officer   See Case officer.

paramilitary operations   Operations undertaken by military forces separate from the regular armed forces of a nation. Often used in an effort to hide source of control.

PHOTINT   Photographic intelligence.

piano   Clandestine radio.

plausible denial   A nice term that basically means if you get caught, we can disown you and deny that you work for the CIA, or other Intelligence agency.

President's Daily Brief   Includes the most exclusive and sensitive items which are summarized succinctly and sent to the President and a highly select list of leaders and White House aides.

processing   Development of collected raw information of possible intelligence value to make it useable for analysis and into a finished intelligence product.

product   The finished intelligence, which is disseminated to those who need it for decision making.

reconnaissance   Observation or patrol missions undertaken to acquire, by various means, useful information about a target of intelligence interest. (The Watergate break-in was *not* one.)

renegade   A person who operates outside of conventional and approved procedures. Also defined by some as a person who has turned on his country in any of a variety of ways.

Research Intelligence   An in-depth study of a specific issue.

Scientific and Technical Intelligence   Information on foreign technologies.

secret   A security classification, second from the lowest, defined as information the unauthorized disclosure of which reasonably could be expected to cause serious damage to the national security. Secret info is more sensitive than Confidential info, but not as sensitive as Top Secret info.

secrets   Generally, anything that a person or organization considers of enough importance that they do not want others to know about them. Various governments and agencies have different levels of secret classifications. These may include Classified, usually the lowest level for keeping control to selected individuals, Secret, Top Secret, Eyes-Only and other special names for specific areas, including nuclear.

security   Measures taken to protect sensitive activities, data, and personal against compromise by foreign intelligence organizations or anyone including business competitors.

Signals Intelligence   Called SIGINT, this is intelligence gained or derived from the interception, processing and analysis of various communications including electronic emissions or telemetry.

Special National Intelligence Estimates (SNIE)   Short formal evaluations which are completed in days or weeks on key topics of urgent national security interest.

spook   A nickname for an Intelligence Officer, operative, or person.

strategic intelligence   Intelligence supporting national and international level formulation of policy, plans and strategy by top government leaders.

sweep   A search for bugs, i.e. concealed electronic listening devices in a building, vehicle or location that are used to transmit conversation or other information to an enemy. Embassies and CIA offices overseas must be swept regularly to prevent bugging.

target   A person, place, or thing against which intelligence operations are organized and directed.

telemetry   Electronic signals given off by missiles, rockets, vehicles, and machinery during operational testing or use.

top secret   Classified information that includes such material of which the disclosure could be expected to cause exceptionally grave damage to national security. Top secret information is more sensitive than either confidential info or secret info.

tradecraft   The methods used by CIA officers, gained from training and experience, to do their special Intelligence work.

undercover operations   See Clandestine operations.

vortex   CIA spy satellite that can listen in to communications on earth from 22,000 miles up.

Warning Intelligence   Gives notice to our policy makers that something urgent might happen that may require their immediate attention.

(See Appendix A for definitions of abbreviations and acronyms.)

Bibliography

History of the Agency

Breckinridge, Scott D. *The CIA and the U.S. Intelligence System*. Boulder, Colorado: Westview Press, 1986.

Cline, Ray. *The CIA: Reality vs Myth: The Evolution of the Agency from Roosevelt to Reagan*. (Revised edition of *The CIA under Reagan, Bush and Casey*). Washington, D.C.: Acropolis Books, 1982.

Colby, William E. *Honorable Men: My Life in the CIA*. New York: Simon and Schuster, 1978.

———. *The CIA Under Reagan, Bush and Casey*. Washington, D.C.: Acropolis Books, 1981.

———. *Secrets, Spies and Scholars: Blueprint of the Essential CIA*. Washington, D.C.: Acropolis Books, 1976.

Darling, Arthur. *The Central Intelligence Agency: An Instrument of Government to 1950*. State College: Pennsylvania State University Press, 1990.

Hersh, Burton. *The Old Boys: The American Elite and the Origins of the CIA.* New York: Charles Scribner's Sons, 1992.

Johnson, Loch K. *The Central Intelligence Agency: History and Documents.* New York: Oxford University Press, 1989.

———. *Secret Agencies.* New Haven, Connecticut: Yale University Press, 1997.

Leary, William M., ed. *The Central Intelligence Agency: History and Documents.* Tuscaloosa, AL: University of Alabama Press, 1984.

Ranelagh, John. *The Agency: The Rise and Decline of the CIA.* New York: Simon and Schuster, 1987.

Rudgers, David F. *Creating the Secret State: The Origins of the Central Intelligence Agency, 1943–1947.* Lawrence, KS: University of Kansas Press, 2000.

Thomas, Evan. *The Very Best Men—Four Who Dared: The Early Years of the CIA.* New York: Simon and Schuster, 1995.

Troy, Thomas F. *Donovan and the CIA: A History of the Establishment of the Central Intelligence Agency.* Frederick, MD: University Publications of America, 1981.

———. *Wild Bill and Intrepid, Donovan, Stephenson, and the Origin of the CIA.* New Haven: Yale University Press, 1996.

Turner, Stansfield. *Secrecy and Democracy—The CIA in Transition.* Boston: Houghton Mifflin, 1985.

United States Department of State. *Foreign Relations of the United States, 1945–1950, Emergence of the Intelligence Establishment.* Washington, D.C.: GPO, 1996.

Waller, John H. *The Unseen War in Europe: Espionage and Conspiracy in the Second World War.* New York: Random House, 1996.

Warner, Michael, ed. *The CIA Under Harry Truman.* Washington, D.C.: Center for the Study of Intelligence, 1994.

Weber, Ralph Edward, ed. *Spymasters: Ten CIA Officers in Their Own Words.* Wilmington, Del: SR Books, 1999.

Westerfield, H. Bradford, ed. *Inside the CIA's Private World: Declassified Articles from the Agency's Internal Journal, 1955–1992.* New Haven, CT: Yale University Press, 1996.

Winks, Robin. *Cloak and Gown: Scholars in the Secret War, 1939–1961.* New York: William Morrow and Company, Inc., 1987.

Biographies

Agee, Philip. *Inside the Company: CIA Diary.* New York: Stonehill, 1975.

Brown, Anthony Cave. *The Last Hero: Wild Bill Donovan.* New York: Times Books, 1982.

Clarridge, Duane. *A Spy for All Seasons.* New York: Simon and Schuster, 1997.

Gates, Robert M. *From the Shadows: The Ultimate Insider's Story of Five Presidents and How They Won the Cold War.* New York: Simon and Schuster, 1996.

Gilligan, Tom. *CIA Life: 10,000 Days with the Agency.* Connecticut: Foreign Intelligence Press, 1991.

Grose, Peter. *Gentleman Spy: The Life of Allen Dulles.* Boston: Houghton Mifflin, 1994.

Kalugin, Oleg. *The First Directorate: My 32 years in Intelligence and Espionage Against the West.* New York: St. Martin's Press, 1994.

Lamphere, Robert J., and Thomas Shachtman. *The FBI-KGB War: A Special Agent's Story.* New York: Random House, 1986.

Mangold, Tom. *Cold Warrior: James Jesus Angleton: The CIA's Master Spy Hunter.* New York: Simon and Schuster, 1991.

Mendez, Antonio J. *The Master of Disguise: My Secret Life in the CIA*. New York: Morrow, 1999.

Montague, Ludwell Lee. *General Walter Bedell Smith as Director of Central Intelligence*. University Park, PA: The Pennsylvania State University Press, 1992.

Morgan, Ted. *A Covert Life: Jay Lovestone: Communist, Anti-Communist, and Spymaster*. New York: Random House, 1999.

Persico, Joseph E. *Casey: From the OSS to the CIA*. New York: Viking Penguin, 1990.

Phillips, David Atlee. *The Night Watch: 25 Years of Peculiar Service*. New York: Atheneum, 1977.

Powers, Thomas. *The Man Who Kept the Secrets: Richard Helms and the CIA*. New York: Alfred A. Knopf, 1979.

Richelson, Jeffrey T. *The U.S. Intelligence Community*. Cambridge, Massachusetts: Ballinger, 1985.

Wise, David. *The Spy Who Got Away: The Inside Story of Edward Lee Howard, the CIA Agent Who Betrayed His Country's Secrets and Escaped to Moscow*. New York: Random House, 1988.

Wolf, Markus. *Man Without a Face: The Autobiography of Communism's Great Spymaster*. New York: Random House, 1997.

Women in Intelligence

Adams-Deschamps, Helene. *Spyglass: An Autobiography*. New York: Holt, 1995.

Bancroft, Mary. *Autobiography of a Spy*. New York: Morrow, 1983.

Lovell, Mary S. *Cast No Shadow: The Life of the American Spy Who Changed the Course of World War II*. New York: Pantheon Books, 1992.

MacDonald, Elizabeth P. *Undercover Girl*. New York: Macmillan, 1947.

McIntosh, Elizabeth P. *Sisterhood of Spies: The Women of the OSS*. Annapolis, MD: Naval Institute Press, 1998.

Rossiter, Margaret. *Women in the Resistance*. New York: Praeger, 1991.

Operations

Alleged Assassination Plots Involving Foreign Leaders: An Interim Report of the Select Committee to Study Governmental Operations with Respect to Intelligence Activities, U.S. Senate. Washington, D.C.: United States Government Printing Office, 1975.

Allen, Thomas, and Norman Polmar. *Merchants of Treason*. New York: Delacorte Press, 1988.

Bakeless, John. *Turncoats, Traitors and Heroes*. Philadelphia, Pennsylvania: Lippincott, 1959.

Barron, John. *Breaking the Ring*. Boston: Houghton Mifflin, 1987.

Blum, Howard. *I Pledge Allegiance*. New York: Simon and Schuster, 1987.

Bowart, Walter. *Operation Mind Control*. New York: Dell Publishing, 1978.

Colby, William E., with James McCarger. *Lost Victory: A Firsthand Account of America's Sixteen-Year Involvement in Vietnam*. Chicago: Contemporary Books, 1989.

Corn, David. *Blond Ghost: Ted Shackley and the CIA Crusades*. New York: Simon and Schuster, 1994.

Conboy, Kenneth J. *Feet to the Fire: CIA Covert Operations in Indonesia, 1957–1958*. Annapolis, MD: Naval Institute Press, 1999.

Davis, Charles O. *Across the Mekong: The True Story of an Air America Helicopter Pilot*. Hildesigns Press, 2000.

Dobson, Christopher, and Ronald Payne. *War Without End: The Terrorists, An Intelligence Dossier.* London: Harrap Limited, 1986.

Earley, Pete. *Confessions of a Spy: The Real Story of Aldrich Ames.* New York: G.P. Putnam's Sons, 1997.

Felix, Christopher. *A Short Course in the Secret War, Second Edition.* New York: Dell Books, 1988.

Godson, Roy. *Dirty Tricks or Trump Cards: U.S. Covert Action and Counterintelligence.* Washington: Brassey's, 1996.

Haynes, John Earl, and Harvey Klehr. *Venona: Decoding Soviet Espionage in America.* New Haven, Conn: Yale University Press, 1999.

Holober, Frank. *Raiders of the China Coast: CIA Covert Operations During the Korean War (Special Warfare Series).* Annapolis, MD: Naval Institute Press, 1999.

Hood, William. *The Mole.* New York: W. W. Norton, 1987.

———. *Mole: The True Story of the First Russian Intelligence Officer Recruited by the CIA.* New York: W.W. Norton, 1982.

Ignatius, David. *Agents of Innocence.* New York: W. W. Norton, 1987.

Kahn, David. *The Codebreakers: The Story of Secret Writing.* New York: MacMillan Publishing Co., Inc., 1967.

Kessler, Ronald. *Escape from the CIA.* New York: Pocket Books, 1991.

Knott, Stephan F. *Secret and Sanctioned: Covert Operations and the American Presidency.* New York: Oxford University Press, 1996.

Lindsey, Robert. *The Falcon and the Snowman: A True Story of Friendship and Espionage.* London: Jonathan Cape, 1980.

Martin, David C. *Wilderness of Mirrors.* New York: Bantam Books, Inc., 1980.

Meyer, Cord. *Facing Reality: From World Federalism to the CIA.* New York: Harper & Row, 1980.

Milano, James V. *Soldiers, Spies and the Rat Line: America's Undeclared War Against the Soviets.* Washington: Brassey's, 1995.

Miller, Nathan. *Spying for America: The Hidden History of U.S. Intelligence.* New York: Paragon House, 1989.

Murphy, David E., Sergei A. Kondrashev, and George Bailey. *Battleground Berlin: CIA vs. KGB in the Cold War.* New Haven, CT: Yale University Press, 1997.

O'Toole, G. J. A. *Honorable Treachery: A History of Intelligence, Espionage, and Covert Action from the American Revolution to the CIA.* New York: Atlantic Monthly Press, 1991.

Polmar, Norman, and Thomas B. Allen. *Merchants of Treason.* New York: Delacorte, 1988.

———. *Spy Book: The Encyclopedia of Espionage.* New York: Random House, 1998.

Prados, John. *Presidents' Secret Wars: CIA and Pentagon Covert Operations from World War II through Iranscam,* rev. Ed. New York: William Morrow, Co., 1986.

Roosevelt, Kermit. *Countercoup: The Struggle for the Control of Iran.* New York: McGraw-Hill Book Co., 1979.

Rositzke, Harry A. *CIA's Secret Operations: Espionage, Counterespionage, and Covert Action.* Boulder, CO: Westview Press, 1988.

Sakharov, Vladimir. *High Treason.* New York: Ballentine Books, 1981.

Schechter, Jerrold L., and Peter Deriabin. *The Spy Who Saved the World: How a Soviet Colonel Changed the Course of the Cold War.* New York: Scribner's, 1992.

Schlesinger, Stephen, and Stephen Kinzer. *Bitter Fruit: The Untold Story of the American Coup in Guatemala.* New York: Doubleday, 1982.

Sebag-Montefiore, Hugh. *Enigma: The Battle for the Code*. New York: John Wiley & Sons, Inc., 2001.

Shevchencko, Arkady N. *Breaking with Moscow*. New York: Alfred A. Knopf, 1985.

Simon, Jeffrey D. *The Terrorist Trap: America's Experience with Terrorism*. Bloomington and Indianapolis: Indiana University Press, 1994.

Suvorov, Viktor. *Aquarium: The Career and Defection of a Soviet Spy*. London: Harnish Hamilton, 1985.

Warner, Roger. *Backfire: The CIA's Secret War in Laos and Its Links to the Vietnam War*. New York: Simon & Schuster, 1995.

West, Nigel, and Oleg Tsarev. *The Crown Jewels*. London: Harper Collins Publishers, 1998.

Wise, David. *Molehunt: The Secret Search for Traitors That Shattered the CIA*. New York: Random House, 1992.

Woodward, Bob. *Veil: The Secret Wars of the CIA, 1981–1987*. New York: Simon & Schuster, 1987.

Analysis

Adams, Sam. *War of Numbers: An Intelligence Memoir*. South Royalton, Vermont: Steerforth Press, 1994.

Ford, Harold P. *CIA and the Vietnam Policymakers: Three Episodes 1962–1968*. Washington, D.C.: History Staff, Center for the Study of Intelligence, 1998.

Haines, Gerald K., and Robert E. Leggett, eds. *CIA's Analysis of the Soviet Union 1947–1991*. Washington, D.C.: CIA History Staff, Center for the Study of Intelligence, 2001.

Helgerson, John. *Getting to Know the President: CIA Briefings of Presidential Candidates, 1952–1992*. Washington, D.C.: Center for Study of Intelligence, CIA, 1995.

Heuer, Richards J. Jr. *Psychology of Intelligence Analysis*. Washington, D.C.: Center for the Study of Intelligence, 2000.

Katz, Barry M. *Foreign Intelligence: Research and Analysis in the Office of Strategic Services 1942–1945*. Cambridge, MA: Harvard University Press, 1989.

Kennon, Patrick E. *The Twilight of Democracy*. New York: Doubleday, 1995.

Kent, Sherman. *Strategic Intelligence for American World Policy*. Princeton: Princeton University Press, 1966.

Kuhns, Woodrow J. *Assessing the Soviet Threat: The Early Cold War Years*. Washington, D.C.: Center for the Study of Intelligence, 1997.

Laqueur, Walter. *A World of Secrets: The Uses and Limits of Intelligence*. New York: Basic Books, 1985.

MacEachin, Douglas J. *The Final Months of the War with Japan: Signals Intelligence, U.S. Invasion Planning, and the A-Bomb Decision*. Washington, D.C.: History Staff, Center for the Study of Intelligence, 1998.

Prados, John. *The Soviet Estimate: U.S. Intelligence Analysis and Russian Military Strength*. New York: Dial Press, 1982.

Steury, Donald P., ed. *Intentions and Capabilities: Estimates on Soviet Strategic Forces, 1950–1983*. Washington, D.C.: History Staff, Center for the Study of Intelligence, 1996.

———. *Sherman Kent and the Board of National Estimates: Collected Essays*. Washington, D.C.: History Staff, Center for the Study of Intelligence, 1996.

Technology

Bamford, James. *The Puzzle Palace: A Report on America's Most Secret Agency*. Boston: Houghton Mifflin, 1982.

Beschloss, Michael R. *Mayday: Eisenhower, Khruschev and the U-2 Affair*. New York: Harper & Row, 1986.

Brugioni, Dino. *Eyeball to Eyeball: The Inside Story of the Cuban Missile Crisis.* New York: Random House, 1990.

Burrows, William. *Deep Black: Space Espionage and National Security.* New York: Random House, 1986.

Day, Dwayne, John M. Logsdon, and Brian Latell, eds. *Eye in the Sky: The Story of the Corona Spy Satellites.* Washington, D.C.: Smithsonian Institution Press, 1998.

Johnson, Clarence "Kelly", with Maggie Smith. *More Than My Share of it All.* Washington, D.C.: Smithsonian Institution Press, 1985.

Lashmar, Paul. *Spy Flights of the Cold War.* Great Britain: Sutton Publishing Limited, 1996.

Melton, H. Keith. *The Ultimate Spy Book.* London & New York: Dorling Kindersley, Ltd., 1996.

———. *CIA Special Weapons and Equipment: Spy Devices of the Cold War.* New York: Sterling Publishing, 1993.

Minnery, John. *The CIA Catalog of Clandestine Weapons, Tools, and Gadgets.* Fort Lee, New Jersey: Barricade Books, 1990.

Pedlow, Gregory W., and Donald E. Welzenbach. *The CIA and the U-2 Program, 1954–1974.* Washington, D.C.: History Staff, Center for the Study of Intelligence, 1998.

Peebles, Curtis. *The CORONA Project.* Annapolis: Naval Institute Press, 1997.

Pocock, Chris. *Dragon Lady: The History of the U-2 Spyplane.* Shrewsbury, UK: Airlife Publishing, 1989.

Richelson, Jeffrey T. *America's Secret Eyes in Space: The U.S. Spy Satellite Program.* New York: Harper and Row, 1990.

Rich, Ben R., with Leo Janos. *Skunk Works: A Personal Memoir of My Years at Lockheed.* New York: Little, Brown and Company, 1994.

Ruffner, Kevin, ed. *CORONA: America's First Satellite Program.* Washington, D.C.: CIA History Staff, 1995.

Singh, Simon. *The Code Book: The Evolution of Secrecy from Mary, Queen of Scots to Quantum Cryptography.* New York: Doubleday, 1999.

Sontag, Sherry. *Blind Man's Bluff: The Untold Story of American Submarine Espionage.* New York: Public Affairs, 1998.

General Interest

Alexander, Martin S. *Knowing Your Friends: Intelligence Inside Alliances and Coalitions from 1914 to the Cold War* (Cass Series-Studies in Intelligence). London; Portland, OR: Frank Cass, 1998.

Andrew, Christopher. *For the President's Eyes Only-Secret Intelligence and the American Presidency from Washington to Bush.* New York: Harper Collins Publishers, 1995.

Andrew, Christopher, and Vasili Mitrokhin. *The Sword and the Shield: The Mitrokhin Archive and the Secret History of the KGB.* New York: Basic Books, 1999.

Bath, Alan Harris. *Tracking the Axis Enemy: The Triumph of Anglo-American Naval Intelligence.* Lawrence, Kansas: University Press of Kansas, 1998.

Benson, Michael. *Encyclopedia of the JFK Assassination.* New York: Facts on File, 2002.

Blight, James G., and David A. Welch. *Intelligence and the Cuban Missile Crisis.* London; Portland, OR: Frank Cass, 1998.

Breckinridge, Scott D. *The CIA and the U.S. Intelligence System.* Boulder, CO: Westview Press, 1986.

Dulles, Allen. *The Craft of Intelligence.* New York: Harper and Row, 1963.

Dziak, John J. *Chekisty: A History of the KGB.* Massachusetts: D. C. Heath and Company, 1988.

Fialka, John J. *War By Other Means: Economic Espionage in America*. New York: W. W. Norton & Company, 1997.

Fischer, Ben B. *A Cold War Conundrum: The 1983 Soviet War Scare*. Washington, D.C.: Center for the Study of Intelligence, 1997.

———. *At Cold War's End: U.S. Intelligence on the Soviet Union and Eastern Europe, 1989–1991*. Washington, D.C.: Center for the Study of Intelligence, 1999.

———. *Okhrana: The Paris Operations of the Russian Imperial Police*. Washington, D.C.: Center for the Study of Intelligence, 1997.

Godson, Roy. *United States Intelligence at the Crossroads: Agendas for Reform*. Washington: Brassey's, 1995.

Gordievsky, Oleg, and Christopher Andrew. *KGB, The Inside Story of its Foreign Operations from Lenin to Gorbachev*. New York: Harper Collins, 1990.

Grose, Peter. *Operation Rollback: America's Secret War Behind the Iron Curtain*. Boston: HoughtonMifflin, 2000.

Jeffrey-Jones, Rhodri. *The CIA and American Democracy. New Haven:* Yale University Press, 1991.

Kessler, Ronald. *Inside the CIA*. New York: Pocket Books, 1982.

Koch, Scott, and Brian D. Fila. *Our First Line of Defense: Presidential Reflections*. Washington, D.C.: Center for the Study of Intelligence, 1996.

Kohler, John O. *Stasi: The Untold Story of the East German Secret Police*. Boulder, Colorado: Westview Press, 1999.

Lee, Martin A., and Bruce Shlain. *Acid Dreams: The CIA, LSD and the Sixties Rebellion*. New York: Grove Press, 1985.

Lowenthal, Mark M. *Intelligence: From Secrets to Policy*. Washington: Congressional Quarterly Press, 2000.

Marchetti, Victor L., and John D. Marks. *The CIA and the Cult of Intelligence*. New York: Knopf, 1974.

Marenches, Count de Alexandre. *The Fourth World War: Diplomacy and Espionage in the Age of Terrorism*. New York: William Morrow and Company, 1992.

Marks, John D. *The Search for the "Manchurian Candidate"*. New York: Dell, 1988.

McAuliffe, Mary S. *Cuban Missile Crisis 1962*. Washington, D.C.: Center for the Study of Intelligence, 1992.

Mitrovich, Gregory. *Undermining the Kremlin: America's Strategy to Subvert the Soviet Bloc, 1947–1956*. Ithaca, NY: Cornell, 2000.

Newman, John M. *Oswald and the CIA*. New York: Carroll & Graf, 1995.

O'Toole, G. J. A. *The Encyclopedia of American Intelligence and Espionage*. New York: Facts on File, 1988.

Pedlow, Gregory W., and Donald E. Welzenbach. *The CIA and the U-2 Program 1954–1974*. Washington, D.C.: Center for the Study of Intelligence, 1998.

Pinck, Dan C., Geoffrey M.T. Jones, and Charles T. Pinck. *Stalking the History of the Office of Strategic Services: An OSS Bibliography*. Boston: The OSS/Donovan Press, 2000.

Polmar, Norman, and Thomas B. Allen. *Spy Book: The Encyclopedia of Espionage*. New York: Random House, 1997.

Prados, John. *Keepers of the Keys: A History of the National Security Council from Truman to Bush*. New York: William Morrow & Company, Inc., 1991.

Riebling, Mark. *Wedge: The Secret War Between the FBI and CIA*. New York: Alfred A. Knopf, 1994.

Robarge, David. *Intelligence in the War for Independence*. Washington, D.C.: Center for the Study of Intelligence, 1997.

Rose, P.K. *Black Dispatches: Black American Contributions to Union Intelligence During the Civil War.* Washington, D.C.: Center for Study of Intelligence, 1999.

Shannon, Elaine, and Ann Blackman. *The Spy Next Door: The Extraordinary Secret Life of Robert Philip Hanssen, The Most Damaging FBI Agent in U.S. History.* New York: Little, Brown and Company, 2002.

Shulsky, Abram N. *Silent Warfare.* Washington, D.C.: Brassey's, 1991.

Snider, Britt. *Sharing Secrets with Lawmakers: Congress as a User of Intelligence.* Washington, D.C.: CIA History Staff, Center for the Study of Intelligence, 1997.

Steury, Donald P. *On the Front Lines of the Cold War: Documents on the Intelligence War in Berlin, 1946–1961.* Washington, D.C.: CIA History Staff, Center for the Study of Intelligence, 1999.

Tarrant, V.E. *The Red Orchestra: The Soviet Spy Network Inside Nazi Europe.* New York: John Wiley and Sons, 1995.

Thompson, Robert Smith. *The Missiles of October: The Declassified Story of John F. Kennedy and the Cuban Missile Crisis.* New York: Simon and Schuster, 1992.

Warner, Michael. *The Office of Strategic Services: America's First Intelligence Agency.* Washington, D.C.: CIA History Staff, Center for the Study of Intelligence, 2000.

Watson, Bruce W. *United States Intelligence: An Encyclopedia.* New York: Garland Publishers, 1990.

For Kids

Blassingame, Wyatt. *The U.S. Frogmen of World War II.* New York: Random House, 1964.

Dawidoff, Nicholas. *The Catcher Was a Spy: The Mysterious Life of Moe Berg.* New York: Pantheon Books, 1994.

Edwin, John, and Katherine Bakeless. *Spies of the Revolution*. Philadelphia, PA: Lippincott, 1962.

———. *Confederate Spy Stories*. Philadelphia, PA: Lippincott, 1973.

Ellis, Rafaela. *The Central Intelligence Agency*. New York: Chelsea House, 1988.

Epstein, Sam and Beryl. *The First Book of Codes and Ciphers*. New York: Franklin Watts, 1956.

Fleming, Fergus. *Tales of Real Spies*. EDC Publications, 1998.

Grey, Vivian. *Moe Berg: The Spy Behind Homeplate*. Jewish Publication Society, 1997.

Haswell, Jock. *The Magnet Book of Spies and Spying*. London: Methuen Children's, 1987.

Healey, Tim. *Spies*. London: Macdonald Educational, 1978.

James, Elizabeth, Carol Barkin, and Joel Schick. *How to Keep a Secret: Writing Talking in Code*. New York: Lothrop, Lee & Shepard, 1978.

Kent, Graeme. *Espionage*. London: Batsford, 1947.

Kronenwetter, Michael. *Covert Action*. New York: Franklin Watts, 1991.

Mahoney, M. H. *Women in Espionage: A Biographical Dictionary*. Santa Barbara, CA: ABC-CLIO, 1993.

Megros, Phyllis. *All About Ciphers*. London: Collins, 1943.

Melton, H. Keith. *The Ultimate Spy Book*. New York: DK Publishing, 1996.

O'Toole, G.J.A. *The Encyclopedia of American Intelligence and Espionage*. New York: Facts on File, 1988.

Platt, Richard. *Spy: Discover the Secret World of Espionage from Early Spymasters to the Electronic Surveillance of Today*. New York: Alfred A. Knopf, 1996.

———. *Eyewitness: Spy.* New York: DK Publishing, 2000.

Seth, Ronald. *How Spies Work.* London: G. Bles, 1957.

Surge, Frank. *Famous Spies.* Minneapolis, MN: Lerner Publications, 1969.

Thomas, Paul Bernard. *Secret Messages, How to Read and Write Them.* New York: Alfred A. Knopf, 1928.

Travis, Falcon. *The Spy's Guidebook.* London: Osborne Publishing, 1978.

Travis, Falcon, Judy Hindley, and Colin King. *The Knowhow Book of Spycraft.* London: Osborne Publishing, 1975.

Periodicals

Battaile, Janet. "C.I.A. Says It Ousted Officer After a Search of House Unit's Files." *The New York Times*, June 18, 1979. Regarding CIA Liaison Officer Regis Blahut who allegedly rifled the files of the House Select Committee on Assassinations.

Beinart, Peter, "To Save the CIA." *New York Post*, November 5, 2001, p. 35.

Bimmerle, George. "'Truth' Drugs in Interrogation." *Studies in Intelligence*, Volume 5, Number 2, Spring 1961, pp. A1–A19.

"Bin Laden Faces U.S. Justice: Secret CIA Squad was on his tail for 4 years." *New York Post*, December 24, 2001, p. 4.

"CIA feared overseas Bill kill plot." *The Daily News*, March 31, 2000, p. 23. Story involves plot to kill President Clinton.

Crewdson, John M. "Rockefeller Unit Said to Check Report of CIA Link to Kennedy Assassination." *The New York Times*, March 8, 1975, p. 11.

Crile, George. "The Mafia, the CIA, and Castro." *The Washington Post*, May 16, 1976, p. C4.

———. "The Riddle of AMLASH." *Washington Post Outlook*, May 2, 1976, p. C1.

Day, Dwayne A. "Corona: The Birth of Satellite Reconnaissance." *Military Technical Journal*, June 1997, p.25–27.

DeFrank, Thomas M. "CIA: Worst Attacks Won't Come by Missile." *The Daily News*, January 12, 2002, p. 9.

DeFrank, Thomas M., and Corky Siemaszko. "Farewell at Arlington for CIA officer." *The Daily News*, December 11, 2001, p. 5.

Fensterwald, Bernard, and O'Toole, George. "The CIA and the Man Who Was Not Oswald." *New York Review of Books*, April 3, 1975, p. 24.

"For your eyes only: secret CIA spy toys." *The Daily News*, February 18, 2002, p. 23.

Gordon, Michael R. "C.I.A. Warns That Afghan Factions May Bring Chaos." *The New York Times*, February 21, 2002, p. A5.

Gries, David. "Intelligence in the 1990s." *Studies in Intelligence*, Volume 35, Number 1, Spring 1991, pp. 5–11.

"He Lived and Died a Hero: CIA man buried amid praise for doing 'what was right.'" *New York Post*, December 11, 2001, p. 3.

Horrock, Nicholas M. "CIA Data Show 14-Year Project on Controlling Human Behavior." *The New York Times*, July 21, 1977, p. 1. About the MK/ULTRA mind-control program.

———. "CIA Documents Tell of 1954 Project to Create Involuntary Assassins." *The New York Times*, February 9, 1978. Real-life Manchurian Candidates?

"Invisible Ink: The Spy's Favourite Solution." *Eye Spy*, Issue 6, 2001, pp. 31–33, 82.

Kutta, Timothy J. "SR-71 Blackbird: High-flying Lockheed spy plane." *Military Technical Journal*, June 1996, pp. 6–9.

Latham, Niles. "CIA launches campaign to end Saddam's reign." *New York Post*, March 1, 2002, p. 12.

Meyer, Lawrence and Joel D. Weisman. "Giancana, Linked to CIA Plot, Slain." *Washington Post*, June 21, 1975, p. 1.

Mossberg, Walter S. "U.S. Intelligence Agencies Triumphed in Gulf War Despite Some Weak Spots." *Wall Street Journal*, March 18, 1991, p. A-10.

Myers, Laura. "Mob offered to kill Castro for free: Kennedy's CIA approved plots." *New Orleans Times-Picayune*, July 2, 1997, p. A1, A8.

Novak, Robert D. "The CIA Won't Play Scapegoat." *New York Post*, December 20, 2001, p. 37.

"Nuke probe widens on tip by CIA." *The Daily News*, December 10, 2001, p. 4.

Orin, Deborah. "U.S. spy drone spots a 'significant figure' who might be Osama." *New York Post*, January 4, 2002, p. 7.

Ricks, Thomas E., and Alan Sipress. "Spy Planes Seek Out Philippine Guerrillas." *Washington Post*, February 21, 2002, p. A1.

Risen, James. "Secret C.I.A. Site in New York Was Destroyed on Sept. 11." *The New York Times*, pp. B1, B6.

Sisk, Richard. "CIA hails a lost hero: First American to be killed in Afghan action." *The Daily News*, November 29, 2001, p. 3.

Sweetman, Bill. "The Aurora Files: Mach 6 over Area 51?" *Military Technical Journal*, April 1996, pp. 67–69.

Thomasson, Dan K. "The Intelligence Gap." *New York Post*, January 4, 2002, p. 29.

Venter, Al J. "Combating insurgency with 'Eye-in-the-Sky' Surveillance." *Military Technical Journal*, August 1997, pp. 66–71.

Welzenbach, Donald E., and Nancy Galyean. "Those daring Young Men and Their Ultra-High-Flying Machines." *Studies in Intelligence*, Volume 31, Number 3, Fall 1987, pp. 103–115. About early U-2 flights.

Wills, Garry. "JFK slaying probe: CIA, FBI had secrets to keep." *New York Post*, November 23, 1993, p. 19.

Index

B

C

J

K

N

O

P–Q

S

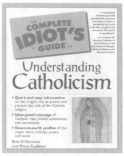

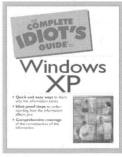